EDUCATIONAL OBJECTIVES AND NATIONAL ASSESSMENT

ASSESSING ASSESSMENT

Series Editor:
Harry Torrance, University of Sussex

The aim of this series is to take a longer term view of current developments in assessment and to interrogate them in terms of research evidence deriving from both theoretical and empirical work. The intention is to provide a basis for testing the rhetoric of current policy and for the development of well-founded practice.

Current titles

Sue Butterfield: *Educational Objectives and National Assessment*

Caroline Gipps and Patricia Murphy: *A Fair Test? Assessment, Achievement and Equity*

John Gray and Brian Wilcox: *'Good School, Bad School'*

Christopher Pole: *Assessing and Recording Achievement*

Malcolm Ross *et al.*: *Assessing Achievement in the Arts*

Harry Torrance (ed.): *Evaluating Authentic Assessment*

Alison Wolf: *Competence-based Assessment*

ASSESSING
ASSESSMENT

EDUCATIONAL OBJECTIVES AND NATIONAL ASSESSMENT

Sue Butterfield

Open University Press
Buckingham · Philadelphia

Open University Press
Celtic Court
22 Ballmoor
Buckingham
MK18 1XW

and
1900 Frost Road, Suite 101
Bristol, PA 19007, USA

First Published 1995

A catalogue record of this book is available from the British Library

ISBN 0 335 19418 4 (pbk)   0 335 19419 2 (hbk)

Library of Congress Cataloging-in-Publication Data
Butterfield, Sue, 1948–
    Educational objectives and national assessment/Sue Butterfield.
      p.   cm. — (Assessing assessment)
    Includes bibliographical references and index.
    ISBN 0–335–19419–2.— ISBN 0–335–19418–4 (pbk)
    1. Education—Great Britain—Aims and objectives.
    2. Educational evaluation—Great Britain.   3. Education and
state—Great Britain.   4. Curriculum change—Great Britain.
I. Title.   II. Series.
LA623.B89   1995
370′.941—dc20
                                      94–23672
                                        CIP

Typeset by Colset Pte Ltd, Singapore
Printed in Great Britain by St Edmundsbury Press,
Bury St Edmunds, Suffolk

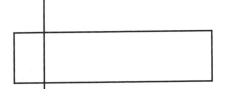

CONTENTS

SERIES EDITOR'S INTRODUCTION

Changing theories and methods of assessment have been the focus of significant attention for some years now, not only in the United Kingdom, but also in many other western industrial countries and many developing countries. Curriculum developers have realized that real change will not take place in schools if traditional paper-and-pencil tests, be they essay or multiple choice, remain unchanged to exert a constraining influence on how teachers and pupils approach new curricula. Similarly, examiners have been concerned to develop more valid and 'authentic' ways of assessing the changes which have been introduced into school syllabuses over recent years – more practical work, oral work, problem solving and so forth. In turn psychologists and sociologists have become concerned with the impact of assessment on learning and motivation, and how that impact can be developed more positively. This has led to a myriad of developments in the field of assessment, often involving an increasing role for the teacher in school-based assessment, as more relevant and challenging tasks are devised by examination agencies for administration by teachers in schools, and as the role and status of more routine teacher assessment of course work, practical work, group-work and so forth have become enhanced.

However educationists have not been the only ones to focus much more closely on the interrelation of curriculum, pedagogy and assessment. Governments around the world, but particularly in the UK have also begun to take a close interest in the ways in which assessment can influence and even control teaching, and in the changes in curriculum and teaching which could be brought about by changes in assessment. This interest has not been wholly coherent. Government intervention in the UK has sometimes initiated, sometimes reinforced the move towards a more practical and vocationally-oriented curriculum and thus the move towards more practical, school-based assessment. But government has also been concerned with issues of accountability and with what it sees as the maintenance of traditional academic standards through the use of externally set tests. The overall effect has been that as certain sorts of responsibility for assessment have been devolved to school level, the parameters within which such responsibility can be exercised have been more tightly drawn.

It is precisely because of the contradictions and complexity inherent in current developments that the present series of books on assessment has been developed. Many claims are being made with respect to the efficacy of new approaches to assessment which require careful review and investigation. Likewise many changes are being required by government intervention which may lead to hurried and poorly understood developments being implemented in schools. The aim of this series is to take a longer term view of the changes which are occurring, to move beyond the immediate problems of implementation and to interrogate the claims and the changes in terms of broader research evidence which derives from both theoretical and empirical work. In reviewing the field in this way the intention of the series is thus to highlight relevant research evidence, identify key factors and principles which should underpin the developments taking place, and provide teachers and administrators with a basis for informed decision-making which takes the educational issues seriously and goes beyond simply accommodating the latest policy imperative.

Sue Butterfield's book is particularly relevant to this task. In it she brings together areas of discussion of assessment which are often, indeed usually, treated separately. In particular she reviews and integrates curricular, technical and political discussions of assessment in order to generate an overview of what is happening at the present time and why. She explores how the language of educational objectives has been developed over time with respect to curriculum development and student assessment, and how it has been co-opted into a discourse of management accountability in the service of political control. She reviews these issues at a general level and also with particular reference to the different ways in which they have been realized in action through the successive developments of GCSE, National Curriculum Assessment, National Vocational Qualifications, and debates over school effectiveness.

However the book is not simply a critique of government interventions. Its strength also lies in the fact that it takes much of the government's critique of educational professionals seriously. The rationale for government intervention – that the 'producers' of education and educational assessment have been unresponsive to consumer needs – is acknowledged as a significant source of concern. In turn some of the implications of new developments, which offer opportunities for re-examining the nature of professional power and how it is exercised *vis-à-vis* individual student learning needs, and indeed the social and economic needs of the wider community, are examined sympathetically. However Butterfield concludes that such opportunities are likely to be lost if the imperatives of market competition simply mean that the power of professional inertia is replaced by the power of educational managers pursuing commercial survival. Overall, the book is intellectually ambitious in the breadth of its review but also very thought-provoking with respect to the opportunities as well as the problems which it highlights in current developments.

Harry Torrance

LIST OF ABBREVIATIONS

APEL	Assessment/Accreditation of Prior [and] Experiential Learning
APU	Assessment of Performance Unit
AT	Attainment Target
BGC	Bishop Grosseteste College
BTEC	Business and Technician Education Council
CAT	Credit Accumulation and Transfer
CATE	Council for the Accreditation of Teacher Education
CATS	Consortium for Assessment and Testing in Schools
CEE	Certificate of Extended Education
CSE	Certificate of Secondary Education
DES	Department of Education and Science
DFE	Department for Education
ED	Employment Department
ENCA	Evaluation of the National Curriculum Assessment at Key Stage 1
ERA	The Education Reform Act 1988
ESRC	Economic and Social Research Council
FE	Further Education
FEU	Further Education Unit

GAIM	Graded Assessment in Mathematics
GASP	Graded Assessment in Science Project
GNVQ	General National Vocational Qualification
GOML	Graded Assessment in Modern Languages
GCE	General Certificate of Education
GCSE	General Certificate of Secondary Education
GM	Grant Maintained
HEQC	Higher Education Quality Council
HMI	Her Majesty's Inspectorate
HMCI	Her Majesty's Chief Inspector of Schools
ILEA	Inner London Education Authority
INSET	Inservice Education and Training
IT	Information Technology
LEA	Local Education Authority
LEAG	London and East Anglian Group
LMS	Local Management of Schools
MEG	Midland Examining Group
NATE	National Association for the Teaching of English
NC	National Curriculum
NCA	National Curriculum Assessment
NCES	National Center for Education Statistics
NCVQ	National Council for Vocational Qualifications
NEA	Northern Examining Association
NFER	National Foundation for Educational Research
NRA	National Record of Achievement
NROVA	National Record of Vocational Achievement
NVQ	National Vocational Qualification
PACE	Primary Assessment, Curriculum and Experience
PRAISE	Pilot Records of Achievement in Schools Evaluation
QTS	Qualified Teacher Status
RoA	Record of Achievement
SoA	Statement of Attainment
SAT	Standard Assessment Task
SCAA	School Curriculum and Assessment Authority
SEAC	School Examinations and Assessment Council
SEC	Secondary Examinations Council
SEG	Southern Examining Group
SOCEET	Social, Economic, Environmental and Technological (aspect of Chemistry)

STAIR   Standard Tests and Assessment Implementation Research
TA   Teacher Assessment
TECs   Training and Enterprise Councils
TEED   Training Enterprise and Education Directorate
TGAT   Task Group on Assessment and Testing
UCCA   Universities Central Council on Admissions
VQ   Vocational Qualification
WO   Welsh Office

INTRODUCTION

The context of this book is the period of rapid – and imposed –
change in education in the UK, particularly following the election
of the first Conservative Government under the leadership of
Margaret Thatcher in 1979. The changes are far reaching across
education. A new system of examining at 16+, the General Certificate of Secondary Education, introduced for 1988, replaced
two previously separate systems. The Education Reform Act 1988
introduced a National Curriculum and assessment arrangements for
England and Wales. Alongside these statutory curricular changes
for the years of compulsory schooling, there have been new vocational qualifications – National Vocational Qualifications. There
are debates of course about how far any of these arrangements are
truly 'national': the developments in Northern Ireland and in
Scotland run parallel to, but are not identical with, those in
England and Wales, and the independent school sector is exempt
from the National Curriculum. Nonetheless, the desired emphasis
of government on standardized national approaches to qualifications and to assessment signals an important trend in policy –
towards centralization of educational control and shifting balances
of power.

There are considerable questions raised by comparable educational changes across the world about the location of power in education. Skilbeck, in a report for the Organization for Economic Cooperation and Development, traces a number of comparable trends across countries, linked to governmental restructuring of their economies: 'Mainly in the Anglo-Saxon countries, there are very definite moves towards central control and direction of the broad outlines of curriculum and assessment.' These trends he sees 'In a broad sense' as 'political, inasmuch as their focus is control, the criteria against which control will be exercised, and the hands in which control will be vested' (Skilbeck 1990: 23). In the UK, the means of that control, the means of more closely managing education at a national level, has been through the close specification of objectives – the actual learning objectives of classrooms and by the establishment of national testing for 7-, 11- and 14-year-olds, with the intention (still unrealized in the face of opposition from teachers and from some parents) of the publication of results in a form that would allow comparisons to be made between schools.

Aronowitz and Giroux's (1986) analysis of *Education under Siege* locates the problem of power not only between government and schools, but between society and profession. Centralization of education cannot, in their analysis, be viewed solely in terms of single political agendas, nor can the success of centralizing policies be attributed merely to the skill of individual politicians. There are fundamental social issues at stake in the changes in education. Difficult arguments about student entitlement and public information co-exist with what appear to be mere vote-catching rhetorical nostalgia about 'standards'.

At the centre of this tension is assessment. Assessment can be argued to provide learners with better information about progress, and better understanding of the pathways of learning. Assessment provides bridges into further formal stages of learning, and students deserve protection from gatekeepers who may be biased or inadequate in their judgements. Students are therefore entitled, it would seem, to rigorous and comparable assessment of their achievements. Alternatively, assessment can be seen as a political tool, to suppress the professional power of teachers for the ideological end of creating a market economy unfettered by professional interference, or to give more direct governmental control over what is an increasingly electorally sensitive item of public expenditure.

The changes are most sharply felt by teachers and 'educationists'. Centralization seeks to change the location of power, and this necessitates changing the nature of teachers' work and their means to control the cultural capital of knowledge. Michael Apple has charted the de-skilling, technicization and intensification of teachers' work (1982, 1986). His study is set in the USA, but the processes described resonate with changes elsewhere. Cohen sees 'blatantly political agendas being imposed upon schools in the USA, UK and Australia . . .' (1990: 33) characterized by agitation about 'standards' and given technical credibility by psychometric claims about measurement of performance.

It is that conjuncture of technical legitimation and political intent which is the starting point for this book. Its case study is the major shift in concept and control of curriculum and assessment in the UK. The General Certificate of Secondary Education (GCSE), the National Curriculum and National Vocational Qualifications (NVQs) have certain important features in common. They all involve identification and use of specified objectives; they are all assessment initiatives designed to bring about curriculum change, and they all institute a different relationship between government, the public and the providers of education and training.

These changes in assessment therefore make technical, curricular and political claims: firstly, that they are able to provide accurate and reliable measurement of individual learning; secondly, that they have curricular, or content, validity; and thirdly, that they provide the basis of a different relationship between teachers and society, consisting in greater accountability for the expenditure of public money and greater entitlement for students.

These considerable claims require evaluation in themselves. Moreover, they require evaluation side by side since they are not discrete claims. The validity and reliability of individual educational measurements bear directly upon the appropriateness of making judgements about parts of the education service on the basis of such assessments. The power of assessment to drive educational activity may, moreover, be used to legitimate rather than to question imposed definitions of curriculum. Therefore, the issue of whether assessments have content validity cannot be separated from the ideological arguments about curriculum content and curriculum process.

A holistic evaluation of the educational and social impact of change seems to be necessary. Yet the changes have the potential to fragment educational activity and educational enquiry, particularly because of the competitive view of education which they sustain. They co-exist in the UK with a developing market economy in education, which is to be driven by assessment results. This market economy depends upon the notion of small cost centres: the school or college, the subject teacher, the individual student. Schools and colleges will (so runs the plan) be chosen by parents and students on the basis of results, subject teachers can be judged on their results, and students will supposedly be motivated to perform better by more overt frameworks of assessment. Assessment thus becomes a key part of a policy of fragmentation, of 'divide and rule' by government over the system as a whole.

Centralization of curriculum and assessment may wrest power from teachers and educationists, but it is unclear where power will then reside. At least at a rhetorical level, the Government claims greater entitlement for learners through its changes. However, reducing the power of teachers is not a means automatically of increasing the power of students. If centralization merely places power with the centre, a fragmented education service has no means to take action, or to articulate the issues surrounding student entitlements. It is, moreover, unclear who is to evaluate the changes. A feature of the centralization through fragmentation policy is that it supports a wholly untheoretical view of educational activity, and the erosion of independent and university-based educational research. It therefore creates the conditions in which evaluation outside the terms of government policy becomes increasingly unlikely.

It is the tension between a policy of fragmentation and the need to retain a holistic and integrative view of current change that is the rationale for this study. Two policy strands are particularly important in addressing this issue: the use of objectives to make educational performance more measurable and comparable; and greater student entitlement (or, within the market discourse, greater consumer rights). How far these principles can be realized in action, and how far they are truly integrated visions for education or rather devices to fragment educational activity, are fundamental questions. The first strand relies predominantly upon technical claims about the possibilities of assessment, and seeks to present a view that educational objectives can be politically prescribed. This raises a central issue of the tension between educational objectives and political objectives. The second strand offers the justification for increasing the role of assessment, and raises the question of the relationship between opportunity and control within an objectives-led system.

These strands provide dimensions of the definition of the field of 'assessment' within the new policy context. Of the three current curricular initiatives, the National Curriculum provides the major example of governmentally imposed change, since it affects all pupils of compulsory school age in state schools in England and Wales. Substantial parts of the curriculum, and the assessment of core subjects, have already been implemented. The National Curriculum therefore provides a major case study for examining the principles and practices of the new education policy.

The central argument of this study is that assessment (or perhaps more truly management) by objectives is a key strand of government policy for social and educational change, and as such requires a central place within the research community of education, rather than a fragmented series of enquiries. Assessment as an area of study is argued to comprise technical, ideological and political elements. The policy context of the current assessment initiatives seeks to divide the activity of education into specific, pragmatic and centrally controlled units. Further, it seeks to create divisions between the discourse of 'educationists' and practitioners, and divisions within each of those groups. Educational enquiry becomes divided between that which can attract funding by working within the terms of reference of government policy and that which retains an independent stance. Practitioners are intended to be restricted to increasingly narrow subject focuses, and therefore in the contribution they are able to make to broader curriculum debates.

Chapter 1 considers the issue of 'learning objectives', and the extent to which these are actually and necessarily an educational – as opposed to a political – issue. So much depends upon the means by which the objectives are identified, and the kinds of power relations which they support, that it is difficult to talk of objectives as though they can be reduced to a technical issue about the design of learning.

Chapter 2 explores the policy context in which the current assessment initiatives operate. It considers the extent to which it is reasonable to see a coherent strategy of control of education running throughout the three major initiatives, and how far this control is designed, and/or likely, to fragment educational activity and enquiry.

The following three chapters (3 to 5) provide an outline of the characteristics and the policy context for GCSE, the National Curriculum and NVQs, respectively. The General Certificate of Secondary Education as introduced in 1986 is important in this context because it had origins in theoretical work related to curriculum and to objectives, and therefore demonstrated at that point a possible marriage between theory and policy. It also took a unified approach to subjects, seeing comparable learning and assessment objectives running across school curriculum subjects. It therefore represents an attempt at a holistic view of the learner in its continuity between subjects, and of the relationship between educational research and the state.

The National Curriculum is set against that particular vision, as representing an intentionally fragmented view of subject areas, and of knowledge as describable within discrete statements of attainment. Those statements, moreover, were generated by individual subject working groups and without any over-arching theoretical foundation for the work. The National Curriculum therefore represents the policy of fragmentation: between subject areas, between teachers within those subject areas and between educational theory (the traditional province of Higher Education) and classroom practice.

National Vocational Qualifications are outlined to illustrate the thorough-going approach to objectives-led assessment which is now characterizing (imposed) activity in education and training. Further, NVQs seek to alter the relationship of parts, at least, of Further and Higher Education to their work, and therefore illustrate the extent of plans for central control. That central control, again, is argued to depend upon reductions in professional power and autonomy, and hence a fragmentation of previous relationships. Most specifically, in relation to education, an NVQ approach could be adopted to reduce or remove the involvement of Higher Education in teacher training, thereby further dividing the phases of education and separating educational theory from educational practice.

Chapters 6 and 7 focus upon two kinds of conflict which underlie current change: firstly, in relation to ideas about curriculum which are unresolved within the current attempts to make everything look standard and bureaucratically manageable. Even within the Government's policies there are considerable tensions between a view of curriculum as a means of imposing uniformity, and as a means of creating flexibility, choice and self-determination. Moreover, the means of disseminating 'curriculum', its commodification as something that can be centrally devised and then 'delivered', ignores the realities of dissemination and curriculum processes. Chapter 7 looks at the meanings and relationships which the mode of introduction of a prescribed curriculum and assessment have established. It looks, for example, at the effects of cascade training in establishing a putative hierarchy of expertise in education, and implications that teachers' work is semi-skilled, technical and readily measurable. This matters too in the discussion of student empowerment. Again, are the messages of the mode of introduction absorbed by students as empowerment or disempowerment? Do learners gain in a technical view of teachers' work, or are learners simply positioned at an even lower level in the 'cascade' of expertise?

Chapters 8 and 9 consider what are sometimes cast as technical aspects of assessment. Chapter 8 argues that criterion referencing may be a very productive educational philosophy – but far too illusory as a technical system to build national procedures for curriculum, assessment and comparative league tables upon. Again, the message seems to be that it is impossible to divorce the technical and the political. So much depends upon the context and purpose of criterion referenced assessment as to whether it produces valid – and educationally useful – information. Chapter 9 looks at the issues surrounding comparison of performance. At the centre of the current changes in assessment and qualification structures is the contention that comparability of standards can be sufficiently accurate to provide the management and market information to drive the new-model education system. Underlying this contention are a very wide range of issues. The chapter reviews past studies of comparability of results, as well as the arguments for and against the so-called 'value-added' comparisons of progression. It argues that the political agenda of comparison has outrun the technical claims for assessment to underpin such comparison.

Chapter 10 considers the ways in which the focus on 'assessment results' threatens to focus narrowly the questions about school effectiveness and educational standards. It identifies dangers in divorcing technical arguments about effectiveness data from the inherent worth of the data, and from the effects of data gathering itself upon educational processes.

Research into GCSE, the National Curriculum and NVQs demonstrates a growing restraint upon the scope of research and the brief to which it can work. Research is increasingly being used (by the Government and its agencies) as an instrument for fine-tuning Government policy, rather than as a means for informing or changing policy. Chapter 11 gives some overview of the issues that have been raised by research into the National Curriculum and its assessment, as well as considering the problems of research, and its vulnerability to subversion to serve particular policy ends. The suppression of the influence of education departments in universities (a significant location of educational research), particularly through legislation in progress to have Education Departments funded differently from other parts of Higher Education through an agency with very specific funding directives, is entirely in line with the general fragmentation-for-centralization of education.

The juxtaposition of issues about curriculum, about power and politics in education, and about technical aspects of assessment is not easy, because the disciplines and discourses around these areas are already habitually separated in education. It is, however, a necessary bringing together. For just as parts of the education service are being set in competition against other parts, and there is a danger of fragmentation in that sense, so also there is a danger that the separation of different areas of study within education leaves significant problems about how to retain a whole picture. How can school effectiveness data be based on assessment results that derive from unevaluated curricular and assessment practices?

There are some very large issues which it is hard to address within the scope of this book. The nature of democracy, and the role of university-based educational research within a democratic society, must hover somewhere around the margins. This book finds reasons for not letting go of education as an area of study within the universities, but is conscious that in debates about power, universities are themselves at issue.

EDUCATIONAL
OBJECTIVES

It is difficult to attempt to address all the possible meanings of the term 'objectives' at once. On the one hand, there are the objectives of policymakers for the education system itself; on the other, there are the more specific learning objectives that teachers and students might be working to in particular lessons or sequences of lessons. Some layers of meaning, such as the overtly political, are addressed in other chapters. This chapter attempts to confine its discussion to learning objectives, and to identify some of the issues surrounding these. It questions, however, whether these issues can be divorced from political issues about power, relationships and control, particularly in a situation where the specific learning objectives are seen as the means at a national level of bringing about fundamental change within and around the education system.

The new interest of UK governments in education exists on at least two levels. Firstly, there is the large policy agenda of how the education system is to be brought under public (or governmental) control. At this level the concern is with accountability for expenditure, and with changing the relationship between society and its education professionals to create direct lines of accountability. Secondly, there is concern about the nature of what is taught and how this might be influencing society in relation to the wishes of policymakers. These two areas are interrelated in the increasing intervention in curriculum content by the Government since 1988 – intervention heralded by Callaghan's Labour Government in 1976. Governmental involvement, both with the broad canvas of the education system and with the details of its curriculum have taken the form of curricular prescriptions based upon specified objectives and learning outcomes. Such objectives are to provide the means by which education gives an account of itself, through measurement of how far objectives have been met. They also provide the tool for government intervention – at a very detailed level – in the content of curriculum. Besieged by measurement and with curriculum prescriptions arriving (and changing) at a rapid rate, the work of teachers is very significantly constrained by objectives used in this way, and thus a fundamental change in the 'professional' role is signalled in detailed prescription at the level of learning objectives.

All this has been imposed upon the education – and training – systems, without any historical evolution. The 'objectives movement' has had limited impact in the UK prior to governmental prescription in the National Curriculum. Its attraction for government is as a way of bringing about rapid and measurable change – a means of management of education.

In England and Wales there are four major curriculum innovations – each shaped by assessment through objectives – which illustrate a dramatic and historically unprepared shift in educational practice in this country. GCSE assessment objectives, National Curriculum attainment targets and statements of attainment, student profiling and the Units and Elements of competence of the NVQs are at the centre of current educational change. Each of them, in ways which will be explored further in later chapters, is based upon objectives.

In order to explore the question of curriculum objectives it may be helpful first to consider them in their oppositional light, as alternatives to other organizing principles for curriculum and learning, and further to consider what value positions are inherent in either the 'objectives movement' or its alternatives. In other words, the attempt here is to explore what is at stake in adopting or rejecting particular objectives models of education.

Objectives as the alternative to rote learning

This is perhaps the most clearly 'educational' context in which the objectives debate may be considered. The tenacity of content-laden curricula and rote-learning is a well-established educational concern, and the search for alternative principles, though not necessarily called objectives, can be found well before the advent of the National Curriculum. In 1580, Montaigne lamented many aspects of his contemporary pedagogy such as the celebration of bookishness at the expense of application of knowledge. Men 'stamped with the mark of letters,' he says, 'are wonderfully acquainted with Galen, but not at all with the disease of the patient' (Hazlitt 1952, Essay 24: 59). He argued for education that recognized the many contexts of learning, even during what appeared to be play, and for expectations in the evaluation of learning that went beyond mere repetition: 'Tis a sign of crudity and indigestion to disgorge what we eat in the same condition it was swallowed' (Essay 25: 65).

Herbert Spencer's discussion of the desirable emphases of learning may be credited with marking the beginning of the modern debate about educational goals. It maps a method of progression in teaching, from concrete to abstract, and questions the assumption that the rules and principles of a subject are the appropriate starting points for learning: rather these principles should be 'disclosed, as they are in the order of nature, through the study of cases' (Spencer 1861: 30). He favoured a rational curriculum, based upon decisions about 'the relative values of knowledges' (1861: 7) and a classification of the activities of human life.

Dewey stressed the need for aims in education, and made a number of distinctions which still have important resonance. An aim, he advocated, is not merely a result but is an end, a deliberate and intended goal; the aims of educators should be educational aims, not issuing 'from some outside source' (1916: 121); the formulation of aims should take account of 'the present state of experience of pupils' and an aim 'is experimental, and hence growing constantly as it is tested in action'. He introduced the distinction between an aim and an object, the latter being a 'means of directing the activity' (1916: 123).

Despite a long history of curricular discussion, the dominance of secondary education in the UK by particular models of examination at 16 tended, until the 1980s, to emphasize content. Syllabuses for public examinations were expressed in terms of the topics to be covered, but not in terms of the learning objectives of the course. Many examinations were dependent on timed essays showing recall of factual material. There are plenty of implicit assessment objectives in such examinations – about recall and speed of writing. What was lacking were overt objectives concerned with what was actually to be learned and applied through the ingestion and repetition of content.

The GCSE introduced an objectives model as an alternative to content-based examination syllabuses which had preceded it. By stressing objectives, it made an important break with the traditions of examining, and opened the way for a wider and more relevant curriculum, and for the identification of underlying cross-curricular objectives. This might be seen as a significant shift and reform in educational practice. Its main impact, however, was upon the two years of secondary schooling prior to public examinations at age 16, the years to which the assessment applied. Nor did GCSE shift the locus of control in education. Although it was at first seen as an unprecedented piece of governmental intervention in the examining systems (previously under the control of university matriculation boards and Local Education Authority consortia), it gave in practice increased endorsement to a professional model of control, not least through the introduction of coursework assessment as a component of final results. The shift that did occur was from a classical humanist view of knowledge absorption to a liberal humanist view of relevance and the personal meaningfulness of learning. This change posed no threat to professional power overall, though it may have altered the balance of power within the teaching profession.

Objectives as alternatives to liberal humanist consensus

Liberal humanism rests on the fundamental assumption 'that human nature is universally and eternally the same' and is closely identified with the traditions of western education, traditions which may no longer answer 'the legitimate needs of the modern world' (Durkheim 1977 [1938]: 321). Liberal humanism proceeds on assumptions of consensus and tradition and can be seen as ill equipped to address the problems of modern societies. It is embedded in the 'habitus' of education which may be at the roots of its reproduction of existing social order (Bourdieu and Passeron 1970) and hence can be accused of perpetuating inequality of access and achievement.

There are a number of ways in which liberal humanism may be challenged through the stating of curricular objectives:

Objectives and the logic of production

The systematization of the curriculum mapped by Bobbitt (1918, 1924) took its inspiration from industrial processes and began a trend not only towards utilitarianism but also towards increasing specificity and proliferation of objectives. It is from the manufacturing terminology of Bobbitt that the terms process and product have passed from the factory to the school, becoming in later discussion of objectives associated with enabling objectives (the process) and terminal objectives (the product).

Objectives and a science of education

Tyler's rational model of curriculum planning (Tyler 1949) restored a level of generality to the notion of objectives. His model of curriculum planning depends on goals, content, methods and evaluation, and offers a model within which identification of more specific goals of content and method can be decided at the level of the institution or the teacher. The model is essentially that advocated for School Development Planning (Hargreaves and Hopkins 1991: 5) with the added emphasis that planning is cyclical not linear, and that the evaluation stage also informs decisions about purposes. It also bears relation to the personal target-setting and review processes of the National Record of Achievement. While Tyler offers a rational model for looking at educational planning which can be adapted to a number of levels of planning – personal, institutional and beyond – he recognized the filters through which the decisions about goals must pass. There need to be philosophical judgements, and interpretations of learners' needs, as well as attention to the needs of society. These filters are, in

Tyler's view, provided by professional judgement – so what Tyler offered is a way of acting systematically within a framework that was still in practice dominated by liberal consensus.

The work of Bloom and his associates (1956) placed objectives in the context of a theory of cognitive development and is based upon classification. Their taxonomy of objectives does not claim a hierarchy as such, but does give the areas a ranking in so far as each successive stage is seen as a prerequisite for the next, so that knowledge precedes understanding and understanding precedes application of understanding and evaluative analysis. Bloom and co-workers attempted to illustrate how this model could be applied to various established disciplines (academic subject disciplines). What was proposed was something of a science of cognitive education. Their contention of general principles governing the cognitive learning across subject areas is, however, problematic, and perhaps underplays the essentially different nature of different academic disciplines. 'Synthesis' for example (dependent according to Bloom on knowledge and understanding) may occur in written composition without explicit 'knowledge' of the kinds listed in the taxonomy (Wilkinson *et al.* 1980: 48). Very young children can synthesize simple events into a story long before their comprehension skills are particularly well developed. Questions arise as to whether across different subject areas the categorizations truly represent the same degree of complexity, a 'circumplex', with variations only in content (Seddon 1978). Despite the detractions from this attempt at a categorization of learning goals, the taxonomy has provided an anchor for a number of research projects into examinations and assessment in the UK (Willmott and Hall 1975; Biggs and Collis 1982; Pollitt *et al.* 1985). Likewise, the knowledge, understanding, application and evaluation framework is that adopted, in different degrees, by GCSE subjects 1986–93, but not by the National Curriculum planners.

The taxonomy of the affective domain (1964) is, as Bloom and co-workers acknowledge, entering an even more problematic area than the cognitive, and one which is far less readily susceptible to assessment (Eisner 1985; Aspin 1986). Like the behavioural approaches which depended upon such classifications, the taxonomers may divorce educational activity from moral contexts:

Bloom misses the opportunity to introduce the necessary

'logical' considerations into his classification of objectives in the affective domain. He acknowledges frequently enough that 'at all levels of the affective domain, affective objectives have a cognitive component' but he fails to see that this cognitive component (the 'judgement', or 'the way someone "sees" the object of feeling') is the crucial factor in determining whether an affective response is desirable or not ... Otherwise we are left with questions like 'commitment to what?'

(Gribble 1970: 14–15)

Technocracy and meritocracy – the behavioural objectives alternative to liberal traditions

Behaviourism, deriving from the work of Pavlov and Skinner, and advocated by Mager (1962) as a basis for designing instruction, offered what seemed a new and more rigorous approach to the processes of teaching and learning. If objectives were expressed only in terms of 'observable behaviours' then programmes of instruction could be designed which would be based upon logical sequences of learning and the readiness of each learner to pass forward could be ascertained without subjective judgement about unseen mental processes, but by reference to the actual observed evidence of learning. A behavioural objective should specify the conditions in which the behaviour is to be demonstrated and the criteria for successful fulfilment. Mager (1962) provided a manual of how to construct such objectives. Gagne (1965) developed an elaborated theory of learning hierarchies and task analysis of prerequisite skills and concepts for a given learning outcome. The role of the teacher becomes one of task analysis and ensuring mastery of prerequisite steps in learning. Computers can, in theory, play a very effective part in such models of learning. If each task can be analysed into common paths that all learners will take, the computer program would be better able to provide that structure while ensuring an individualized pace of learning than the teacher. In this way behavioural approaches seem to offer a highly rational, planned approach to learning. Mastery learning places great emphasis on individual pace of instruction. Computer-based instruction removes the problem of a teacher being unable to give sustained, individual attention to 20 or 30 pupils. The technical approach removes the high degree of (teacher) subjectivity in decisions about the style of teaching and the relationships established – which may or may not be beneficial to learning. The classroom becomes a more scientific environment in which personality clashes and alternative value systems are – supposedly – eliminated by the carefully controlled focus on planned learning pathways and outcomes.

The behavioural objectives movement has been open to a number of critiques. It supplants important questions about what should be taught and why, with questions only about task analysis and ordering of instruction. It also raises problems about the level of a behavioural objective and how far each task has to be analysed for the model to provide support to instruction. Eva Baker points out that merely following the formula of a behavioural objective does not in itself 'present sufficient cues regarding what a teacher should alter in instruction'. The example adduced is: 'Given a lyric poem, the student will be able to write a 450-word essay on the theme and tone' (Baker 1976: 11).

Chanan (1974) addresses the difficulties of setting objectives in the humanities, and concludes that the greatest difficulty lies in those objectives that are tacit because they are embedded in the value systems of our society. These exemplify the implicit objectives of education. Emergent objectives (i.e. those which are not pre-specified but are identified during a process) are almost a defining characteristic of creativity. Eisner (1985) distinguishes between expressive and instructional objectives. Moreover, 'the assumption that objects [objectives] can be used as standards by which to measure achievement fails, I think, to distinguish adequately between the application of a standard and the making of a judgement' (Eisner 1985: 91).

Specific objectives, particularly in their association with behaviourism, appear to present a reductive and mechanistic view of the complex processes of human learning. Behaviourism is a development in some ways from the movements outlined above which sought to associate education with industrial process, or to apply the principles of science to curriculum planning.

However, it is perhaps too easy to forget the Utopian aspirations of the technicist vision. A life governed by rationality can be proposed as an alternative to existing social orders in which patronage and privilege are rarely subject to scientific, rational challenge. The all powerful individuality of the teacher is channelled into a rational analysis of specific learning tasks. Assessment is focused on specific tasks rather than clouded by generalized views of 'ability'. Viewed from this perspective, measurable objectives represent an attempt to alter the basis of control in education: to reduce the social, personal and social class features of education and to systematize it in such a way as to remove these interference factors. It is in this sense parallel to other attempts to make education more accessible to greater numbers, by removing some of the traditional, consensual and hence unspecified customs of the classroom, school or system. It makes the curriculum explicit and hence open to scrutiny.

However, there are problems about the larger structural messages of technocracy. It implies obedience, orderliness and rationality, and could be seen as a means to produce a subdued population. It cannot be assumed that the governmental attraction to objectives is located in a meritocratic reorganization of society. It may be that the larger technocratic messages are attractive to holders of power, along with the reduced (and replaceable) role of teachers in a technicist curriculum model.

United Kingdom contexts

The Schools Council research in curriculum development came increasingly to associate itself with school-based development and with action research by teachers. Stenhouse advocated a process model in opposition to the objectives model for thinking about curriculum: 'The improvement of teaching is not the linear process of the pursuit of obvious goals. It is about the growth of understanding and skill of teachers which constitutes their resource in meeting new situations ...' (Stenhouse *et al.* 1980: 244).

Her Majesty's Inspectors of education (HMI) were working throughout the 1970s and the first half of the 1980s on more explicit and comprehensive curriculum guidance. Their work on this was published in a series of so-called 'Red Books'. The Red Books sought to establish a very broad framework: 'We believe that there are general goals appropriate for all pupils, which have to be translated into curricular objectives in terms of subjects/disciplines/areas of learning activity.' They suggest that diversity in organization in secondary schools could be mitigated by more national agreement about these objectives (DES 1977: 5).

The level of specificity of such goals is not suggested: the report's development of the idea of 'areas of experience' (DES 1977: 6 ff.) suggests that the general goals might also be conceived at a cross-curricular level. The notion of a common curriculum is established by this report, which is broadly consonant with some of the developments into GCSE, and which is essentially liberal humanist in its identification of areas of experience which are to frame the curriculum.

The Assessment Objectives of the GCSE (1986–93) were to be expressed in terms of the 'observable and measurable behaviour which the achievement of the educational aims of a course in the subject brings about' (DES 1985b: 20). Given the limited currency of the behavioural objectives movement in this country, it is difficult to know what model was here intended. In the great majority of cases the objectives of the subject criteria do not conform to this definition of Assessment Objectives, and with no generally accepted precedent, nor might they be expected to. The introduction of the National Curriculum for England and Wales marked a very different level of prescription for assessment by objectives from GCSE. The liberal humanist model of GCSE, with considerable scope for interpretation and judgement at teacher level (exemplified particularly by coursework assessment), was replaced by something closer to behavioural objectives. Chapters 3 and 4 will look in more detail at the kinds of difference between the GCSE model and the National Curriculum model which supplanted it. The point to be made here is simply that the National Curriculum initially indicated a significant break with traditions of professional control, and its statements of attainment – its learning objectives – were the key to the enactment of change.

By 1993 the need for a review of the National Curriculum and its assessment arrangements was recognized by the Government. The factors underlying this review will be discussed later. In relation to objectives it is important to note that the review moves away from an objectives model as first conceived for the curriculum:

A simple reduction in the number of statements of attainment may not be the best way to deal with the problems currently being experienced. The opportunity might, rather, be taken to gather the main statements into clusters to create a more integrated description of what a pupil must know, understand and be able to do at each level.

(Dearing 1993b: 7.9)

The 'gathering' into 'clusters', and the 'integrated description' are very different approaches to 'objectives' from the attempt in the original statements of attainment to be as precise and discrete in the identification of achievement as possible. This is no small difference. It marks a move from a would-be technically measurement-led system, towards an approach to assessment objectives closer to that established formerly by GCSE. It implies much more use of judgement (professional judgement) in looking at achievement against integrated statements where a general view of achievement will be taken, and where decisions will need to be made on a case-by-case basis about how to weigh strength in one part of the description against relative weakness in another. There may be a loss of diagnostic information, which closely defined objectives can be argued to provide. The real significance of such a change, however, is the movement back to assessment processes in which professional experience is more prominent; and in which, some might argue, professional 'mystification' (DFE 1992a) is able again to intervene between government and classroom.

Alongside the development of the National Curriculum for compulsory schooling, there has been a development of NVQs. The characteristics and rationale of these qualifications will be outlined in Chapter 5. Here they deserve mention since they are very clearly within the behavioural model of objectives. For each occupational area covered by the qualifications, competencies are specified, to be assessed wherever possible by actual job performance in specified conditions. General NVQs (GNVQs) concentrate on the assessment of core skills alongside units of occupational assessment.

The National Record of Achievement provides a further example of the application of objectives. Designed to be a continuous personal record from school to training and into work, the Record incorporates achievements in National Curriculum and where applicable in NVQs. It also, however, is to be used as a means of encouraging reflection on wider achievements, and in supporting a process (with teacher/mentor help) of personal profiling and target setting.

There are, then, a number of different objectives models co-existing in the current work of teachers – though the general drift towards specified objectives can be seen as a common theme. Moreover, all these models seek to provide new bases for assessment. However, there may be considerable differences in the way in which objectives operate, depending on factors such as who is identifying them, how precise they are, and what they are used for in terms of assessment processes. Very different power relations may be established by the different models, between government and teachers, between teachers and the public, between teachers and students – much depends on who is setting the agenda, and with what constraints.

Dimensions of the 'objectives' issue

General curricular aims

There are differences, as discussed above, in the nature of objectives in use. The terminology across the current assessment systems varies, and the concepts differ too. Although the GCSE stated general aims for each subject, the National Curriculum does not have such general curricular aims. While the political aims of the National Curriculum in terms of the role it is to play within a restructuring of education may be clear enough, there is a noticeable absence of any philosophy of what is to be achieved overall by the study of a particular curriculum subject, beyond that is the contribution that subject makes to the undefined notion of 'balance'.

The contrast might be illustrated by some examples from the earlier GCSE model. Subject specific aims include the development of the ability of students to:

> develop a feel for number, carry out calculations and understand the significance of the results obtained
>
> [Mathematics para. 2.1] (DES 1985b)

> understand themselves and others
>
> [English para. 1.1.4] (DES 1985b)

to prepare students to participate more fully in decision making processes as consumers, producers and citizens
[Economics para. 1.1.3] (DES 1985b)

to promote the development of curiosity, enquiry, initiative,
ingenuity, resourcefulness and discrimination
[Craft, Design and Technology para. 3.6] (DES 1985b)

These few examples give some flavour of the tone and stance of
the original GCSE objectives, and indeed of the liberal humanist
traditions from which they derived. This is the stance – but also
the layer of educational intention – which the National Curriculum
significantly omits.

The aims of personal profiling are part of the National Record
of Achievement (NRA). The early aims for this were outlined by
the working group looking at records of achievement in the school
context: recognition, motivation and self-awareness, curriculum
evaluation in relation to pupils' potential, and providing a document of record (DES 1984). These aims have carried forward into
the wider application of NRA into the post-16 vocational qualification routes. The general aims of the NRA seek to provide some of
the coherence that may be lacking across the curriculum, particularly in an objectives-led model of subject development in
schools, or of vocational training as occupational competencies.

Level of specification

There are wide variations in interpretation of how specific objectives should be. Here again there are wide variations between the
1986 GCSE and its sequels. The assessment objectives of GCSE
were expressed at a very general level. Teachers were left with
much interpretation to do and much professional experience to
bring to bear in making these objectives meaningful. Mixed lists
of GCSE 'aims' and 'objectives' were actually hard to tell apart.
There was no very clear policy of distinguishing the two, nor of
putting into practice the guidance of the General Criteria that
objectives should specify that which is measurable. The National
Curriculum marked a more definite step towards a behaviourally
defined curriculum – though even its proliferation of strands and
statements of attainment prove in use to require considerable

'professional' interpretation of the kind it was intended to reduce. NVQs have the most clearly behavioural model, replicated through the assessor and verifier awards which establish an elaborate technical pyramid of assessment. The assessors and verifiers must themselves reach behaviourally defined standards of competence.

An inherent feature of specifying objectives is proliferation. The more specific the objectives the more there have to be, and each layer of objectives begs the question: but what does that actually mean? It appears to be a process of endless self-replicating fission, a chain reaction – a sort of splitting of the atom of 'professional judgement'. It is as yet unclear whether the energy released by this process is destructive or constructive.

Statutory authority

The purposes of setting up an objectives-led curriculum are represented in the degree of legal authority that the curriculum has been given. The minimalist legal framework for curriculum established under the Education Act 1944 is in sharp contrast to the number of statutory powers over curriculum and assessment given directly to the Secretary of State by the Education Reform Act 1988 (Chitty 1993). These are not general powers or areas of responsibility, but powers to prescribe very specifically, hence the legal weight behind the very details of the Attainment Targets. Secretaries of State for Education now have the power to influence very precisely – through specified objectives – the content and ordering of the curriculum in individual classrooms. Vocational Qualifications and Records of Achievement rest upon different dynamics, mainly those of market and funding. The Training and Enterprise Councils (TECs) rely for continued funding upon meeting targets in numbers of NVQ awards, and therefore have a material interest in pushing forward the new qualifications. Either way, the introduction of the National Curriculum and of NVQs carries considerable government authority and the move to objectives make these very highly prescriptive.

Whose objectives?

There is emphasis in the first HMI Red Book on teacher involvement in the processes of reaching national agreement: 'There is a lot to be said for all those concerned with the drawing up and teaching of curricula defining their aims and objectives' (DES 1977: 5). An assumption is made that there is in fact a degree of common understanding about the degree of specificity (including behavioural specificity) which might be appropriate. HMI saw teachers as collectively and collaboratively involved in identifying their objectives.

Gribble (1970) celebrates the act of classification because of the opportunity then to expose and reject suspect educational goals. Nuttall outlines many of the positive functions that objectives may serve across the whole range of education, but stresses that the model adopted by the National Curriculum – of national specification – negates those benefits:

> There is a growing amount of evidence that suggests that the target-setting model of education, reductionist though it may be, has led to the improvement of standards and demystified the educational process for many young people, by clarifying the nature of what they are learning and how it is to be assessed. In my opinion, though, it is the giving of responsibility to individuals to set their own targets and the giving of freedom to negotiate that are perhaps more potent ingredients than just the act of setting targets. I strongly believe that negotiable targets are more helpful than fixed targets, handed down by government committees to 25,000 different schools.
>
> (Nuttall 1988: 234)

A process-oriented view – that the identification of objectives is in itself an important activity for the participants – could, of course, be applied to behavioural task analysis or non-behavioural curriculum discussions. What matters from this perspective is not the model of learning objectives which is adopted, but whether it is meaningful and 'owned' by those using it.

Intensification of workload

One function which objectives are fulfilling is that of intensification of teachers' work – a process that has been described and illustrated by Apple (1986). The tendency for objectives to proliferate has, in practice, greatly enlarged the curriculum content and added to the complexity of curriculum process in all areas affected – hence plans for simplification in the Dearing review (Dearing 1993b). Thus objectives appear to provide an integrated answer to forcing through change in education and to replacing professional with governmental control. Not only do objectives allow very high degrees of bureaucratic, central (and ultimately political) control, they have in their very nature a tendency to increase workload, and render those who might object to such shifts in control too busy to protest effectively.

Overview

In the discussion of objectives, it might be possible to see four broad categorizations of views of objectives emerging:

The deconstructive

The identification of underlying purposes is a process for altering the social systems which have rested on consensual assumptions and have perpetuated the dominance of particular groups or social classes. In such a view the National Curriculum and NVQs bring into the open the nature of the curriculum: students are better informed about what is expected of them, and teachers' powers are reduced. Bernstein's theory of control (1977), however, would suggest that since the National Curriculum is highly classified (i.e. divided into distinct subjects), and likely to encourage increasingly framed (teacher-dominated) pedagogic modes, then it is operating counter to student empowerment. How this operates in practice – either to empower or control – may depend upon the extent to which students actually participate in the deconstructive activity. Are they involved in discussion of where curriculum comes from or why? Processes such as self-assessment do not automatically involve students in the deconstructive process if the targets and objectives are already a given of the situation in which students find themselves. 'Negotiated assessment', particularly associated with the NRA and profiling, is at an interesting point of interface between a personal empowerment and a market perspective. The language of 'negotiation' seems derived from worker–employer relations of the post-war period and may have resonances which suggest a balancing of power positions in a market framework. In an educational context where traditional power lies with the educator, it could be seen as a term so vague as to allow the existing order to continue, with an extension of liberal principles rather than a radical shift in power.

The bureaucratic

The categorization of educational objectives will enable monitoring or 'quality control' in education and training. This might describe the interests of the DFE in meeting their responsibilities to gather information about educational spending and performance. An objectives model of curriculum might appear superficially to allow the work of teachers to be carefully measured in terms of pupil performance and for success rates to be matched against expenditure. It takes power away from teachers, but does not necessarily divert it directly to students.

Schön's identification of a technicist, bureaucratic takeover of education acknowledges that radical critics might side with bureaucrats in trying to take power away from teachers. However . . . 'There is something inconsistent about a demystification of professional expertise which leads to the establishment of a breed of counter-professional experts' (Schön 1983: 342).

The market

Explicit goals will provide better information to 'customers' about the 'product' of education. Employers in this context will be able to see a more direct link between money spent on training and precise occupational skills. In relation to compulsory education, the National Curriculum plays a key role in the market economy established by the 1988 Act. The role is, however, ambivalent since a more thorough-going vision of a market in education might have left curricular decisions to the market-place. That, however, would have been too drastic for the traditionalists within government who would see standards as embodied in the curriculum structure of their own experience. There is also a market argument for public information and quality control (the food-labelling argument) which would require that educational performance could be reduced to a limited number of readily assimilable statistics, and that schools could be compared on their results just as customers might choose between brands on the shelf depending on weight and price. Objectives would appear (in a very simple model of education and training) to satisfy the need for simplification of information, and hence simple comparability.

The liberal humanist

Educational achievement is too complex and too varied to submit to classification at anything other than a fairly general level. The more precise objectives of teaching are a matter for individual teachers and schools. Professionals achieve best when they are given freedom to interpret and judge for themselves. This position, defended by HMI until the advent of the National Curriculum, and in their contributions to the 1986 GCSE, can be seen clearly in their wish expressed in the education Red Books for teachers to agree through a national consultation process on the general objectives of the curriculum, while leaving the processes of interpreting general objectives to individuals and schools. Such a process is essentially a professionally dominated view of educational control. The alternative as represented by National Curriculum and assessment appears to have produced a near-unworkable and certainly unwieldy system. In practical terms, the professional view seems to have survived some of the bureaucratic challenge. It has been, however, weak in addressing issues of student power, parental choice and the rights of the wider community in relation to the education. The strength of liberal humanism is that it draws on tradition and existing relationships. Its weakness is its tendency to protect existing powers, to claim consensual agreement, and to limit explicit information.

The arguments around objectives are not single or simple. 'Education' – if that term can be taken to embrace both a social process and a broad professional group – has not always made its longer term or its specific learning objectives clear. The defence of any lack of clarity would lie in complexity of the educational enterprise, and the problems associated with attempts to reduce education to a more scientific process. There may also, however, be ways in which objectives are central to a discussion of professional power, since power may be seen to reside in the unspoken, the unexplicit. The challenge to education is to address the power and privilege it has held, as a profession and within individual classrooms, through the tacitness of curricular objectives in the past. Defence of the intuitive, the personal, the complex in human learning, does not directly address the issue of what education is about or what access the learner has to that metaknowledge.

Objectives may be seen as inhabiting an important area, along with assessment with which they are a close partner, in the erosion of professional, and dominantly liberal humanist, values and governmental intention to erode that power. The unspoken and closed processes of professionals are also at odds with claims for social change which arise from positions quite different from those of government. To characterize the current imposition of objectives as merely party political, or as simply discreditable because of associations with behaviourism, might be to underestimate the degree of social change which it implies, or the different agendas for change which it might ultimately serve. If the 'breed of counter-professional experts' that Schön speaks of are not suitable arbiters of a new order, then it seems that education has itself to take a more proactive role in discussing, publishing and justifying its objectives, and in deciding on the kind of objectives which are appropriate to carrying through its aims.

THE POLITICAL
CONTEXT OF
ASSESSMENT

Changes in assessment are inextricably a part of wider political change; indeed assessment is an important means by which such change is to come about. Broadfoot's claim that at the 'macro-level', 'assessment practices are one of the clearest indices of the relationship between schools and society, since they provide the means of communication between the two' (Broadfoot 1979: 11, 27) is here judged against the current changes in assessment. This chapter firstly reviews the move towards greater centralization and accountability in education, and then analyses the specific ways in which educational activity is fragmented through the erosion of its professional bases. This fragmentation is closely linked to assessment practices.

The current context of educational change is identified by Chitty (1989) as having two important focal points, in 1976–87 and in 1987–88, the first of these marking a key point in the centralization of educational control. The year 1976 saw the beginning in the UK of the so-called 'Great Debate' on education, in the wake of the then prime minister Callaghan's speech at Ruskin College, calling for greater accountability of the education service. The year 1987–88 saw the passage of the Education Reform Act which introduced local management of schools whereby schools would substantially manage their own budgets. The Act allowed for open enrolment so that student numbers would no longer be controlled by Local Education Authorities (LEAs) and put in place an elaborated procedure for schools to become grant maintained and opt out completely from the control of LEAs. The first, but by far the sketchiest parts of the Act have to do with the new National Curriculum and assessment arrangements. The Act outlined the provision in general terms and gave sweeping powers (as in other areas of the Act) to the Secretary of State for Education to introduce the detail. Ranson (1988) sees social and economic change of the 1960s and 1970s as creating a context for questions about consumer rights and educational accountability.

James Callaghan's Ruskin speech of 1976 sets the scene for a more centralized control of education, and the accountability of education is by then the dominant concern. Metaphors of secrecy and growth signalled by David Eccles' concern about the 'secret garden of the curriculum' into which 'from time to time we [Parliament] could, with advantage express views on what is taught in schools and in training colleges' (*Hansard* 21 March 1960: cols 51–52) were replaced by the 1980s and 1990s with metaphors of consumerism, of 'quality', 'choice' and 'accountability' (DFE 1992a: 2–5). The 'Demystification of education' (1992a: 8) becomes an explicit part of the project.

The Thatcher Government from 1979 extended the demands for accountability, and however inadequate the evidence for relating national prosperity to details of educational provision, the search had begun to find ways of making education and training more effective (though the criteria of effectiveness have not, it will be argued, been clearly defined) without continuing to increase the cost.

One strand of accountability has been the need for education better to meet the demands of employers. The complexity of the labour market in post-industrial society appears to consist of two dominant features. One is high levels of unemployment as old labour-intensive industries decline and disappear. The other is a shortage of a highly skilled (and often transitorily required) workforce to staff new industries. The response to both has been to place increasing emphasis upon preparation for work among the young, which suggests that the problem rests not with the nature of social change but with the individuals in the labour market and with the systems of provision of training (Gleeson 1989: 2). Critiques of academic qualification routes as having limited relevance to productive work identify the enduring dominance of qualifications by traditionally privileged sectors of society (Dale and Pires 1984: 51–65). The cultural and social reproduction identified by Bourdieu and Passeron (1970) as the effect of education, may be illustrated in the characteristics of vocationally oriented provision, with 'not only differences in status, but also in teaching relations, curriculum and career opportunities' in tripartite Further Education (Gleeson 1989: 37).

There are tensions and polarities, then, operating within the labour market itself, and in attempts to relate employment and education. There are polarities too within the formulation of Conservative policy in the 1980s. Simons (1987: 4), Quicke (1988: 5–20), Whitty (1990: 24–8) and Chitty (1989: 211–19) draw attention to the neo-liberal and neo-conservative elements operating within Conservative policy. In education and training these markedly different strands of opinion have emphasized different approaches. The neo-conservatives have been centrally concerned with maintenance of standards (the term 'standards' is so variously used in educational discussion that a section of Chapter 10 is devoted to it) by which they often mean a stratified provision dividing academic and vocational education (Ranson 1984: 239). The neo-liberals have been concerned with creating more effective conditions for the operation of a competitive market in education.

Both of these approaches are currently identifying themselves as consistent with the use of specific educational objectives. Such objectives are compatible with assessments which may serve either the purposes of neo-conservatives or of neo-liberals, or indeed, both at once.

> The interesting point about the role of assessment, or more accurately, testing, in a New Right discourse, is that it bridges between a neo-liberal free-market concern, for the making of comparisons between schools and teachers, in order to facilitate informed parental choice, and the neo-conservative distrust both of teachers and of new teacher-based forms of assessment.
>
> (Ball 1990: 52)

In a fixed, 'standards'-led conception of education and training, objectives exist to ensure that past notions of acceptable performance are met. In some subject areas the cultural value systems are very visible. The National Curriculum in English, for example, has enshrined notions of standard English, cursive handwriting, the study of Shakespeare and explicit knowledge about language (DES 1990d). The National Curriculum history presents English history as the culmination and centre of its construction of the subject (DES 1991a). These content decisions have been acknowledged as produced under a close commentary from the Secretary of State (Cox 1991: 3–13), and derive to some extent from traditional constructions of subject content. A 'standards' model (in a neo-conservative sense) uses objectives primarily as a vehicle for influencing content, with the most readily inferred purpose being to slow (or even arrest) the pace of social change.

By contrast, in a market model, objectives may be (though in Ball's analysis cited above, are not) part of a motivational system, where content is less important than skills. The neo-liberal agenda includes increasing participation in education and training, fostering flexibility and an 'enterprise' culture. These policies, though focused upon the market, are not inconsistent with improvements in access and equal opportunities policies. The 1980s saw the development of the Technical and Vocational Educational Initiative (TVEI). This was overseen by the Manpower Services Commission as part of the Employment Department. Its introduction was interesting in a number of ways. As an initiative that was to attract schools it marked part of a struggle between the Department of Education and Science and the Employment Department for influence in the school sector. Its introduction was announced by Margaret Thatcher herself (Chitty 1989: 46) which may be taken to indicate the importance the administration attached to it – and perhaps Thatcher's own level of approval of the initiative. Furthermore, although the introduction of a strongly vocationally oriented scheme into the school system (with categorical funding to attract schools in) was initially viewed with distrust, there were very productive developments at local level. Dale (1990: 42–66) suggests that the implementation of TVEI demonstrated a tension between diffuse and centralized models of structure and between educational and occupationalist ideologies. He suggested that the interaction between the Manpower Services Commission Model and the sites of implementation had considerable effects in how these tensions were resolved in practice.

Similarly, Morrison and Ridley (1989: 41–9) and Ball (1990: 70–99) identify two distinct strands in vocational education. One is concerned with training for specific occupational activities in a utilitarian, instrumental paradigm; the other reconstructionist, fostering transferable, problem-solving skills. Ideally the objectives are then part of an individual's motivational or target-setting system. It is the process of setting of objectives that is important. The difference between a system driven by 'specified objectives' and one where objectives are 'identified by those working directly with them', is approximately parallel with that suggested between quality control and quality development in education (Whale and Ribbins 1990: 167–79).

There may be tensions within the neo-liberal position, between competition on the one hand and enterprise on the other. A competitive view would foster comparable results to inform and drive the market-place, whereas an enterprise view would favour personal motivation and individual target-setting. Translated into practice, a competitive emphasis would favour testing in education as a means of providing consumers with information about school performance, whereas an enterprise emphasis would favour self-awareness as in the processes of drawing up a personal record for the National Record of Achievement document. It is then possible to see two dimensions within the neo-liberal positions of market. One strand of the neo-liberal approach finds expression in enterprise initiatives where process is the keynote. The other, like the neo-conservative approach, becomes intertwined with a bureaucratic, data-gathering function for the Department for Education. Collection of statistics is made possible by 'measurable' objectives.

The way neo-liberalism and neo-conservatism relate is by no means straightforward. The extent to which league tables of school results are a part of a market or conservative vision is unclear, though it could be argued that the purely market argument would allow schools to flourish or decline solely according to popularity without insisting on comparative data to guide that popularity. League tables of raw data are likely to favour the schools which form the traditional elite: selective schools and those in socially advantaged areas. Such tables may be used to legitimate traditional content and methodologies. An enterprise approach – as seemed to be suggested by Local Management of Schools (LMS) – might have fostered experimentation and development and allowed more responsiveness to consumer wishes. The prescription of curriculum and assessment under the 1988 Act ensured that such freedoms could not exist and laid the path for comparative league tables.

A move to consumerism has implications for other traditional bases of power, such as the professions. An important element in Thatcher Government policies was the erosion of professional power in general, and this can be seen operating in relation to teachers (Grace 1987; Grundy 1989; Grace 1991b: 3–16): ... 'concepts such as "directed time" have shattered the historical professional ethic . . .' (Grace 1991b: 8). Professions pose a threat to the market economy because of their internal systems of accountability and their monopoly of essential services. Making schools directly accountable to educational 'stakeholders' is one of the main effects of the Education Act 1988. 'Changing relationships are a characteristic of the impact of schemes [for LMS] at the boundary between schools and external interests' (Thomas *et al.* 1989: 7).

Higher Education, and its professional power, is also the focus of current change. Duke analyses a new discourse in all areas of universities' work, portrayed by some as a 'crisis' (1992: 15–27). The end of the binary divide between universities and polytechnics paves the way for greater equality in funding between the former sectors, and hence for increased competition. A more competitive teaching and research market has placed pressure upon some universities and departments substantially to increase student numbers to maintain historical levels of funding, and therefore created competition to attract students. The purpose of the changes was to increase participation rates to greater parity particularly with European Community countries, and also to challenge the hegemony of Higher Education. Not only will Higher Education be more responsive to the market, but also to NVQs, which at the higher levels are designed to impact upon its work. NVQs give awarding bodies, rather than institutions, power of award and control over quality. Quality control through NVQ competencies, through performance indicators and through academic audit, introduces objectives models into Higher Education, and extends the vision of a market driven and controlled by stated objectives throughout the whole of education. Much will depend upon which assessment paradigm, that of enterprise or of comparison, accompanies this 'objectives' movement.

All this begins to look like a very coherent, and coercive set of changes for education. At the heart of the opportunities represented by these changes appears to be the possibility of using objectives for personal/institutional motivation, development and self-assessment. At the other extreme is the coercive, external use of objectives, enshrining a set of neo-conservative political principles and enforcing them through bureaucratic data-gathering.

Control of education: the role of assessment in establishing a new order

The education reforms[1] of the Education Act 1988 and the Education (Schools) Act 1992 were designed to address educational control. Outlined here is an argument for seeing assessment, particularly, but not exclusively, in the form of National Curriculum assessment, as the key to the changes in control.

Prior to the 1988 Act it is possible to identify four significant agencies other than central government and the DES having control and influence over the work of teachers: the teacher unions, the Local Education Authorities (LEAs), Higher Education and the various associations representing particular curricular specialisms.

The unions' influence, most manifest in, but not confined to, salary negotiations, was tested by the industrial action of 1984–87. The action is generally regarded as unsuccessful: the 1980s according to Warnock, 'will go down in educational history as one of the most disastrous times in the relationship between the teaching profession and the public' (Warnock 1989: 107). The reasons for failure may be identified with governmental strength of purpose or with weaknesses deriving from disunity among the teacher unions (Pietrasik 1987: 188). An indication of the failure of the action was the unsuccessful call by unions to boycott the new GCSE examinations. The introduction of a new system of examinations with heavy reliance on teacher-assessed coursework intensified teachers' workload but also offered a reform which many secondary teachers considered long overdue in creating a more equitable system for qualifications at 16+. Teachers faced a dilemma of professional conscience. An identifiable period of anxiety in relation to assessment change had begun. It is documented in relation to GCSE by Radnor (1987) and Butterfield (1989) and it continues identifiably through the introduction of National Curriculum assessment (NFER/BGC 1991a,b; ENCA 1992a,b) and through the major changes to GCSE within six years of its inception to conform to the National Curriculum by 1994. The power of assessment anxiety, coupled with rhetoric of curriculum reform for greater equality (DES 1987b), has proved to be an important feature in the reduction of union capacity to organize united action. The competitive context introduced by LMS makes the individual school, rather than the LEA and the union, the unit of responsibility for a teacher; since the competitive market is to be informed and driven by assessment results, it would be possible to see assessment here in a very significant, even central, role in the attempt to remove union influence.

As the employers of teachers, LEAs have had substantial powers and influence. Their powers were reduced by changed representation on governing bodies by the Education (No. 2) Act 1986. The Education Reform Act 1988 was a turning point in the redefinition of the LEA's role (Audit Commission 1989). The White Paper, *Diversity and Choice*, signals a further challenge to the LEAs, anticipating an increase in Grant Maintained (GM) schools, and increased financial delegation to those remaining within LEAs (DFE 1992a: 31–6). As other powers are reduced, their role in curriculum leadership and advice inevitably changes, and central prescription of curriculum defines to a large practical extent the nature of their curricular role. Their training and advisory functions have changed along with new funding arrangements, and a context is now established in which nationally identified priorities will almost entirely guide their curricular work. Their functions in relation to primary assessment are similarly under national guidance, with their responsibilities related to training and coordination of moderation (SEAC 1990b). Their relationship to schools is changed by the need to sell services to individual schools rather than to hold a monopoly of provision and coordination. Thus they are in turn driven by the competitive market existing between schools, and inevitably responsive to the extent to which that competition is articulated through assessment results. Furthermore, they are in competitive situations among themselves, with their own performance in terms of national assessment results published as a national league table (*Times Educational Supplement*, 14 August 1992: 3). Their reduced powers through funding are still further constrained by the narrowly defined field in which they have now to deliver – and the measurement of that delivery will be National Curriculum assessment results.

The influence of Higher Education upon schools and teachers has been threefold. Firstly, the entry requirements to Higher Education exert direct influence over teaching and qualification routes (and resilient systems of prestige) in secondary education, and might also be argued to have insidious effects upon the shape and expectations of primary education. In some ways the current educational changes imposed by the Government present a paradox: they are on the one hand prescribing a secondary-style, academically-biased curriculum upon primary schools; on the other, increased participation rates in Higher Education have implied a competitive market and a need to widen and change the criteria of selection. In such a process there is the possibility of a redefinition of academic success which could have considerable impact in encouraging wider views of school curricula. In view of this paradox, there is no clear pattern emerging of how this strand of influence upon schools is likely to develop. The plan for a retrenchment in Higher Education numbers (CVCP 1993) seems, however, to indicate more than mere parsimony, and possibly signals a victory for a Conservative version of command economics over a market economic model with broader, flexible, consumer-led access.

The second strand of influence is through Initial Teacher Education/Training.[2] Secondary PGCE courses are now required to be increasingly school-based (DES 1992e). The Education Bill published in November 1993 heralded a Teacher Training Agency which will administer state funding for teacher training places. This would remove teacher training from the Higher Education Funding Council, and may indicate a range of policy intentions, ranging from a different (lower?) unit of resource for such training than for other Higher Education provision, to a phased dismemberment of Higher Education through what are initially identified as its out-lying areas. Licensed and articled routes to qualified teacher status have been designed to improve the supply of teachers and to end the monopoly of Higher Education in the preparation of teachers and as gatekeepers to the profession. The rationale for reducing the role of Higher Education is the demand for teachers in shortage areas outstripping supply, the appropriateness of on-the-job trainers and concerns about the progressivism that is sometimes claimed to permeate the existing courses:

> Schools should be free to employ graduates directly on leaving university. The present system obliges potential teachers to spend a year working for the largely worthless Graduate Certificate of Education. . . We should like to see 'educationists' . . . deprived of authority, either to train teachers or to impose their counsels on the classroom.
>
> (Hillgate Group 1986: 10, 15)

Proposed alternatives would be supported by competences, and raise the prospect, as Taylor (1991: 55–7) sees it, of a 'National Curriculum for Teacher Education'.

The third strand of influence is through the in-service education of teachers, in short course provision and through award bearing, usually higher degree, courses. Changes in funding have reduced the opportunity of teachers to participate in such courses (Rudduck 1992: 194), and the scope of provision is likely in future to be increasingly tailored to government-identified priorities and to immediate school needs. The separation of management and teaching as school activities (Mac an Ghaill 1992: 227–8) raises the likelihood of senior staff in schools seeking accreditation of management competencies under the standards drawn up by the Management Charter Initiative, and hence identifying their professional development as lying outside the educational research community, and higher degrees. These changes suggest a very circumscribed future for education departments in Higher Education, if at all, as objectives and assessment driven in tandem with schools and with other parts of the education service.

Professional associations related to areas of education or to school subjects also promote and disseminate ideas about educational practice. They have no automatic voice in current change. Their influence may be tenuous and short-lived. Following through the example of English, the Statements of Attainment allowed for responses to reading to be spoken or written (DES 1990d), which to some extent retains a view of aspects of the subject curriculum as integrated, in line with the central propositions of the National Association for the Teaching of English (NATE 1988). The cost and complexity, however, of devising assessments (other than teacher assessments) which can adequately reach such Statements of Attainments may make them susceptible to review. The tension that might be seen between the professional associations and the current centralization arises not only from different views of curriculum; it is indicative also of a tension between curricular breadth and considerations of convenience in applying 'standard', external assessment.

Overview

This discussion has not attempted to trace all the changes to which education is now subject, nor to be comprehensive in looking at the changing pattern of influence. It has, however, attempted to highlight some of the ways in which assessment (and objectives-based assessment) is a key part of the change. There are dangers in dividing discussion of assessment from the political context, for as Broadfoot pointed out 'the apparently objective endorsement of assessment' may be 'essentially a political act' (1979: 93). Inattention to the 'prevailing policy climate' might result in the incorporation of Records of Achievement into a system of control and surveillance (Broadfoot 1990: 214). 'Only by attempting to develop a deeper understanding of the forces that inform particular policies can we hope to anticipate fully their potential significance and so have a basis for action' (1990: 215). Grace, in commenting upon parallel changes in New Zealand, sees the separation of context and assessment as part of a focused political rhetoric:

> The creation of a moral panic about standards proceeds by a strategy of decontextualising measures of educational achievement from their history and their socio-economic context.
>
> (Grace 1991a: 272)

It is the problem of decontextualization that this chapter has attempted to point up, by suggesting that assessment is a key strategy for the implementation of changes that are not in the narrow sense educational. The changes are intended to have far-reaching consequences for society, in altering the role of at least one professional group and centrally defining their work. The tensions within New Right policies between a direct interventionist approach to curriculum and a market forces philosophy are, in the end, merely explanations of why those working in education are experiencing changes as contradictory and confused. The precise unpacking of which influence is dominant at any one time is probably less important than the net effect of destabilization of the education service and intensification of its workload. Both serve to introduce a fundamental New Right policy of reduction of professional power. It is in this context that assessments based on prescribed objectives (and in many cases limited-focus timed tests) need to be understood. In debates about what constitutes 'standards' and how they are to be raised, the New Right is about as divided as any other section of society. However, standards of education may not be their prime concern. Coercion and control of the education service would appear to be the more reliable effect of their policies.

3

THE GENERAL CERTIFICATE OF SECONDARY EDUCATION, 1986–93

The features of the new examination system were signalled by Sir Keith Joseph in public speeches in the first half of 1984. 'I conclude that it is a realistic objective to try to bring 80–90 per cent of all pupils at least to the level now associated with the CSE grade 4, i.e. at least to the level now expected and achieved by pupils of average ability in individual subjects . . .' There would be, he implied, 'standards of competence' not offered by the existing system, though his use of the term 'objectives' in the speech referred to the objective of raising standards rather than to educational objectives as such. The 'curriculum should be relevant to the real world'; there 'should be differentiation within the curriculum for variations in the abilities and aptitudes of pupils'. Further, 'We should move towards a greater degree of criterion-referencing in these examinations and away from norm-referencing' (Joseph, Speech at the North of England Conference, Sheffield, 6 January 1984). The central objectives of the examination system itself, 'enhancing standards, motivation and esteem' were to be achieved through the use of grade related criteria:

> to define more precisely for each subject, the skills, com-
> petencies, understanding and areas of knowledge which a

candidate must have covered, and the minimum level of attainment he [*sic*] must demonstrate in each of them if he is to be awarded a particular grade.

> (Joseph, Speech to the Assistant Masters and Mistresses
> Conference in Bournemouth, 16 April 1984)

These principles were recorded in *Better Schools*, published in March 1985:

> The Government is confident that the arrangements will improve both teaching and examining in schools and colleges. They will promote a much needed increase in those practical and other skills which will be demanded by the future pattern of employment. They will also improve the motivation of many pupils following examination courses, particularly those who at present may expect only modest results in GCE or CSE examinations . . .
>
> (DES 1985a: 32 para. 98)

A key factor in the relevance and improved achievement anticipated in GCSE was the coursework:

> By comparison with existing examinations, the national criteria place a new emphasis on oral and practical skills and course work, on reasoning and on the application, as well as the acquisition, of knowledge and understanding.
>
> (1985a: 30 para. 97)

Following its official introduction in June of 1985, the new examination system was to be in operation for the summer 1988 examinations, and the first candidates would therefore embark upon their courses in September 1986. A training programme began with the appointment by examining groups of 'subject experts' (Phase 1). The phased training for teachers began in January 1986 (Phase 2), to be followed by school-based in-service training (Phase 3) in July 1986, and syllabus-related training (Phase 4) in September 1986 to run concurrently with teaching for the examinations.

In March 1985, the National Criteria documents (DES 1985b) were published, providing the general criteria which were to govern the examination system, and the subject specific criteria which were to govern syllabuses in 20 subjects, and the subjects for which those were to be a template, as in the case of French which was also to provide the criteria for other modern languages.

The General National Criteria (DES 1985b) lay down the principle of the grading on a seven-point scale:

> Grades A, B and C will be linked to the standards of the previous O-level grades A, B and C; grades D, E, F and G will be similarly linked to CSE grades 2, 3, 4 and 5 ... The standards required in the GCSE examinations will be no less exacting than those required in the previous GCE O-level and CSE examinations. O-level and CSE, taken together, were originally designed for the upper 60% of the ability range by subject. GCSE is not to be limited in that way.
>
> (DES 1985b: para. 7)

Any apparent contradiction in this claim was to be resolved by the grade criteria which were 'being developed . . .' (para. 9). Draft grade criteria in key curriculum areas, English, Mathematics and Science, were subsequently rejected after a research study to attempt to link them to grades (Kingdon and Stobart 1988: 139–40). Performance matrices in relation to individual subjects were attempted, but also abandoned. The research of Good and Cresswell (1988) was essentially into scaling techniques and the relationship between judgemental and statistical scaling in the award of grades. It did not attempt to illuminate the, by then, thorny question of grade criteria.

The new examinations were required to provide both certification of achievement for school leavers at 16 and 'to serve as a basis for further study . . .' (para. 11). Candidates across the ability range must be 'given opportunities to demonstrate their knowledge, abilities and achievements: *that is, to show what they know, understand and can do*' (italics added). The monosyllabic style of this requirement assists it in concealing that it goes to the heart of all educational purposes and is by no means unproblematic in its achievement. 'Differentiated assessment' is the context, but the requirement has implications that are not bounded by differentiation.

The precedent was established of national prescription, and the examination syllabuses were to conform to certain general criteria in order to be accepted by the Secondary Examinations Council (SEC) established in 1983 to oversee the planned programme of examination reforms up to 18 +. The general aims of the course of study had to be stated, such aims defined as 'the educational purposes of following a course in the subject . . .' (para. 21.b). 'The assessment objectives (including a statement of the abilities to be tested)' were recommended to follow (para. 21.c) but were not there further defined. The parentheses prompt a question as to what else the assessment objectives were anticipated to cover, in addition to, or as an umbrella for, the statement of the abilities to be tested. In the Annex to the document, 'Glossary of Terms for a Single System of Examining at 16 +', this definition is given:

Assessment objectives
The term *assessment objectives* is used to describe the skills/ abilities which are measured and recorded for assessment purposes within a particular subject examination. Such *assessment objectives* should be expressed in terms of the observable and measurable behaviour which the achievement of the educational *aims* of a course in the subject is intended to bring about.

The term is defined in its plural only, which might suggest it only had a collective meaning. The use of the word 'describe' in the example above is not wholly clear in its intention, and seemed to prepare the way for something other than the somewhat behavioural definition that followed.

The new examinations were to have certain distinctive features in their assessment, particularly related to the assessment objectives: 'the scheme of assessment must reflect the assessment objectives . . .' (para. 19.e.ii); 'the principle of fitness for purpose must be observed' (para. 19.e); and accordingly, since the examinations are not to be designed only to test recall, but also understanding and skills, 'the scheme of assessment should normally offer an appropriate combination of board-assessed components and centre-assessed course work' (para. 19.e.iv).

Other principles which should govern all syllabuses and assessments would be the avoidance of 'political, ethnic, gender and other forms of bias' (para. 19.h); the bearing in mind of 'linguistic and cultural diversity' (para. 19.i); the use of 'clear, precise and intelligible' language in all parts of question papers (para. 19.j); and 'Awareness of economic, political, social, and environmental factors relevant to the subject should be encouraged wherever appropriate' (para. 19.k).

There were also requirements relating to the processes of

moderation, and to the inclusion of grade descriptions. Some of the requirements, as has been suggested above, are internally problematic, some are problematic in terms of how they were to be translated into syllabuses, and how they were to be monitored.

The assessment objectives were a central feature of the new examining system. It was the emphasis of the assessment objectives upon 'abilities' and 'skills' which determined the need for a coursework element, and which marked the greatest departure from the emphasis upon recall of knowledge and upon timed, written examinations. The assessment objectives were not, however, at the inception, seen to be the means by which the candidates were to be assessed, but rather guiding principles in devising suitable syllabuses and assessment procedures. The grade criteria were to provide the yardsticks for assessment and the problems in devising such criteria will be argued in Chapter 4 to have contributed to the demise of the 'Keith Joseph GCSE' of 1988, and the success of the Hillgate pressure group in establishing its model of a National Curriculum.

The history and context of the General Certificate of Secondary Education

It is possible to give an account of the history of public examining at 16+ which makes the introduction of GCSE seem a logical and unproblematic development.

Deriving from the University of London matriculation examinations introduced in 1838, and the considerable influence of universities upon schools, the GCE O-level examinations introduced in 1951, like the School Certificate Examinations from which they evolved, were dominated by tests of recall and written response. The narrow range of skills limited curriculum development, and gave inadequate recognition to the needs of those who would not enter Higher Education. The limited expectations of examination systems is reflected and perhaps lamented in this classification of purposes: 'a means of maintaining standards, . . . an incentive to effort . . ., an administrative device and . . . a tool of social engineering' (Morris 1961: 1–43). The Beloe Report of 1960 recommended that certification be introduced through a new examination for a larger group than the 20 per cent capable of the pass grades of the GCE O-level. A further 20 per cent might take four or more subjects in a new examination and the next 20 per cent might take one or more subjects (Secondary Schools Examinations Council 1960). In 1963 the first candidates began preparing for the Certificate of Secondary Education examinations, and in that year the *Examinations Bulletin*, Number 1 recorded that: 'The education service has accepted, though with mixed feelings, the inevitability of the Certificate of Secondary Education.' The fear was that the 'formalising effect' of examinations would damage the curricula of the Secondary Modern Schools (Secondary Schools Examinations Council, 1963: 1).

Despite the opportunities created by Mode 3 schemes (designed and assessed by teachers in schools) and the greater scope for involvement of teachers in the work of the CSE examination boards, the CSE was always in danger of being unduly shaped by the GCE, and had to compete with it for credibility. Studies which concluded that a CSE grade 1 might be harder to obtain than an O-level pass standard (Nuttall 1971; Willmott 1975) had little impact on popular images of the two examination systems. Examinations across a wide ability range were now dominated by recall, and little had been done to address vocational relevance. Moreover, widespread amalgamation and reorganization of schools along comprehensive lines in the 1970s exposed many problems in a dual system of examining in both the administrative and pedagogic spheres.

Matters of standards and comparability tended to dominate the study of examinations, whether it were the reliability of examinations within one examining system, as in the study of the effect of question choice in O-level examinations (Willmott and Hall 1975), or studies embracing both O-level and CSE (Willmott 1977). Monitoring standards over time, or between different examinations, by the use of reference tests, raises questions about the applicability of those tests at different periods of time, or their inclination more to the kinds of abilities relevant to one examination than another. Having an examination system with certain common features, and with stated 'assessment objectives' for each central subject area could open the way to more meaningful comparisons.

A Joint Examinations Sub-Committee of the Schools Council reported in 1975 and the Waddell Committee, established to explore any remaining problems, reported in 1978 (DES 1978). It was optimistic about the feasibility of a single system, but on its analysis of pilot 16+ schemes was in favour of differentiated examinations. Differentiation, it felt, would be essential for a system common to all public examination candidates, unlike the 16+ examinations which were attracting disproportionately few of the most or least able of the examined population and so could not provide satisfactory evidence in support of undifferentiated examinations. This was not an uncontroversial contention, and the Examining Groups are still exercised in monitoring differentiation.

In 1980 the GCE and CSE Boards Joint Council for 16+ National Criteria began its work, publishing draft subject criteria in 1981 and 1982 as the basis for a consultation exercise, and essentially laying the foundations that were to become, in many cases with little additional superstructure or alteration, the National Criteria of 1985. The Cockcroft Report (DES 1982) urged many of the educational reforms that opponents of existing examinations had long advocated, and doing so in the central area of Mathematics opened the way for change elsewhere. It endorsed assessment of 'perseverance' and 'inventiveness': 'Work and qualities of this kind can only be assessed in the classroom . . . over an extended period' (1982: 161). Sir Wilfred Cockcroft was appointed in November to the Secondary Examinations Council in the first stage of a restructuring exercise that abolished the Schools Council (formerly the Secondary Schools Examinations Council), signalling government commitment to change and to a more rapid, less research-oriented period of educational change.

The General Certificate of Secondary Education (GCSE) was introduced by an announcement to the House of Commons, on 21 June 1984, by the then Secretary of State for Education and Science, Sir Keith Joseph. It was to replace the Ordinary level General Certificate of Education examinations and the Certificate of Secondary Education examinations and was to be a common examination system for the great majority of the 16+ plus age group.

This is the relatively 'unproblematic' history of GCSE: a response to the unwieldiness of a dual system that, in any case, only sought to certificate 60 per cent of the school population, and a response to the difficulty of freeing the secondary curriculum from rote learning, transmission teaching and repetitive writing under the existing examination systems.

The more problematic history of GCSE is of greater relevance in discussing and explaining some of its internal inconsistencies. Despite what appears to be a long period of preparation, rumours were strong in April and May of 1984 that the plans for the new examination were to be abandoned. Agencies considered to have influence upon the Government's thinking had criticized the plans. The Centre for Policy Studies advocated the retention with minor amendments of 16 + examinations, and regarded the sweeping aside of all existing examinations for the age group as unnecessarily costly and extreme. The Centre was reported as dissatisfied with the speed with which satisfactory national criteria were supposed to have been identified, and was opposed to the compulsory course work elements (*The Times* 2 March 1984: col. 6c). Right-wing opponents of GCSE saw it as 'the natural result of comprehensivisation and the destruction of the grammar schools' (North 1987: 12), and 'actually the creation of educationists' (Worthen 1987: 27). Keith Joseph was regarded as either having allowed his concern with 'relevance' to have outweighed the arguments of his more traditionalist colleagues, or to have bowed directly to pressure from the education lobby. However, the concern with differentiation – another central tenet of Joseph's education policies – meant that GCSE required, across most subject areas, choices to be made about appropriate level of entry for each candidate. While the GCSE appeared to be a development of the common examining system that many teachers had argued for and examination boards had been preparing for several years, it also had certain features which appeared to satisfy the Secretary of State that standards could be more effectively monitored and raised.

Other than the most immediate and political circumstances that accompanied its introduction, questions arise as to how this 'objectives-based' and 'criterion-referenced' examination system should be viewed in relation to a history of educational objectives, and this opens up further perspectives.

The Assessment Objectives of the GCSE were not so drawn that they can be discussed solely or adequately within recognized studies of educational objectives. Their relationship to the curricular frameworks developed by HMI are further developed in Chapter 6. Their relationship to the taxonomy developed by Bloom and co-workers is developed in Chapter 4. Such analyses, however, offer only one dimension for understanding the ways in which an examination system articulates with ideas about education.

The assessment objectives of the GCSE (of 1988) do not exist
in isolation from ideological positions about education, and they
represented, for a time, the dominance of HMI's general vision of
curricular coherence and breadth. Their generality of expression
retained a liberal humanist view of curriculum and teaching: the
wider objectives of the system for greater participation are also
broadly liberal in intention and style. GCSE effectively placed more
reliance upon teachers by emphasizing course work: it was essentially a professional vision of curricular change. There were discor-
dant notes. The cascade training derived from 'fundamentally a
rational model that had validity for transmitting purely technical
information in a well-defined, stable and consensual context. For
GCSE both the task and the context were rather different' (Radnor
1987: 55). 'The pathway link between the "edifice" at the top of
the mountain – the panels and committees of the Examining
Groups and the SEC that collectively produced the ideology, the
philosophy and the syllabuses – and the field stations in the
valley – the chalk face – would appear to have been roughly hewn'
(1987: 65). There were tensions then apparent between a professional and a rationalizing vision for education, that were, along
with other elements of influence, to be worked out in the introduction of the National Curriculum.

The official monitoring which accompanied the introduction of
GCSE and its first examination in 1988 was generally favourable
in its conclusions. HMI acknowledges 'difficulties' in assessment of
oral work and other forms of course work (DES 1988a: 20), but
is generally sanguine about the curricular improvements facilitated:
'There has been considerable enrichment of the curriculum in years
4 and 5 . . .' (1988a: 16). Although 'urgent consideration and
action' is recommended for aspects of the examination system,
there is little evidence that developments in question style or
examining approach are in the minds of the Inspectorate. It is the
'system' that is under consideration (1988a: 37–8). The 'criteria'
for the construction of syllabuses are a matter of general approba-
tion in the report, and the assessment objectives not mentioned in
any context that seeks to analyse their role. 'Mark allocations
usually reflected the published assessment objectives, though there
was a tendency to give an undue proportion of marks for factual
knowledge as opposed to evaluation or other higher order skills'
(1988a: 23). The subordinate clause could be taken to signal the

relative unimportance that HMI proposed to attach to the weightings supposedly at the heart of reform. One of the final duties of the Secondary Examinations Council was to monitor and report upon the implementation of GCSE. It was unlikely that as custodian of itself on this occasion it would have found much to censure. It fell to the School Examinations and Assessment Council (SEAC) to produce the Report to the Secretary of State. SEC, we learn, hosted conferences for examiners (SEAC 1988: para. 16) with an important training dimension (para. 42). The Joint Council for the GCSE was active in setting up working parties and individual Examining Groups all have improvements in hand (1988: paras 6–14). It is the teachers who were to bear the burden of criticism: 'problems were said to arise, too, from the failure of some teachers to build assessed coursework into normal classroom activity or to consider, with their colleagues, the cumulative impact on pupils of individual subject demands' (1988: para. 22).

The GCSE remains in the National Curriculum context as the main vehicle of assessment at Key Stage 4. Its assessment objectives from 1994 in core subjects must conform to the National Curriculum attainment targets: 'For syllabuses in the foundation subjects, the question papers taken together must sample sufficient statements of attainment/strands at all levels to ensure valid and reliable assessment' (SEAC 1992c: para. 31). Differentiation by task becomes obligatory: 'Each scheme of assessment must involve papers – individually or in combination – targeted at different ranges of levels (tiers) in the 4–10 range. Candidates enter for a single tier in a syllabus in a particular examination sitting, unless subject criteria specify otherwise' (1992c: para. 14). For no identifiable reason of validity of assessment, the course work element is restricted: 'Each scheme of assessment must include an externally set and externally marked terminal examination. This examination must be allocated a weighting of at least 80% (at least 50% in modular syllabuses) except where subject criteria or other SEAC guidance indicate otherwise' (1992c: para. 10).

The changes required in GCSE, from 1994, represent something of the embattled context from which it came, and its attempts to reconcile different sets of influences. Its vulnerability was that it met the demands of no group adequately, although it won increasing support from teachers, and it did produce steadily improving examination results. This played into the hands of the standards lobby who claimed that improvements in results could only be at the expense of lowered standards of assessment. The 1992 GCSE results and the controversy around them will be discussed later in relation to the comparison of standards of performance. Such controversy provides further evidence of the extent to which the assessment of individual students has become inseparable from the larger politics of assessment.

4

THE NATIONAL CURRICULUM AND ASSESSMENT

The Education Reform Act 1988 established for England and Wales the outline of a statutory curriculum, and endowed the Secretary of State for Education with extensive powers (in this matter as in others covered under the Act) over the curriculum: 'to establish a complete National Curriculum as soon as it is reasonably practicable ... and to revise that Curriculum whenever he considers it necessary or expedient to do so' (Education Reform Act 1988: 4.1). Moreover, the Act gives an indication of the level of detail that is to be prescribed centrally, as well as the interrelationship between the Curriculum and its assessment: 'The Secretary of State may by order specify in relation to each of the foundation subjects: (a) such attainment targets; (b) such programmes of study; and (c) such assessment arrangements; as he considers appropriate for that subject (Education Reform Act 1988: 4.2). The Act therefore gives a very high level of detailed control of the Curriculum to central government, with each new Secretary of State (of whatever political persuasion) having statutory powers to make specific or widespread changes on no more than the grounds of 'expediency'.

The initial discussion of this chapter will be based upon the design and detail of the curriculum as created by the 1988 Act and by the original sets of Statutory Orders issued under the Act. The short history (to date) of the National Curriculum has also been a history of rapid revisions, and at the time of writing the curriculum and its assessment is undergoing a fundamental revision, following the Dearing review of 1993. The need for this revision is in itself important, in that it can be seen as reflecting upon the processes by which the National Curriculum and assessment have been introduced, and on the policy intentions themselves. The details of the revision, likewise, cast light on some of the conceptual flaws of the Government's intention to produce a readily measurable set of standards of performance without sufficient initial consultation. The latter part of the chapter will consider these revisions.

Characteristics of the National Curriculum

The characteristics of the National Curriculum itself can be broadly divided into its shape as a system of progression (most closely linked to the arrangements for assessment), its shape as a grouping of subject areas (linked to assessment and curriculum audit), its claimed social effects and its claimed educational characteristics.

The shape of the National Curriculum is essentially described through the model proposed by the Task Group on Assessment and Testing (TGAT) and it was their Report on assessment which determined the working characteristics of the curriculum. TGAT proposed a model of 10 levels within each of the subjects proposed by the Education Bill. They also proposed that the Attainment Targets be grouped into profile components for reporting rather than simply aggregated overall for each subject (DES 1987c: paras 93–122). The levels would be assessed on an on-going basis by teachers, and at Key Stages (defined by ages 7, 11, 14 and 16, and laid down for TGAT in their terms of reference).

TGAT's proposal was linked to graded objectives, and the idea that levels can be clearly defined within any given area of attainment. This is a notion linked to behavioural and mastery learning approaches. SEAC training materials published in 1989 for primary schools use the term 'mastery', though there is also a disclaimer of 'mastery learning' as such (SEAC 1990a: 56–7). The

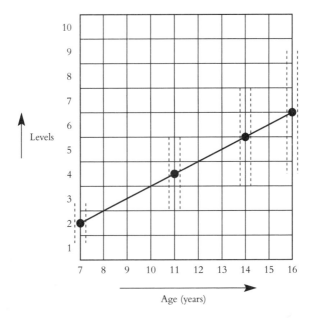

Figure 4.1   Task Group on Assessment and Testing model of progression in the National Curriculum. Sequence of pupil achievement of levels between ages 7 and 16. The solid line gives the expected results for pupils at the ages specified. The dashed lines represent a rough speculation about the limits within which about 80 per cent of the pupils may be found to lie. *Source:* DES 1987c.

grouping of Attainment Targets into profile components is conso-nant with the approach advocated in Records of Achievement, and in vocational profiling, that stated objectives provide a disag-gregated account, which is inherently different from aggregation into a grade or mark, or holistic reporting of overall qualities. The aggregation of levels is logically inappropriate and therefore raises a number of practical problems in working examples, by obscuring differences between students, by losing diagnostic information about strengths and weaknesses and by creating situations where some Attainment Targets contribute nothing to the overall score.

TGAT claimed that their model could provide diagnostic/formative information about individuals, as well as summative information, and evaluative information about the work of classrooms, schools and LEAs. The notion that their model, or any single model, is capable of fulfilling those requirements through one and the same set of processes has been questioned (Nuttall 1988; Gipps 1990: 98).

The basic curriculum was prescribed in terms of subjects by the 1988 Act. It comprised Religious Education, the core subjects of Mathematics, English and Science, and the foundation subjects of History, Geography, Technology, Music, Art and Physical Education (Education Reform Act 1988: 3). Within each subject, the Secretary of State has powers to prescribe the Attainment Targets, programmes of study and assessment arrangements.

The claimed social effects of the National Curriculum are summarized in the Consultation Document (DES 1987b), where there is emphasis on matters relating to entitlement: on transfer between schools; more explicit and appropriate expectations; 'access to the same good and relevant curriculum'; and 'checking on progress' for diagnostic purposes (1987b: 3). It is also to increase the accountability of schools and to raise 'standards'.

The issues are individual educational issues as well as social issues, and the introduction of the National Curriculum and assessment has been accompanied by a number of studies which have attempted to evaluate the effects upon particular groups of students. Those identified as being vulnerable are students with special educational needs, students whose first language is not English, pupils at Key Stage 1 who have not reached the age of seven (i.e. who are young among their year group), students who are socially disadvantaged (NFER 1991b; ENCA 1992b) and pupils at Key Stage 1 who have not had nursery experience (ENCA 1992b). Since these features of low achievement belong to a different social and political agenda from that prevailing within the introduction of testing, the influence of such findings may be limited.

The Consultation Document includes in its justification of a National Curriculum the importance of 'entitlement': 'ensuring that all pupils study a broad and balanced range of subjects . . . ensuring that all pupils, regardless of sex, ethnic origin and geographical location, have access to broadly the same good and relevant curriculum' ... (DES 1987b: para. 8). The claims around this require two main kinds of investigation: firstly, in terms of whether the National Curriculum actually establishes such entitlement or not, and secondly in terms of whether the mode of control of curriculum does or does not support entitlement. The first issue is being widely addressed in research and evaluation studies, and some of these will be outlined in Chapter 11. The second issue is inherently more difficult to research, because it cannot be measured in terms of whether individual pupils are achieving appropriately against the given curriculum. It involves rather the effects on learners of the central control of curriculum and assessment, and of the operation of a market in education. Within that context, the wider messages of 'assessment' and the implications of those messages for teachers and learners may have as much role to play in student entitlement as any particular details of curriculum. Assessment, based upon stated and behaviourally conceived objectives, has been the fulcrum of both central control, and the operation of a market economy in education.

History and context

As with the GCSE, there are various levels at which the historical context of the National Curriculum can be discussed. It may be historically located within the policy of a particular government, or as a resolution of differing views within a particular administration (Whitty 1990; Chitty 1989; Lawton 1988, 1989) and as a continuation of a thread of post-war centralization policy in education spanning Conservative and Labour governments (Ranson 1988). It marks a significant stage in the attempts to remove education from academic control and influence, along with a reduction of the political influence of Local Education Authorities. As such, the particular centralization that it indicates has profound political origins, and may be located in a period of major post-industrial change, as well as within the particular party political context of current governments. It can also, however, be seen as refocusing fundamental educational problems, particularly about progression, breadth and relevance.

The diversity of schools within the state sector, in terms of size and organization, was an issue for HMI in the 1970s. Such diversity may be seen as justifying the kind of work carried out by HMI, as a flexibly operating, liberally oriented inspectorate (Thomas 1986). Lawton (1986) contrasts the professional framework of HMI with the bureaucratic, centralizing interests of the DES. Curriculum 5–16 (DES 1985c) offers a framework which suggests that diversity can be sustained provided there are common characteristics in curricula. This document outlines the curriculum characteristics of breadth, balance, continuity, relevance, differentiation and progression. *Aspects of Secondary Education* (DES 1979) also stressed coherence. These characteristics could be seen as providing one of the dimensions of the HMI curriculum, the quality dimension to adopt one mode of description. It complements the other curricular dimension advocated by HMI, which might loosely be called the content dimension, outlined in curriculum 11–16 (DES 1977) as the eight areas of experience – later nine[3] (DES 1985c) which should be covered in the curriculum available to all pupils. The dimensions are not of course separate, since curricular breadth, for example, is to be achieved through a coverage of the areas of experience. These areas are not elaborated in detail, and this could be seen as a strength within a professional consensual framework, but a weakness in a more bureaucratic model.

HMI's thinking is fundamentally different from that which emerged in the Education Act 1988. Nonetheless, HMI had established a language which was sufficiently general (and liberal) to be adopted for other purposes and colonized with other meanings. Claims of commonality (DES 1977), breadth and balance were to attach to the National Curriculum model. In this transition of language, the weakness of the liberal humanist model, as proposed by HMI, is revealed. Its language and concepts are loosely defined and capable of co-option and distortion. The inadequacy of assuming that there is a national consensus about what constitutes balance in the curriculum is evidenced by the ease with which claims of balance could be used in other documents, with other purposes. HMI intended that agreement would emerge through discussion among professionals: they suggested that 'agreement could be reached nationally' (DES 1977: 5). Such professional process is necessarily slow; the speed of introduction of the National Curriculum and assessment appears to render that model inoperable. The DES's language implies continuity with HMI's proposals while in fact establishing a radically different model.

James Callaghan's Ruskin College speech expressed concerns which have explicit resonances with the Education Act 1988. The speech signalled a more pragmatic relationship with industry, particularly in the claim that Science should be more technological and less academically oriented (Moon *et al.* 1989: 273). The questioning of poor participation of girls in non-compulsory Science signals the move towards a compulsory/entitlement curriculum. The questioning of the full subscription of Humanities courses as against undersubscription of Science and Engineering courses in Higher Education indicates unease about the liberal underpinnings of the educational establishment. Informal teaching methods are questioned (1989: 273), and there is a call for accountability to specific groups of stakeholders: 'To the teachers I would say that you must satisfy the parents and industry ...' (1989: 276). Its suggested remedies are a 'basic curriculum' with 'universal standards' and it raises the possibility of a separate non-academic post-16 curriculum. The speech urged the need for a 'debate' (1989: 274) though in retrospect it appears to have set the agenda for change. Its clear links with the National Curriculum, and with the development of vocational qualifications, make it a landmark in the surface history of current educational change.

A further, related factor which lies behind the introduction of the National Curriculum was dissatisfaction with the GCSE. This came from groups which might be seen as representing both neo-conservative and liberal educationist concerns. The former found expression in a book published in 1987 called *The GCSE: An Examination*. This attacked the move away from traditional subject descriptions and what was called the 'politicisation' of education in that subjects such as Science were related to social, economic and environmental factors (North 1987: 171–98). On the other hand, the GCSE was also criticized for its failure to promote the equality that it had promised (Radnor 1988: 37–48).

There were other features of the original GCSE which made it vulnerable. Its criterion-referencing was to a broad set of (liberal humanist) assessment objectives in each subject, and these reflected in turn a broad set of principles about common learning experiences. Hence there is no hierarchy of objectives: what might be regarded as higher level achievements – such as evaluative judgement – are where appropriate to the syllabus, general assessment

objectives across the grades. The breadth of the necessary interpretation of assessment objectives, to encompass the wide range of
achievement from the highest to lowest grade award, made it possible to argue that this was not in any meaningful sense criterion-
referencing. It was intended at the outset to develop more detailed
criteria for each grade (DES 1985b: para. 21 h). However, the
initial work on this demonstrated that the lists would be unworkably long (a lesson that seems to have been overlooked by government in setting up the National Curriculum). GCSE therefore
continued to use its loosely-framed grade descriptions, and
therefore did not provide the more detailed information about
the meaning of grades that the public and employers had been
promised. It did not penetrate, therefore, the professional control
of educational standards in the way that its introduction had
intended, and course work assessment actually increased the direct
control of teachers over the examining process.

> In this respect the National Curriculum can be viewed as a
> reaction against GCSE, with weaknesses in GCSE used as one
> excuse for an attack upon the notion of a common examina-
> tion system. Because GCSE was identifying assessment objec-
> tives which described cognitive (and sometimes affective and
> psychomotor) achievement rather than subject content, it also
> opens questions about a common curriculum not only in
> terms of the subject curriculum itself, but also in terms of the
> kind of commonality that underlies experience across the
> curriculum.
>
> (Butterfield 1992: 202)

GCSE may have increased professional control, but that control
was being used in ways that did not necessarily inhibit the opportunities of students. It placed a renewed emphasis upon study skills,
use of library and other resources for learning, upon independent
learning with teacher as facilitator and upon students becoming
more questioning and active in their learning. The focus was much
more on transferable skills than was the case with GCE and CSE
examinations, and the kind of learning associated with GCSE was
not logically isolable within individual classrooms or subject boundaries. Much of this resonated with the changes occurring in
response to the development of the Technical and Vocational

Educational Initiative. The two innovations developed in tandem in the second half of the 1980s.

GCSE had its role to play in opening up interdepartmental discussion within schools. At a practical level, departments have needed to cooperate to determine timing of respective project work to avoid overload in the final weeks of the course. More fundamentally, GCSE appeared to raise large issues about the nature of the secondary Curriculum by altering the status of subject knowledge within the definition of subjects and of assessment objectives. Opponents responded: GCSE was accused of a 'more or less wholesale abandonment of the idea of education as an initiation into existing forms of worthwhile knowledge and understanding' (O'Hear 1987: 117). Such objections also expressed themselves in the successful political lobbying, particularly by the Hillgate group, seen as instrumental in establishing the statutory National Curriculum (Quicke 1988; Chitty 1989: 216; Whitty 1990: 26).

A further context for the National Curriculum is the integrity of the 1988 Act. Maclure identifies the National Curriculum with the kind of control needed to balance the move to a competitive market in educational provision:

> The argument behind the 1988 Act is that it is only possible to take the risks inherent in setting schools free of the local authorities' leading reins if there is a clearly defined National Curriculum in being, and if the Secretary of State has the power to prescribe and police it.
>
> (Maclure 1989: xi)

The tension between a competitive system and central control is, in this analysis, resolved by the National Curriculum. Similar, and more detailed analyses are suggested by Whitty (1990: 24–8), in sketching a tension between neo-conservative opposition to progressivism and neo-liberal wishes to create a market economy for education. The conservative elements of the National Curriculum are linked back to the revised code of 1862 by Moon (Brighouse and Moon 1990: 13) and to the 1904 Board of Education's prescribed syllabus for secondary schools by Aldrich (1988: 22). Lawton (1989: 47–52) sees two strands within contemporary Conservative party thinking (privatization and minimalism/segregation) as having been particularly influential in bringing pressure on the then Secretary of State for Education, Kenneth Baker, in the drafting of the Reform Bill. While the privatizers 'in a fairly extreme form would advocate the dismantling of the whole state education service or gradually privatising the system', the minimalists 'support a state education service which concentrates on the basics . . . suspicious of frills such as art and music, and hostile to political and economic awareness seeing them as potentially subversive' (Lawton 1989: 48–50).

These analyses draw upon political, not educational accounts of the National Curriculum, for the obvious reason that the genesis of the National Curriculum does not have an 'educational' history. It was not the product of evolving thought about the curriculum. Indeed it ran counter to the principles that HMI had been developing in their Red Books. It was designed to take education out of the hands of 'educationists' and to free it from 'theory'. The National Curriculum is primarily meaningful as a resolution of competing policy claims within government, and the language but not the meanings of HMI have been adopted by the DES to describe its characteristics. The assessment arrangements similarly reflect the atheoretical policy model: 'there is no empirical basis for this model; no theory of learning, no theory of curriculum was invoked to justify any of these figures – they are, to an extent, arbitrary' (Nuttall 1988: 231).

A tension has existed through the history of the National Curriculum between the policy of control and the policy of markets, and the attempts to maximize the educational/diagnostic potential of the Task Group on Assessment and Testing proposals. The development of Standard Assessment Tasks at age seven (Key Stage 1) was put out to tender and three agencies were involved in the first pilots using different models but all developing materials which would sample widely through the attainment targets, provide detailed profile information and have high degrees of construct and content validity. The aim was that such materials would not only be suitable for calibration of teacher assessments, since they were close in kind and range to the activities which teachers were likely to assess as they worked through the programmes of study, but also that they provided staff development opportunities (Robinson 1990).

The SAT run at Key Stage 1 in 1991 provided evidence of a number of issues. The results of the evaluation suggested that there were differences between SAT results and teacher assessments

(NFER 1991a and 1991b; ENCA 1992a and 1992b) and this has been used as an argument against giving more weight to teacher assessments in order to reduce the volume and range of SATs used, which would have been one option in order to simplify the task and reduce the time required. The discrepancies between SATs levels and teacher assessments could have been explained by teachers' unfamiliarity with the work and the levels in the first year of the National Curriculum assessments, and by the fact that there was inevitably a time lag between the carrying out of the teacher assessments and of the SATs.

Colin Robinson, as Head of Evaluation and Monitoring with SEAC, described there as being 'an almost universally held view that the amount of time that teachers are having to give to the SAT assessment is too great – possibly twice as much as would be reasonable', and he outlined the following possible strategies:

> a reduction in the number of Attainment Targets addressed in the SAT
>
> or
>
> a reduction in the number of Statements of Attainment addressed in the SAT
>
> or
>
> a reduction in the number of pupils assessed in the SAT
>
> or
>
> a reduction in the number of contexts used
>
> or
>
> a combination of some or all of the above.
>
> (Robinson 1990: 4)

He went on to say that 'manageability . . . is currently our highest priority' (1990: 5).

Each of the options outlined by Robinson has very different implications for the relationship between teacher assessments and testing, and for the relationship between a professional model of educational assessment and a model of governmental control. These are as follows:

To sample more selectively across Attainment Targets (ATs)

This would retain the sophistication of the pilot SATs but might, depending on exactly what model was adopted, place more reliance on teacher assessment. This would mean that some ATs were left entirely to teachers to assess, possibly those that required careful classroom observation. This might lead to the neglect of some areas of the curriculum, if teachers began to 'teach to the test'. To support curricular breadth, a continuing high level of support and in-service training would be needed and a strong procedure for moderation of teacher assessments other than through SATs. The model for moderation proposed by TGAT could have been adapted for this.

To sample across children

The SATs would then become a moderating device. Again the SATs could retain sophistication and content and construct validity. They could cover more ATs than in the first option. Again this would, in practice, throw greater reliance upon good teacher assessment, but it would be more comprehensively moderated across ATs than in the first option.

To alter the SATs to make them easier to administer by reducing the number of contexts used

This has some consonances with the first option since any simplification of SATs implies a reduction of the ATs which they can validly sample. (In practice this was addressed by altering the curriculum documents in Mathematics and Science, reducing the number of ATs, so that sampling across ATs appeared more comprehensive with less actual penetration of the full range of curricular activity.)

The option chosen was the third, which is a control, rather than an educational, option since it reduces the role of teacher assessment, and retains a view of assessment as relatively unproblematic and capable of external standardization. In practice the SATs at seven had an increasing proportion of written response in 1992 and 1993 than in 1991, and Key Stage 3 tests in 1993 were written in response mode and in presentation mode. This move towards recall, writing and de-contextualized application can be seen as further evidence that the fundamental intention of the National Curriculum is not about development or better diagnosis. The reduction of curricular validity of the assessment is consistent with an unsophisticated information-gathering exercise for the publication of 'results' and the creation of league tables of schools. The restriction of the influence of teacher assessment upon the aggregated 'result', in relation to the TGAT proposals and in relation to the possible options available to redress problems with the 1991 pilots, was consistent with a philosophy of control of professional work. A related (but reductive) argument is that teachers could not be making fair judgements of pupils when the survival of their schools and their own jobs depended upon the outcomes.

The option of sampling across children might best have matched the needs for wide curricular validity and for manageability. This possibility could have drawn upon the past work of the Assessment of Performance Unit (APU), established in 1974 by the DES to monitor the achievement of school pupils in England, Wales and Northern Ireland. Its surveys used carefully developed testing materials, often requiring observation of pupils carrying out tasks rather than paper-and-pencil modes of presentation and response, in order validly to assess the component parts of what constituted particular parts of the curriculum. Some of the testing was therefore time-consuming (the cost of valid assessment) and only appropriate for light sampling. The rejection (to date) of sampling procedures of this kind to endorse teacher assessment for the National Curriculum reflects a wish for blanket testing more than a wish to retain a broad curriculum supported by appropriate assessment arrangements. That blanket testing arguably serves a dual policy role. It reduces the status of teacher assessment and provides a superficial appearance of rigour in modelling the patterns of traditional examinations. It is not, however, necessary to achieving the claimed educational purposes of the National Curriculum assessments, which could be more validly assessed by a combination of teacher assessment and light sampling across pupils using moderation tasks.

Manageability, then, could have been achieved in other ways, without sacrificing aspects of curricular coverage. 'Manageability' begins to look like a coded message about something else: less about concern with classrooms and more about concern with central management control of the education system. The emphasis on the management possibilities of the National Curriculum is also signalled in the then Secretary of State's wish to 'give a clear incentive for weaker schools to catch up with the best and the best will be challenged to do even better' (Secretary of State's Speech to the North of England Conference, 6 January 1989).

In looking at the intended characteristics of the National Curriculum, there are multiple dimensions, and the issue arises of whose intentions are being considered. On the one hand, there is the Government's policy of control realized through DFE information gathering about performance based on a set of objectives. For the DFE the priority may be fulfilling its function of being able to gather statistical information about education, and for the Government, the priority may be the creation of a market as a policy view about how standards are raised. For those working in education a different set of intentions, about entitlement and progression may have priority, but these have been difficult to sustain because they belong to the legitimating rhetoric of the introduction of National Curriculum, and not to its actual policy intentions. Whitty speaks of the governmental view that "'the liberal establishment'" had been 'culpable for pulling a fast one over the government with the GCSE' (1990: 25). The history of the National Curriculum suggests a more determined governmental attitude that educational arguments – those from education professionals – shall not prevail over policy intentions of central control and professional accountability.

A little fine-tuning?

The pilot SATs at Key Stage 1 demonstrated that the curriculum in Science and Mathematics was overelaborate in its structure of Attainment Targets. Subsequently, the number of Attainment Targets in Science was reduced from 17 to four, and in mathematics from 14 to five. If overload and the difficulty of assessing across so many targets was the most visible problem, it was by no means the only one. By 1993 a major review was undertaken, leading to new Orders for each of the National Curriculum subjects. The review of the National Curriculum (Dearing 1993b) reflects the political tensions underlying processes of coercion of teachers by government-imposed change. Dearing acknowledges – at least as a technical issue – the problem of communication between the centre and the schools (Dearing 1993a: 62). The almost total boycott of Key Stage 3 tests in Mathematics, Science,

English and Technology in 1993 represented the largest stand against the Government by teachers since the industrial action of the mid-1980s. Trade union law made it essential that the teachers' case be presented in terms of unreasonable workload, rather than fundamental weaknesses in the curriculum and testing. Therefore, 'slimming down of the curriculum' becomes one way of meeting the overt cause of dissatisfaction and to some extent, of diverting attention from deeper problems – of both curriculum and coercion. Manageability is again the keynote of the Secretary of State's concerns about assessment arrangements (Dearing 1993a: 47).

However, some central areas of the curriculum design (and, indirectly, issues about curriculum control) come under the scrutiny of the review. The National Curriculum progression model based upon 10 levels and 10 ages from seven to 16 gives what speciously appears to be a graph of progress, defined by the Statements of Attainment (SoAs). This is not drawn from any evidence, as Nuttall (1988) has pointed out, nor does it represent, as the Task Group acknowledged (DES 1987c: para. 93), any theoretical model or research findings about changes in cognitive functioning that occur during those ages. In practice there are considerable differences between a *developmental* model and this one. There are, moreover, areas where the development required between one putative level and another is considerable; others where the levels are defined only by differences of content, and not by any developmental factors as such.

A number of considerations inform Dearing's discussion of the 10-level scale, not least that to move away from it at this point would be a (further?) step into the unknown and

> a move away from the scale could prejudice the implementation of the new Orders . . . The timetable for this introduction . . . is . . . very tight indeed. I regard the task of slimming the curriculum down and freeing up time to be used at the discretion of the teacher as the fundamental outcomes of the review. This task must be completed quickly in order not to protract debilitating uncertainty.
>
> (Dearing 1993b: para. 7.59)

All in all, Dearing's vision is of a more teacher-controlled curriculum and perhaps in that context the 10-level scale, so necessary surely to emphasize the differences in achievement that the Government wishes to publish, seems a less crude instrument. An important distinction that Dearing makes is between the kinds of problems that are caused by ,the scale itself, and the problems caused by the very large number of statements of attainment within each attainment target:

> The problem lies, rather, with the attainment targets and the statements of attainment. [However] A simple reduction in the number of statements of attainment may not be the best way to deal with the problems currently being experienced. The opportunity might, rather, be taken to gather the main statements of attainment into clusters to create a more integrated description of what a pupil must know, understand, and be able to do at each level.
>
> (Dearing 1993b: para. 7.24/7.29)

The other emphasis of Dearing 'freeing up time to be used at the discretion of the teacher' is a highly significant move away from the heavy central prescription. Its strongest effects are likely to be experienced at Key Stage 4, where flexibility is introduced through the notion of 'short courses' in Technology and Modern Languages as alternatives to full National Curriculum subjects. History and Geography become optional at this level,

> absorbing and valuable subjects. But I cannot see a reason, either nationally or in terms of the individual student, why these subjects should, as a matter of law, be given priority in this key stage over others, such as the creative arts, a second foreign language, home economics, the classics, religious studies, business studies or economics.
>
> (Dearing 1993b: para. 5.25)

The other effect of 'freeing up', apart, that is, from allowing more space in the curriculum for wider academic options, is the greater opportunity for vocational routes. Significant too, is where Dearing locates this new curriculum power: 'These are general recommendations. Specific decisions on choice of pathways and subjects are best left to students, parents and schools' (Dearing 1993b: para. 5.27).

It is also important to consider some of the problems not identified by the Secretary of State for review. The National Curriculum

ATs and SoAs are pragmatically derived; they are based on a functional analysis approach. However this analysis was not carried out 'in the workplace'. It did not involve observation of students and teachers. Even though its objectives may not be individually unreasonable, the pragmatic approach breaks down because it has included more than can reasonably be done all together. The tendency of users of even rigorous functional analysis to add to the analysis has been documented by Webster (1991), in relation to the drawing up of NVQ competencies. At the other end of the age range, evidence from the USA suggests that pressure on performance and screening in early grade classes is causing 'continued escalation of curriculum' (Shepard and Smith 1988: 135). There is known to be a direct link between the prescription of objectives and a tendency to overload. This may in part be addressed by Dearing's move to level descriptions which is potentially a significant shift from an objectives model, back to something more closely resembling the original GCSE model of, in that case, grade descriptions.

The objectives are not operating within any overall statement about educational purpose. The National Curriculum has no overarching statement of its educational aims, nor is there any statement of the educational contribution each subject area is intended to make. It appears to be an entirely descriptive (and prescriptive) curriculum account. The ATs define what the subject is but not its purpose. This is again in keeping with a pragmatic model, and a conservative model based on existing practice. It does not make use of the objectives model for what is one of its major potential functions, to explore purpose and intention and to make closer matches between those and curricular activity.

The less than satisfactory ordering of ATs in some cases may represent the novelty of this kind of approach, the multiple requirements placed upon working parties and inherent features of the subject areas (Cox 1991: 113). Also, the difficulties of integrating a supposedly progressive series of levels with a content-based curriculum and the overall arbitrariness of a 10-level framework. The implications of this arbitrariness become more serious in relation to the levels being used as a basis for judgements about teaching and schools, and possibly for the placing of pupils in particular teaching groups. The loss of information involved has been outlined by Cresswell and Houston (1991) who recommend a profile-reporting system as more valid than current aggregation and similarly by Brown (M. Brown 1991) who suggests that the inaccurate picture of achievement gained through reporting the median of achievements levels across ATs leaves nothing to be gained by aggregated reporting prior to Key Stage 4.

The move from a dominant concern with curricular validity to the 'manageability' of the current test developments for National Curriculum, at both Key Stage 3 and Key Stage 1, suggests that the proposed educational meaning of an objectives structure is largely being abandoned. The analysis of the curriculum into objectives is now being replaced by a resynthesis into the kinds of assessment traditionally associated with written activities and single grades.

Chapter 11 considers how these issues are being studied and evaluated. A major concern, however, must be the different kinds of question and issue raised by the National Curriculum assessments, which are at one and the same time making large technical claims for validity and reliability of assessment and operating within a highly charged political context. It is difficult, as Dearing has demonstrated, to carry out a review which looks purely at curricular and assessment issues, without acknowledging such factors as the locus of control in education. On the other hand, there is a danger that problems with the National Curriculum and assessment come to be seen only as 'local', matters relating to specifics about the design or content of subject curricula, or to the 10-level scale. There is then a view that what is needed is more experience or some fine-tuning. That does not address the larger questions of where the National Curriculum is aiming in educational terms. This curriculum – and most of all its assessment arrangements – rests on one central tenet: that it is the relationship between education and other parts of society (government on the one hand; consumers on the other) that must be changed. Studying the details of the curriculum and assessment in practice does not necessarily keep that larger claim in focus.

5

NATIONAL VOCATIONAL QUALIFICATIONS

A National Council for Vocational Qualifications (NCVQ) was set up by the Employment Department following the publication of a White Paper *Working Together* (DES 1986b). The Council has established two new qualifications: National Vocational Qualifications (NVQs), designed to be operational in 1991 and to cover '90% of the work-force occupations by the year 1995' (FEU 1994: 20) and General National Vocational Qualifications (GNVQs), piloted for some occupational areas in 1992 and designed to cover the main occupational areas by 1996.

Although these two qualifications have some major similarities in their overall conception – particularly in that they are built on a principle of credit accumulation for individual units, and assessed according to specified outcomes, there are also differences between them which may make their introduction – and possibly their effects – distinct. Whereas NVQs have as a very important principle workplace-based assessment, GNVQs 'are designed for delivery in full-time education with limited access to the workplace' (NCVQ 1993: 5). And whereas NVQs are specifically geared to competencies within a specified occupational area, GNVQs are concerned with 'general skills, knowledge and understanding which underpin a range of occupations' (1993: 5).

Both NVQs and GNVQs represent a change in assessment in the vocational field running concurrently with the National Curriculum in schools. Like the National Curriculum, these qualifications have specified objectives as their basis, and like the National Curriculum, they are built on the idea of identifying levels. In the case of NVQs there are five levels planned (with Level 3 being designed to be comparable to A-level and Level 5 postgraduate), and in the case of GNVQs there are currently plans for four levels.

There are, as well as these surface features of similarity to the National Curriculum, more significant similarities. The new vocational qualifications, too, introduce changes in assessment which are part of a larger social and political agenda and in which there are very difficult tensions in the extent to which there are opportunities or further controls. Just as with the National Curriculum the claim of creating greater entitlement cannot simply be dismissed as expedient rhetoric, in the introduction of the new vocational qualifications there are debates to be had about whether the utilitarian surface of the qualification structure is necessarily operating as a mechanism of control.

This chapter outlines the key features of the new vocational qualifications and the tensions that exist between the behavioural framing of competencies and the opportunities created by the recognition of experiential learning that a competency framework facilitates.

The identification of competencies provides the clearest example to date of the deconstructive possibilities of an objectives model, and the use of such a model to drive social change. The wider access to qualifications that may be facilitated is twinned with a challenge to the traditional powers of education at all levels, and particularly to the autonomy of the universities. Industry Lead Bodies and awarding bodies for NVQs at the higher levels pose a challenge to traditional academic qualifications, particularly if political decisions were to drive the shift to vocational qualifications through funding allocations. A likely area for a testing of the NVQ model at higher levels is in education, both for initial teacher training and continuing professional development. This would represent an important area of the disputed territory of education between the Department of Employment and the Department for Education[4].

The field of vocational education and training is the site of two main tensions: firstly between academically and non-academically oriented provision; and secondly between providing individual opportunity and meeting the demands of the labour market. The categorically funded curriculum initiatives, CPVE and TVEI (the Certificate of Pre-Vocational Education and the Technical and Vocational Education Initiative) introduced in 1985 provided a focal point for that debate. These initiatives were sponsored by the Employment Department through the Manpower Services Commission. They drew schools into new relationships with each other (as TVEI consortia) and with industry. They were designed to make inroads into the enclosed territory of schools and to address the problem that high status work in schools was linked to academic subjects. There are different views of how this initiative worked. Dale sees its most significant effect as the change it brought about in 'control':

> The TVEI story might be judged a success story indeed. However, . . . much the greatest successes and consequences of TVEI are to be found in its effects on the control and processes of schooling, rather than in its effects on the curriculum or on the young people who experienced it . . . TVEI altered fundamentally and irrevocably the administration and control of education. It represented an unprecedented, unanticipated, unwelcome and entirely novel intervention into the previously self-controlled world of the secondary schools by a body that not only had no previous record there, but that symbolized values that were anathema to many people working in schools.
>
> (Dale 1990: 3)

Dale sees the means of introduction of TVEI as the basis for the centralization of educational control of the Education Reform Act 1988. Other commentators acknowledge the alien nature of TVEI to the culture of schools but regard it as having been used to drive empowering change for students (Harland 1987: 38–54; Jamieson 1990: 130ff.).

Target-setting and personal profiling were inherent features of the negotiated learning of TVEI. These processes may have provided opportunities to foster self-awareness and new relationships between learners and teachers. Morrison and Ridley summarize what they see as the two ideologies emphasizing the society-focused (rather than knowledge-focused) view of education. On the one hand, 'instrumental ideologies – instrumentalism, revisionism and those stressing economic renewal – emphasize the need for education to fit learners into society ...' On the other,

> are more radical society-oriented educational ideologies. Figuring high at times of social rebuilding or social upheaval ... reconstructionism posits a view of education as a major force for planned change rather than stability in society ... Society in need of reconstruction requires an educated populace whose curriculum has a strong social core with a stress on citizenship, egalitarianism, democracy and participation in decision-making. In this world teachers are catalysts and guardians of social change. There are dangers in this approach. Such a vision is potentially unstable as it is always looking to the future ... it relies on high levels of control – running the risk perhaps of centralization or even indoctrination.
>
> (Morrison and Ridley 1989: 45–8)

According to that analysis, the introduction of TVEI could be seen as representing a struggle between instrumentalism and self-awareness in vocational training/education, and between teachers as agents of social change, and teachers as centrally directed.

Earlier, the Certificate of Extended Education (CEE) was a contested ground. The first conception of the CEE was of a course and certificate at 17+ which could bring a wider group within the available academic qualifications at 18+. The Keohane (1979) and Mansell (1979) Reports offered two further perspectives, but both essentially suggested different tracking for some students. Keohane recommended a separate subject examination, and Mansell an integrated curriculum, but both saw the function of the qualification as vocational. Ranson (1984) discusses the Keohane and Mansell proposals in terms of Bernstein's collected and integrated codes, and traces within the CEE development three assumptions which he sees underlying the extending central control of education: vocationalism, rationalization and stratification.

Now, for an increasing proportion of young people the practical, the familiar and immediate, common sense and everyday knowledge, become the subject of the curriculum,
displacing the analytical and the cognitive, the unusual and
distant, the universal.

(Ranson 1984: 232)

Atkins, addressing the CPVE, weighs possible functionalist analysis: 'a coherent scheme of skills-training to be offered to those best
suited to it' with neo-Marxist perspectives, which she suggests
would identify vocational education as a removal from the more
prestigious educational routes of certain groups, a continuation
of class-based curriculum differentiation, limitation of economic
power, and an increase in the power of staff through the scrutiny
of personal factors within the integrated code. She also suggests
that teachers and lecturers have a further kind of dilemma, because
high unemployment levels (which form a rather confusing part of
the rhetoric about vocational education, since it is unclear whether
vocational education will in itself increase the number of employment opportunities) are variously argued to be either a temporary
phenomenon or a permanent feature of society (Atkins 1987:
46–9). The hidden vocational curriculum can be at least as much
a part of the system of control, as the overt curriculum. Wolpe
presents a bleak picture of classroom messages.

The concern of the teachers was with the present and that is
controlling the class. The messages they were transmitting
were ones on behaviour – being quiet, good, sitting still,
listening, settling down to work ... the emphasis was
on a vague and unspecified level of attainment to prevent
unemployment.

(Wolpe 1988: 239)

Concerns about vocational education as related to control, both
at the classroom level, or at a societal level as suggested in the
analyses above of Atkins and of Ranson, may seem to have been
exemplified in the introduction of NVQs. Just as the introduction
on the National Curriculum is largely atheoretical and seeks to
sweep aside the academic debates about learning and about opportunity, so too the NVQs are pragmatic and instrumental. Far from
addressing concerns about difference between traditional academic

and vocational education, they offer a vocational model which is a radical alternative to existing academic curricula.

National Vocational Qualifications

NVQs were introduced in 1988 for operation from 1991, under the general frameworks laid down by the NCVQ. They are specifically geared to making vocational training relevant to the workplace and thus they potentially, fundamentally change the nature of Further and Higher Education. They mark a radical shift in the nature and location and timing of vocational qualifications. The break with tradition is explicitly signalled in the Council's own training materials as outlined in Table 5.1.

The shift from courses to 'standards' is very significant demonstrating defined levels of *competence*, rather than *attendance* on a

Table 5.1 Vocational qualifications continuum

Traditional	NVQ
Course based	Standards based
Specific learning route	Any mode, pace, length of study
Created by a syllabus	Derived from industry-defined standards of competence
Concerned with a subject	Concerned with one or more occupations
Pre-entry requirements	No specific pre-entry requirements
Access to qualifications via a course	Open access to assessment
Acquire vocational qualification or not	Credit accumulation of competencies and units achieved
College-based	Use the workplace for learning
Only pass/fail	Continuous assessment
Covers skills and knowledge	Covers skills knowledge and their application

Source: NCVQ *Looking at Competence* (1989: 37)

course or the demonstration of *knowledge* or *understanding*, becomes the key to a qualification. Thus the curricular and assessment assumptions that have underpinned previous educational provision are radically changed. The definition of standards by Industry Lead Bodies for *occupational* sectors places an important element of control with employers, rather than with providers of training within the education sector. The competencies are (notionally at least) derived through functional analysis of what a specific job entails, and not through educational/theoretical models of learning.

The levels of NVQ seek to match and relate to academic levels of educational attainment and therefore to provide a basis for parity of esteem between vocational and academic qualifications. This in itself suggests a challenge to the prevailing assumptions in education. That challenge is further sharpened by the very different form that the vocational qualifications take from current post-16 academic routes. Very specific areas of competence are further defined through units, subdivided into elements. The elements of competence are then supported by associated performance criteria. The aim is for very precise specification and a technical view of occupational competence. In behavioural tradition, mentalistic notions of understanding – and requirements that underlying knowledge be demonstrated in itself – are subsumed by the requirement for demonstration only of the discrete behaviours identified with the elements of competence. The strong occupational emphasis also means that valid assessment of some competencies can only occur in the workplace. Thus it shifts the centre of activity, from a college into the workplace.

This very technical vision of post-compulsory education is somewhat oddly counterbalanced by some of the processes which are its logical extensions. Since the emphasis is not on courses, but on what someone can actually do, then assessment of prior and experiential learning (APEL) becomes a significant part of any NVQ assessment. In practical terms, the importance of experiential learning – and of all prior learning relevant to the competencies of any given qualification – has generated a need to devise procedures for its assessment and accreditation. This prior learning may take the form of learning as part of a course of study, or learning which occurred through employment, or elsewhere. The example below, taken from the USA (Commission for Educational Exchange,

Alternative Education in the United States), gives an illustration of the variety of prior experiential learning which might provide relevant evidence for accreditation:

Alternative Education

1 Work: including typing, filing, accounting, inventory control, financial management, computer programming, editing, sales . . .

2 Home-making: including child-raising, child psychology, interpersonal communication, gourmet cooking.

3 Volunteer work: community activities, political campaigns, service organizations, health care . . .

4 Non-credit learning in formal settings: company courses, in-service training, workshops, clinics, conferences, conventions, lectures, courses on radio and television, non-credit correspondence courses.

5 Travel: study tours, vacation and business trips, living for extended periods in other countries . . .

6 Recreational activities and hobbies: musical skills, aviation skills and training, acting or other community theatre work, arts and crafts, fiction and non-fiction writing, public speaking, gardening, etc.

7 Reading, viewing, listening: any subject area in which a person has done extensive reading and study, other than for college credit.

8 Discussions with experts: significant, extensive or intensive meetings with such people may also earn credit.

The assessment and accreditation of prior learning has several far-reaching implications. Firstly, it potentially changes the nature of much of the work of Further and Higher Education. It removes their traditional control of knowledge and their rights of transmission of knowledge. Skills – or competencies – gained elsewhere can be accredited, and Further and Higher Education, if they wish to remain players in the qualifications field, become increasingly assessors rather than purveyors. Evidence of prior learning may be gleaned in a variety of ways. The traditional interview has always sought to assess prior experience and present skills. Some competencies may be assessable through written tests. However, much prior learning requires different kinds of evidence: more detailed than an interview can obtain, and more wide-ranging than can be tested in restricted conditions. Portfolios of evidence, requiring the compilation of a range of previous experience and evidence provides the most important new medium for assessment of prior learning. The preparation of portfolios, however, requires fairly sophisticated understanding of what constitutes relevant evidence, and more than that, of the underlying frameworks of competence that evidence is adduced to illustrate. Some of the work of Further and Higher Education may shift from provision of courses, to guidance and career counselling, to support for the preparation of portfolios, and to assessment.

Secondly, APEL logically removes some of the restriction that education has traditionally placed on double-counting of qualifications, in the case of prior learning that is already certificated. The NVQ framework does not preclude competence gained in one area from being counted in another. All that is required is evidence. If a qualification (academic or vocational) is able to provide evidence of certain competencies, then there is no logical reason – within an NVQ – why these competencies cannot be counted towards another award in which the same competencies apply. This model could be argued to be fundamentally different from academic award models, but is likely to raise challenges to the academic systems. Some Higher Education provision now includes modules which can be counted towards either diploma or degree awards; the logic of allowing a module only to count towards one or the other may be difficult to sustain in the view of radical shifts in thinking about the nature of qualifications, created by NVQs.

Thirdly, prior and experiential learning may shorten or by-pass any period of training/study. If this is happening in the vocational areas, there are likely to be market-led demands – if not governmental demands – for a re-examination of course length in academic areas, and whether courses should be uniform in length and provision irrespective of the entry qualifications and experience.

Fourthly, access to qualifications should be increased by the recognition of a far wider range of routes. In broad social terms, accreditation of prior and experiential learning redistributes the definition of work and learning, and brings some groups formerly marginalized in employment into a potentially more central position in employment training. This may be especially true for women with family and other experiences, but without previous formal occupational recognition. The extension of this into academic qualifications would have considerable consequences in terms of increasing access, and in causing radical shifts in the pattern of university work, concurrent with incentives to take increasing numbers of part-time students.

A complementary strand in the development of NVQs is the National Record of Vocational Achievement (NROVA) now replaced by the National Record of Achievement (NRA) also available to schools. The Records and NVQs together make up 'the emerging model of vocational education and training' (Jessup 1989: 65ff.). This kind of record serves the more indeterminate function of vocationalism: what Gleeson (1989: 53) describes as 'mass vocational literacy'. Its ideals are personal growth, within a construct of vocational growth. In drawing the learner into a metarelationship with learning it provides a balance to the mechanistic aspects of a behavioural framework.

According to the Employment Department Consultative Document *Quality Assurance of the National Record of Achievement* (October 1991):

> individuals must be involved (preferably on a one to one basis with their mentor) in the assessment of their own learning;
> individuals should be able to discuss/contribute their own view of progress and attainment;
> individuals should have the opportunity to identify, express and reflect on their development . . .

The NRA and the NROVA offer opportunities for personal target setting and for relatively open-ended reflections on learning and achievement, in addition to recording achievement on pre-specified competencies of NVQs (or Attainment Targets in the National Curriculum). The total model for vocational education and training thus attempts to integrate different models of vocational education identified by Morrison and Ridley (1989: 46–7) as either instrumental or reconstructive.

Issues surrounding NVQs

There are a number of technical issues surrounding the nature of NVQs and the competency framework, and a number of social issues surrounding the way in which they will in fact relate to employment, to opportunity and to the traditional areas of educational control. It is likely that many of these issues will become conflated and that, as with the GCSE, some objections which are social/political may be presented as technical or as theoretical. The various kinds of issue do not exist entirely separately: the definition of statements of competence – like all statements of objectives beyond the most restricted – depends upon socially negotiated meanings. The issues in dissemination of curriculum and assessment change are further discussed in Chapter 9. For the purposes of this discussion, however, some attempt will be made to identify the different types of issue, as well as the ways in which the issues articulate with each other.

Competencies arguably present a narrow framework for thinking about the kind of competence required by any employment. Analysis may distort and simplify. It sacrifices a holistic picture of competence for an analytic picture of separate competencies (Otter 1992: 6–7). This argument is parallel to the problems that behavioural objectives have always raised. A related matter is the level of specificity, and the practical difficulty of assessing any individual across a large number of separate statements, in this case Units and Elements.

NVQs present partly a process and partly an outcome model. The emphasis on transferability means that an entirely outcome-based model would be inadequate. This mixed model represents some of the complexity of matching performance standards with range, but may render NVQs vulnerable, not as too simple a model, but as too sophisticated.

Occupational knowledge and understanding have been the assumed underpinning of qualifications in the past (Wolf 1989: 39–52; Debling 1989: 85–8). The NVQ model places practical performance at the centre of its qualifications and does not require any direct attempt to assess knowledge or understanding. This is a fundamental shift. Liberal education has rested upon the claim that transferability is dependent on a broad base of knowledge and comprehension. NCVQ's Director of Research acknowledges the difficulty: 'Fundamental issues, such as the overall structure of knowledge, understanding and cognitive skills and how they support competent performance, need to be addressed' (Jessup 1989: 3).

The usefulness of the functional analysis by which the competencies were specified will depend upon the suitability of the contexts in which it was carried out (Webster 1991). Moreover, functional analysis for illumination or reflection by practising workers may produce different sets of competencies from those which provide a suitable basis for training. Looking purely at what an effective manager, florist, or trainer actually does in his/her job is not, for example, able to access information about the kinds of knowledge – or the attitudes to work – which may underpin that practice. The robustness of practice based only on competencies – with no evidence of an underlying rationale for action – remains in question.

There are additionally many practical difficulties in carrying out NVQ assessments. The assessment and accreditation of prior learning, which may be the key to opportunity within the NVQ model, proposes in fact a very complex set of assessment dimensions. Verification of prior and experiential learning by assessors must depend upon indirect evidence, and much depends upon the ability to present that evidence effectively and relevantly.

The procedures associated with APEL, which logically becomes a key feature of NVQs, are sophisticated and may require levels of resourcing at least as great as former qualifications and courses. Moreover, it is difficult to separate out cognitive and other competency in the assessment of portfolios of evidence. The ability to interpret, order, organize, prioritize, explain, justify and evaluate APEL becomes as important in portfolio presentation as the other learning experiences that are represented. Claims that NVQ's drawing on APEL will only be focusing on the targeted competencies may be hard to sustain. Much of the traditional role of education in facilitating comprehension and judgement may be supported by the need for portfolios. While that may sustain educational traditions, and make the innovation more acceptable to traditional providers, it may also weaken the opportunities for social change through APEL.

The opportunities presented by NRA are complementary to NVQs in the more personal framework for reflection offered. However, if target-setting and reflection are entirely bounded by NVQ competencies then the Record serves a limited function as a Unit Credit record. The experience of Records of Achievement in schools has been that motivation of staff and students is a very significant factor (PRAISE 1988: 175–6) particularly since the processes which lie at the heart of the usefulness of such Records are time-consuming. The lines between surveillance and oppor-tunity (Hargreaves 1989: 133–43) between control and effective learning (Broadfoot 1990: 214) and between form-filling and personal growth may be too narrow to maintain in a climate of denigration of educational work.

The impact of NVQs upon Higher Education is limited at present, with staff in continuing education departments (still largely seen as discrete parts of universities) more conscious than others of the possibilities and challenges (Duke 1992: 26). A Lead Body for education is still under discussion. At the time of writing, its relationship to the Teacher Training Agency, to the Department for Education, to Local Education Authorities and their increasingly privatized curriculum advice/INSET/professional development units, and to Higher Education is unclear. Work on competencies for teacher education has so far been tentative and largely controlled from within the profession. The ESRC-funded, 'Modes of Teacher Education Research Project' reports that

> On 47 courses, competences [though not, of course NVQ competencies] were being used as a basis for course planning or for defining aims and objectives ... They were also frequently used to assess students' individual needs ..., or to assess teaching practice ... Twenty-two courses were using competences in order to evaluate course provision and on three courses competences were being used to improve working practices between HEIs [Higher Education Institutions] and schools and therefore develop the notion of 'partnership'.
> (Barrett *et al.* 1992: 52)

Eraut argues that there is little relationship between the NVQ model of competency and any current PGCE courses. Moreover, he suggests that 'personal theories' properly underlie the work of teachers, and that part of the process of teacher education (as distinct from NVQs) is to bring these personal theories under 'critical control' (Eraut 1989: 184).

While a Lead Body for education would be likely to include the groups with a professional interest in education, the NVQ framework suggests a very different balance of power in the control – and possibly in the award – of qualifications from the previous dominance by Higher Education. Qualified Teacher

Status (QTS) might come within the NVQ model, offering a professional-occupational example of the model and at the same time breaking the circle of academic influence in education. It would be a logical extension of current policy. Articled and licensed teacher schemes, as well as the move towards increased school-based training PCGE students, all signal a workplace-based training and assessment policy. The next logical step would be to remove time requirements, so that qualified teacher status could be more closely linked to the demonstration of requisite competencies rather than to a given period of training holistically assessed.

The other power base of university Departments of Education is in the provision of award-bearing in-service education, mainly in the form of taught higher degrees for serving teachers. This is significant in terms of influence upon the way in which senior staff in schools frame their developing careers and understandings, and in terms of allowing, through funding, 'academic freedom'. At present, that base is diminished by the devolution of funds to schools. In practice, many schools do not have the individual resources to support award-bearing study, nor are they all convinced of the relevance of traditional awards, particularly in an education system which is placing emphasis on narrowly conceived educational outcome, 'results', and financial efficiency.

There are advantages in terms of some strands of the Government's policy in promoting NVQs for initial training and for serving teachers (through the Lead Body – proposed – for Education, through the Training and Development Lead Body and through the Management Charter Initiative). These would provide an alternative, and probably a cheaper alternative, to in-service training as compared with academic awards. They would structurally move teachers into the competency framework and create a logical continuity between the National Curriculum and occupational competencies. They would prove publicly that the work of at least one professional group could be made open to monitoring and account.

The NVQ framework is deconstructive at one level – in that it deconstructs the nature of occupational competence. That deconstruction makes certain values and definitions clearer. It is conducted from a particular ideological standpoint, which questions the dominance of training by academic (and tacit) criteria, and also from a political stance which may seek to diminish the power base of Higher Education. The deconstructive process, however, also makes the values and beliefs explicit. The effects may not be comfortable for Further and Higher Education, but choices remain about response. Options include submission, subversion, colonization, or an open engagement in the deconstructive debate. The last might take the form of investigating the functional analyses on which competencies have been framed, analysing the assumptions of vocational competency, suggesting other models of competencies, and relating the value processes at work in NVQs to the values of individuals within society. If NVQs are subjected to the same processes of 'manageability' as the National Curriculum assessments, rather than to a wider debate, then it is likely that their current insistence on real and varied contexts for assessment could be progressively reduced to restricted, multiple-choice tests. The result would be not only a vocational training structure highly differentiated from the academic (as already looks likely), but also a system of vocational training more clearly related to control than anything previously seen.

General National Vocational Qualifications

A GNVQ consists of mandatory and optional units (different numbers of units for different levels of qualification). The mandatory, or core skill units across Levels 1–3 are communication, application of number and information technology. It is the core skills that allow the GNVQ to claim its general application to occupational areas, and which make it flexible enough to be taught within schools, to mixed occupational groups, and therefore suitable to situations where total student numbers may be relatively small. Its optional units are the occupationally specific units. At Level 1, one such unit is needed for a qualification, at Level 2, two, and at Level 3, four occupational units. Personal action planning, linked to the NRA is seen as an important part of the programme 'delivery'. NCVQ is 'working closely with the Standing Conference on University Entrance to ensure that admissions tutors are fully acquainted with GNVQs' (NCVQ 1993: 11). Government commitment to parity with academic qualifications is also underlined by *Education and Training for the 21st Century*: 'General NVQs should ... offer a broad preparation for employment as well as an accepted route to higher level qualifications, including higher education [and] . . . be of equal standing with academic qualifications at the same level' (DES 1991c: para. 3.8). The White Paper on *Competitiveness* calls Advanced GNVQs 'the new vocational A levels' (President of the Board of Trade *et al.* 1994: para. 4.51).

The main distinct issue attaching to GNVQs, as opposed to NVQs, is the kind of direct impact that they are likely to have on the work and outlook of schools. Further Education has already been significantly affected by the introduction of NVQs and is already very familiar with the kinds of structures needed to support their assessment. Schools are at the beginning of the process of introducing GNVQs. They have not worked before with a vocational qualification for which there is such strong governmental will to create parity of esteem with academic qualifications, or to create the climate (possibly ultimately funding-driven) for accepting vocational qualifications as entry qualifications into higher education. There is also considerable scope offered by the Dearing proposals (Dearing 1993b) to develop GNVQ provision in the 14–16 age group, thereby making considerable changes to a heavily prescribed National Curriculum and academic curriculum. This will almost certainly lead, as Dearing suggests, to changes in GCSE examinations, to incorporate GNVQ units. This would mark a significant shift in the nature of examining at 16, not only because the content of examining would reflect the vocational curriculum more strongly than it has done before, but also because the notion of units and credit accumulation could re-open the development of modular courses that the National Curriculum has thrown into question.

Here we begin to see some very large differences in objectives-based assessment systems; on the one hand used for linear courses in the National Curriculum model, and on the other, used to support a credit accumulation pattern in NVQs and GNVQs. Each has its own implications. While the National Curriculum model establishes some claim to common curriculum (though this definition has already been challenged in Chapter 4), the vocational qualifications present a system of options and individual routes. Does this difference matter? Is it simply the difference between school and work, or between childhood and adulthood that is reflected, or are there fundamental ideological conflicts between the two concerning the nature of the individual's relationship to the state, and the nature of a student's relationship with the teacher?

Both models (the National Curriculum and the GNVQ/NVQ model) pose interesting challenges for all of education and for the work of teachers at all levels in education, as both create new roles for teachers very different from the kinds of control that they had over the curriculum in the past. There are fundamental issues to address about whether education is to be fragmented into different models for different ages, whether it is to prefer one of these models over another, or whether it is to articulate a different vision for education across the vocational and the academic areas.

6

THE CONTESTED GROUND OF CURRICULUM

The assumptions underlying specific developments (GCSE, the National Curriculum and National Vocational Qualifications) are that curriculum can be made more measurable and in some way more effective if it is more closely prescribed. There is, however, as previous chapters have outlined, little evidence that there is a single coherent view guiding the strong arm of government policy in directing curricular change. At present, measurability appears to be the main overall point of agreement among policymakers, or certainly among those whose voices are dominant. It is the perceived need to make curriculum more measurable that has allied recent change so strongly to assessment. It has also imposed upon curriculum certain features (of content, design and overall political structure) that have profound implications for students, for those working in education, and for the way in which education articulates with the wider society.

This chapter looks at ways in which the constraints placed upon curriculum by the current applications of an objectives model, and its accompanying assessment arrangements, is in tension with the wish (also emanating from government) to provide the conditions for a learning society, in which the individual is active in negotiating pathways of life-long learning. The chapter does not seek to engage in the debates about vocational and academic education – they have been outlined in Chapter 5 – which are an important background to the current discussion, but not its focus. This chapter is, rather, concerned to highlight the areas where 'education' could be more active in engaging proactively and with some unity of purpose, to make sense for learners and the community of the contradictions in current government policy.

A subject-based curriculum

The introduction of both the National Curriculum and NVQs (though not General NVQs) entrenches still further within secondary and post-secondary education and training the 'subject' model, or what Bernstein (1977) identifies as the collected curriculum code. The National Curriculum does this through a re-assertion of traditional school 'subjects', and NVQs through the separation of work-related skills into occupational competencies. The existence – and persistence – of the subject model is discussed by Ribbins (1992: 1–20) who locates the explanation for 'subjects' within philosophical and sociological discourses about education, and introduces a possible reconsideration of subjects within the National Curriculum framework. The constructed nature of the subject (Goodson 1987), and its place within the politics of the schools (Ball and Bowe 1992) link it to a number of traditions and interest groups, and thus point to the difficulties of overriding such interests or introducing more integrated views of educational process. The National Curriculum also imposes a secondary model of subjects and assessment on primary education as well, thereby implicitly challenging more integrated curricular models of topic-based and thematic work.

The subject basis of the National Curriculum increases its supposed measurability since the subjects provide the units in which the measurements can be made. The structure of the National Curriculum was initially established by the Task Group on Assessment and Testing (TGAT), which determined the use of a 10-level scale, and the framework of Attainment Targets which each of the Curriculum working groups would have to adopt. This is in itself significant in that it was a clear indication that the assessment was becoming the main shaping characteristic of the curriculum and the definition of curricular progression.

Moreover, far from allowing any diversity of subject development, TGAT imposed a common model for very different subjects, assuming that progression and levels in Science, for example, might look similar in conception to levels in English. Within the general policy intention of competition and accountability, the uniformity thus imposed (or attempted) was to make possible the comparison of schools and of teachers. The aim was to impose a uniformity of organization within which teachers would be competing with each other, thus seeking to exploit the subject as the basis of division between teachers.

The focus of the National Curriculum on subjects, and the focus of National Vocational Qualifications on occupational competencies, both leave very large questions about the underlying processes of education, and about the other kinds of learning that go on around that which can be specified in what are essentially syllabus documents. In the National Curriculum, for example, there was originally no space for careers education and yet this had been an apparent policy priority in the introduction of the Technical and Vocational Educational Initiative, and in the discussion surrounding the introduction of the National Curriculum, which was to enable, the UK 'To compete successfully in tomorrow's world' (Thatcher 1987). The obvious means by which this competition was to be facilitated appeared only, however, to be a 'back to basics' strategy, with a vision of an obedient and drilled workforce rather than a flexible and responsive one. Similarly, National Vocational Qualifications are designed to lead to job-specific skills rather than necessarily adaptable, flexible, self-aware workers. The interpretation of these broad policy aims about competitiveness into education and training systems that would establish competition between education professionals seems to rest on a very simplistic idea that a successful economy will simply be the sum of its parts. In other words, it seems to suggest that if everyone in the UK is forced into a more competitive relationship one with another, the whole economy will somehow become a macro-expression of that competitiveness. The curriculum conception behind this seems to be subservient to its instrumental functions of fostering measurement as a basis for competitiveness. Moreover, there is also a missing link between the kind of dynamism that the country is said to be needing and the static nature of the curricula supposed to address the problem.

The measurable curriculum is a commodified curriculum. Definitions of curriculum as process are ignored and the curriculum becomes reified in the form of documents that are delivered to teachers in schools, and subsequently 'implemented' and 'delivered' to students. The quantity that has been successfully delivered can then be measured, through testing, and the results fed back to the centre and out to consumers.

In the case of NVQs, curriculum is obliterated altogether and assessed competencies become the reification of training, the commodity that can be measured and traded. By-passing the somewhat ethereal notions of learning and curriculum takes away the central professional power of the professional and reduces the erstwhile professional to an assessor, a technically conceived job.

The attack upon 'theory'

There is an absence – a deliberate absence – from the National Curriculum of any theory about how people learn, or indeed what the underlying principles of education should be. TGAT considered that the National Curriculum would be easy to design because of its freedom from theory: 'No difficulties of principle are anticipated in applying this framework to individual subjects: it does not depend upon empirical evidence of a particular linear (or other) pattern of learning for its initial construction . . .' (DES 1988b: 21, para. 7).

The characteristics of the learner are rejected as a basis for curriculum. The model that is adopted is firmly within the subject-based tradition, and far from addressing the need for curriculum to relate more closely to learners it creates a greater distance between them and the prescribed content:

> National Curriculum requirements that reassert traditional subject contents, that excise science from its social context, and that impose ethnocentric interpretations of history and literature: these . . . leave learning disconnected from experience.
>
> (Hargreaves 1991: 250)

Both the National Curriculum and NVQs provide a means for government to distance itself from curricular process, while establishing a framework of prescribed content and outcomes. In so doing the government and the bodies that represent its curriculum policies may retain the appearance of rising above theoretical debates about learning. They thereby also, of course, marginalize such debates. This parallels the move to create a Teacher Training Agency which will manage the funding of initial training based in schools not in Higher Education (on-the-job training). The intensification of teachers' workloads and the nature of testing at Key Stages constrains the kind of curriculum development work and the breadth of discussion that schools can engage in. Curriculum coordinators, who have often taken over large parts of the erstwhile roles of headteachers and deputies, experience their role as technical and administrative rather than having real scope for leadership in curriculum discussions (Butterfield 1993b). Rapid revisions of the National Curriculum in 1992 and currently, mean that teachers are so fully occupied with responding to imposed change that theoretical justification for teaching approaches and methods are challenged by simple instrumentalism.

Central control and narrowly defined curricular objectives are identified as reductive, and the responses to this propose that the political dimensions of curriculum must be acknowledged. Apple calls for a movement away 'from the current "quasi-scientific" and management framework . . . toward a political and ethical structure' (Apple 1979: 105–22). Bernstein sees the initial education of teachers as increasingly technical as 'the specialized disciplines which constituted "education" . . . are weakened as political, cultural and academic sites' (1990: 161).

No curriculum is, of course, genuinely atheoretical. The current technically conceived models simply reflect one set of theories about how people might have their learning organized. The theoretical unity of curriculum is, however, being provided by a theory about the national management and measurement of education and training and not by theory about learning. This leaves fundamental questions unanswered about how and by whom alternative unifying theories are to be proposed.

The inflexibility of national prescription

A governmentally controlled curriculum – whether for schools or for vocational training – is, by virtue of its means of control, monumental. Curriculum which is cast in legislation, or which involves large national frameworks and systems of funding, is inherently inflexible. It is inflexible to local conditions, to particular needs and to rapidly changing general needs. Also, as has been seen in the development of the National Curriculum, particular power groups within government may be influential in pressing one-sided views. The National Curriculum, representing as it does the influence of the Hillgate group at the time of its conception, and therefore dominated by a return to curriculum patterns of the 1930s, is not well matched to the increasing importance of the European Community and the conditions of the 1990s. It is currently undergoing its second major set of revisions since its inception; this is both an indication of its original weaknesses, but also of the kinds of flexibility that curriculum in general needs for constant evaluation in use. It has proved to be far too demanding and cumbersome, a problem that Chapter 1 identified with the use of specified objectives. Its pre-Dearing rejection of vocationalism made it seem a curious anachronism after the developments in vocational education of the 1980s, and very much at odds with the rhetoric of its links to national competitiveness.

The synchronous development of NVQs suggested that while a traditional 'academic' education was the essential grounding before 16, the route for many (ultimately all?) thereafter would be a strongly technicist occupational-related training. Neither part of this curriculum design addresses the interrelationships between personal development, intellectual understanding, attitudes and motivations around jobs, the need to provide answers to unemployment and its personal and social consequences, and the need to create mobility and opportunity within the growing European Community.

Reconceptualizing the learner

Empowerment

In a context of increasing technicization of education, Apple discusses the hegemonic relations which he argues are reproduced through schooling, through the rhetoric of systems management, and through the supposedly consensual decisions underlying the selectivity of curriculum. Conflict is written out and the curriculum transmits 'shared' values through subject definitions, choice about content, and through its processes of selection for higher study (Apple 1979: 105–22). In *Teachers and Texts*, Apple (1986) further analyses the processes of cultural reproduction, using 'texts' to mean not only textbooks but also the kinds of reports and proposals which form public opinion 'about what should be taught in schools and what teachers' jobs should look like' (Apple 1986: 12). Arguably, his concern is the whole range of experiences and values to which teachers give apparent authority and as 'a different sort of text' (1986: 150) he discusses the 'new technology' of computing: 'It embodies a form of thinking . . . [in which] "how to" will replace "why" . . . at the level of the student. This situation calls for what I shall call social, not technical literacy, for students' (1986: 171).

Applying his analysis to the UK context, we might see that although National Curriculum pedagogy is not prescribed, a context of prescription becomes pervasive, and increasingly translated into transmission, rather than encouraging 'social literacy'. 'A culture which reduces pupils to passive receivers of knowledge is likely to reduce teachers to passive receivers of curricula' (Barnes 1976: 188). In the light of recent change, it might be more appropriate to reverse Barnes' statement, in speculating about the effects that a hierarchically disseminated curriculum may have upon teaching and learning.

We might indeed see the process of dissemination as central to the meanings of curriculum, for teachers and students. In the analysis by Raymond Williams of four kinds of communication system operating in societies, it is possible to see many echoes of the current tensions in educational control: authoritarian – for the transmission of the 'instructions, ideas and attitudes of a ruling group'; paternal – involving the exercise of control 'directed towards the development of the majority' ('an authoritarian system with a conscience'); commercial – 'works are openly offered for sale and openly bought'; *and democratic – a system 'we can only discuss and imagine'* [italics added] (Williams 1962: 130–7).

The National Curriculum consultation used the term 'entitlement' to try to define the relationship between students ('pupils') and the curriculum. We might associate the term 'entitlement' more with the paternalistic model proposed by Williams than with a democratic model. The more radical term 'empowerment' seems to promise a fuller role for students and to come closer to an idea of democratic participation – both within and beyond education. Empowerment is concerned with

> giving [students] the mental tools to reflect, to reason, to argue and to solve problems. It is about developing those human endowments, those human qualities, whereby they can understand themselves, the people and the world around them, and therefore assume some measure of control over their own life and destiny.
>
> (Pring 1990: 98–9)

While Pring interprets this in an essentially liberal humanist way – about personal destiny – there may also be a need to consider the wider conditions in which individuals operate. However, there is a considerable gulf between providing the 'strong system of reformed local democracy' (Ranson 1993: 348), and interpreting that into meaningful democracy for students.

The importance of democracy, operating at the level of the individual school or college, is widely identified (see for example, Apple 1986; Ball 1987; Giroux 1989; Harber and Meighan 1989). The term is potentially inclusive of students. Students engaged in democratic procedures have a structural education in citizenship. However, the available definitions of democracy in education and of its implicit objectives suggest models which could be consistent with control as well as with empowerment. The definitions do not imply that the cultural capital of knowledge is owned by the students. In the 'empowered *school*', 'pupils *usually* contribute fresh, positive ideas' when consulted about *possible* priorities' (Hargreaves and Hopkins 1991: 42) [italics added]. The language is marginalizing, and no structure for student consultation is suggested.

Ball's account of the micro-politics of the school ends with the view that '*school democracy*' may be a way of advancing the ideological struggles within schools [Ball's italics]. He concludes, however, that 'that . . . is another story' (Ball 1987: 280). Apple's discussion of democracy (1986) similarly concludes a far-reaching critique of the processes of education. Its assumption appears to be that the democratic functioning of education is a way in which teachers preserve the freedoms that in turn help them to provide similar opportunities for their students: 'our ability as educators to educate ourselves – and hence the later education of our students – is ... more than a little dependent on protecting the possibility of more democratic curricular and teaching practice' (Apple 1986: 178). It is essentially a professional vision, in which the teachers are entrusted with freedoms to hand on. It is a hierarchy of democratic entitlement rather than a radical democratic vision in which students' democratic rights precede those of professionals. Lawton's cultural analysis approach (Lawton 1989) appears to omit the structural level of meanings, and hence does not incorporate a view of the processes of schooling and curriculum as a means to equality of epistemological status between students and teachers.

The democratic school is sometimes equated with collegiality (Fullan 1982; Bush 1986). The problem with the concept is that it is grounded in ideas about colleagues, and is therefore inclusive of the professional group, but exclusive of others involved in processes of education, most notably the students. The 1988 Act presents a challenge to collegiality, along with professionalism, and that challenge chimes in with radical positions of very different origins, which would question how far the student has adequate rights within a collegial vision.

It is unclear how equality, in any full sense, can actually operate without changes in the way teachers and students are related within educational provision. While the imposition of curricula, the technicist nature of those curricula, and the use of the term 'training' rather than education to describe development undertaken by teachers suggest that suppression of teachers may lead to further suppression of students, the alternative visions of democracy are not well formed. A problem lies in that some commentators who resist central control also appear reluctant to, in any way, diminish the powers of teachers, seeing them as an important line of resistance to technicist change. Yet resistance itself is paradoxically related to control in education:

workers resist in subtle and important ways, I believe. They often contradict and partly transform modes of control into opportunities for resistance ... Whatever reproduction goes on is accomplished not only through the acceptance of hegemonic ideologies, but through opposition and resistance.

(Apple 1982: 25)

Such an argument would suggest that the patterns of resistance to the National Curriculum may be as reactionary as the Curriculum itself appears to be.

Opportunities and choice: the learning society

A debate within the UK – not new and not unique – is about the relationship of academic and vocational education. The Further Education Unit report on four European countries, including the UK, was somewhat pessimistic in looking for an end to such division: 'parity of esteem for vocational and academic education may be an unrealistic aim ...' (FEU 1992: 7). However, the kind of divisive specialization that this creates can be seen as having fundamental roots in our culture – and fundamental consequences in preventing cultural change. It also may restrict the evolution of common understandings and discourses for conceptualizing learning:

One consequence of inheriting a deeply divided system in which academic and vocational tracks are so embedded in the institutional and social structure is the absence of any embracing concepts to describe knowledge and skill development.

(Young 1993: 215)

The introduction in 1992 of General National Vocational Qualifications marks a significant stage in the realignment of vocational and academic qualifications. The publication of the Dearing Report, reviewing difficulties encountered in National Curriculum and assessment, similarly marks a possible change in the balance and structure of curriculum, certainly at the later stages of compulsory schooling.

In the light of consultation I have come to the conclusion that it would be desirable to provide somewhat more scope for schools to build a range of options into the curriculum to complement a statutory core of subjects. For very many students, this greater scope for choice would take the form of a selection of GCSEs. Other students would be better served by courses of a more applied character through the programmes overseen by the National Council for Vocational Qualifications as part of a curriculum which retains a significant academic content. This is not to suggest tightly defined alternative pathways, since many students may find a mixture of academic and applied elements both motivating and crucial to future success. Schools ought to be able to offer a wider range of choice. By extending the range of options to include courses with a substantial element of applied knowledge – the so-called vocational courses – schools will be able to provide challenge and motivation across the whole range of student aspirations.

(Dearing 1993b: para. 5.18)

Although the language of 'choice' appears frequently in government discussion of education, for example in the White Paper *Choice and Diversity* (DFE 1992a) its application in Dearing, giving emphasis to student choice and student aspirations is significant, as is the emphasis on flexibility and options in curriculum. In *Choice and Diversity*, 'diversity' was defined by the DFE to mean diversity of schooling through grant-maintained schools (those opted out of Local Education Authority control), City Technology Colleges (business sponsored) or assisted places in independent schools. 'Choice' referred to parents' rights (often more rhetorical than real) to choose schools and 'to choose the form of control for each school' (DFE 1992a: para. 1.17), i.e. either to remain in Local Education Authority control or to 'opt out'. Dearing's emphasis on the individual student (not 'pupil' – the DFE's official term) repositions the power and responsibility in educational choice.

The Dearing Report also opens the door for a consideration of GNVQ credits being gained through GCSE courses, thereby increasing possibilities for modular pathways, and a revision of GCSE syllabuses with reference to frameworks other than simply the National Curriculum. That signals a remapping of the post-14 curriculum, and a reconceptualizing of continuity between the pre-16 and post-16 curriculum.

These trends are further reinforced by a White Paper in 1994, *Competitiveness: Helping Business to Win*, with a significant input from the Department of Trade and Industry clearly signalling its intentions to re-enter the contested curricular ground post-14. The document reflects in its own internal contradictions much of the problem around the prescriptive curriculum and rigid market context for schools, as against the enterprise and autonomy required by adults in rapidly changing working contexts. Among its proposals towards increasing national competitiveness are the establishment of a 'General Diploma' consisting of a grouping of subjects at GCSE level, to include core GCSE subjects in Mathematics, English and Science, and two other GCSEs or 'their vocational equivalents'. The principle of grouping looks like a revival of a 'School Certificate' model dating from 1917. However, the incorporation of status for 'vocational equivalents' in this way is of greater potential significance. The White Paper further proposes the strengthening of A-level and vocational A-level–GNVQ courses, increased support for careers education and guidance, and an additional £23 000 000 over three years for work experience in the last year of compulsory schooling.

The White Paper *Competitiveness* re-echoes in its assertion of government strategy for raising standards much of the kind of discussion that suggests that testing and inspections will be an automatic spur to effort. 'Schools and colleges have been galvanised by an new emphasis on choice, quality and sharp accountability for results' (President of the Board of Trade *et al.* 1994: para. 46). The definition of choice still seems to mean a competitive market between institutions:

> Greater choice is a further stimulus to improvement. There are now over 900 self-governing (Grant Maintained [GM]) schools, with another 150 in the pipeline [note the industrial image] . . . These schools are being encouraged to specialise in particular subjects, such as technology through the new network of technology colleges, as do the 15 City Technology Colleges. GM schools can now also consider introducing

various types of selectivity in admissions arrangements in response to local demand.

(1994: para. 4.14)

Here we see again the conflict in the whole concept of 'choice'. It is to be 'A stimulus to improvement' (presumably for institutions competing to attract students). Yet the paragraph ends with 'selectivity' presumably exercised by those same institutions. The picture here moves between one of schools fighting to attract students, and schools as the arbiters of rights of entry. 'Local demand' is similarly vague: what parts of a local community will close down their own options in order that other members of the community will be selected? If, for example, the 'local demand' is for selective entry according to academic ability, then presumably some majority within the governing body of the schools and the existing parents, will vote for such selection, but that does not address the needs of others within the locality who will have their children de-selected on such a basis.

This discussion around schooling, and around training and college-based provision is crucial to the development of curriculum. It reveals the means by which curriculum specialization is conceived within the current policy framework. Some very loosely conceived local democracy introduces a differential status for different schools and possibly re-introduces a grammar/technical divide, with a number of less-favoured schools in some areas providing for students who have not been selected elsewhere.

However, the tenor of the White Paper shifts as it attends to the 16–19-age group: the language of 'Helping Young Adults to Succeed' (1994: para. 4.16) takes over from a discourse about parents' 'choices' and the *'Parent's Charter'*. The erstwhile invisible student suddenly comes of age, and moves from the power game to be played over her head by schools and 'local demand' to become the young adult making choices of her own. 'At 16 young people are able to choose between or combine courses leading to three main types of qualification, each enhancing the contribution they can make at work and opening up opportunities for further learning' (1994: para. 4.21). GNVQs 'offer young people the opportunity to learn to high standards in a practical and vocational context' (1994: para. 4.23).

There is, it seems, a mismatch between the discussion of the organization of schools and the discussion of the post-compulsory provision. In the account of schooling given in the White Paper as in other documents, such as the *Parents' Charter* distributed to all homes in England and Wales in June 1994, the student as an individual agent is invisible. In the discussion about post-14 education/training and particularly post-16, the student is to become active and independent, exercising choices in a complicated network of qualifications routes, and the language of 'offer' and 'opportunity' begins to dominate.

Does this contradiction matter? It will be suggested that it does, for two main reasons. It matters, firstly, because it does not represent the actual continuity of the learner. Young people are not suddenly awakening at the age of 14 or 16. Their experience is continuous and their ability to make use of opportunities for personal choice at 16 will depend on the extent to which their earlier education has prepared them to do so. To maintain a kind of public rhetoric about compulsory education which suppresses the independent existence of pupils/students is not helpful to establishing continuity and coherence, and implies a passivity of learning prior to 14 which runs counter not only to much educational theory but also to the expressed aims for the post-14 age group.

Secondly, it matters because of the very high degree of personal agency which is implied in post-16 plans for the management of learning, and on which those plans, at a national level depend. 'Lifetime Learning: Learning does not stop when work starts' (1994: para. 4.35). 'The government will help individuals assume greater responsibility for their own development and training throughout their life ...' (1994: para. 4.62). This emphasis on lifetime learning takes us even further into the idea of personal responsibility for learning, and implies what is increasingly coming to be known as the 'learning society' (Husen 1974; Ball 1993). This takes us well beyond arguments about whether there is simply sufficient continuity between the pre-16 and the post-16 curriculum, and into a whole new challenge for the conceptualization of the state, education and training, and the individual.

The development of NVQs proposes in itself a new relationship between learners and providers of training. This has been outlined in more detail in Chapter 5. NVQs remove the 'course' from the definition of learning. Qualifications may now be independent of courses and increasingly flexible in time and place of the learning to which they relate. Accreditation of prior and experiential learning opens up potentially a very wide range of lifetime experience to redefinition as 'learning'. The implications of this are significant, though the reality of a society in which learning can be so fluidly defined may be some way off.

What needs urgently to be addressed in relation to NVQs, and for plans for extension of the flexibility to pre-16 learning, and more widely in plans for a 'learning society', is what the meaning of all this is for individuals. Whereas in traditional education/training provision the course might have been the organizing principle, that principle is now located with the individual outcomes. The individual seeking guidance (recognized to be crucial to this model) needs a high degree of self-awareness to initiate and interact with the sources of guidance. The individual becomes, in effect, the organizing principle of the learning, and the individual pathway through learning exists only with the individual. The National Record of Achievement provides the document in which this pathway can be recorded, and the focus for the individual to reflect upon, discuss, understand and take control of the achievements of learning and the future targets for learning, but that Record is less valuable than the process of reflection and growth that underlies it. The hard-edged (apparently simple) model of targets and assessments, the new vocational model, also involves, at a much more complex level, a conceptualization of individual responsibility and self-awareness.

> Learning requires individuals to progress from the post-war tradition of passivity, of the self as spectator of action on a distant stage, to a conception of the self as agent both in personal development and active participation within the public domain. Such a transformation requires a new understanding from self-development for occupation to self-development for autonomy, choice and responsibility across all spheres of experience ... This implies something deeper than mere 'lifelong education and training'. Rather, it suggests an essential belief that an individual is to develop comprehensively throughout his or her lifetime and that this should be accorded value and supported.
>
> (Ranson 1993: 342)

In this kind of definition, Bernstein's 'collected code' of curriculum demonstrated by National Curriculum subjects or by occupational competencies becomes more marginal to an integrated code in which the individual ultimately is the means by which the curriculum is described.

Teachers also – perhaps most of all – will need to reflect this vision of a learning society, structurally in their own conceptualization of career and personal development. Yet teachers are being cast as functionaries in the delivery of commodified curricula. There are therefore (and the next chapter will develop this theme) considerable contradictions between the new vocational education plans and the way teaching roles (in school education and Further Education) are being defined by prescription and technicization.

There are possibilities of real change within the current proposals, and some major issues which need to be addressed. Indications of a new flexibility seem to open the way for a more genuinely entitled (empowered) student, certainly post-14, and one might anticipate that there will be repercussions in younger age groups. However, the flexible, independent, student of the late 1990s choosing pathways from a number of possible routes through education and training, has an enormous supposed capacity for personal responsibility, a breadth of knowledge about structures and possibilities and the self-awareness to make best use of these options. That implies not only a huge role for those with direct contact with students (teachers, careers officers, student counsellors), but also major shifts in practice to model flexibility and accessibility.

Overview

The restructuring of post-14 curricula in the UK can be seen as having a number of meanings. It replaces the rigidity of government prescription with a more flexible set of options. It places the student at the centre of this framework of options. Choice now becomes associated, not with parental choice of diverse schools competing in the marketplace, but, more directly, student choice, within a number of curricular options. Curriculum becomes the site of choice, rather than schools or colleges.

Restructuring also suggests that there is a continuity between school and working life that the National Curriculum as conceived in 1988 structurally obscured. It allows for that continuity to be firmly established within curricular provision. It therefore allows for vocational education to be embedded within the work of secondary schools. The GNVQ, if that is to be the main form of vocational qualifications for the 14+ age group, is within an integrated rather than collected (subject-based) code, and therefore places a greater emphasis on the individual as the unifying and contextualizing location of knowledge.

Potentially, this does appear to be an empowering vision of education. At its heart, however, there will be problems of individualism, and how far such individualism is a necessary part of creating passive consumers, unable to engage collectively in discourses about the greater whole, and how far it is about genuine autonomy and rights.

A number of initiatives within education – and training – see themselves as involving students more actively in their own learning. The Records of Achievement movement seeks to emphasize the negotiation process between teacher and learner. There is, particularly in reaction to the possible subjection of learners to a testing culture in schools, interest in pupil self-assessment. Such initiatives, however, are readily marginalized in the context of results-driven frameworks of accountability. Yet, at the centre of planning for competitiveness and for a more vocationally relevant curriculum are options and choices which depend entirely upon autonomous, responsible and self-aware learners.

The conditions that might create such autonomy and self-awareness are not automatically provided by the National Curriculum, nor NVQs, nor by the conceptualization of curriculum as a commodity that can be 'delivered', 'implemented' and measured by results that are closely linked to content in defined subject or occupational tracks. Whether we are conceptualizing students moving through a post-modern world of ambiguities and contradictions, or whether we conceptualize them as informed consumers and producers in the marketplace, the conclusion about the kinds of skills and understandings they would need is probably similar, in terms of the level of personal responsibility they will need.

Much of the foregoing discussion has focused on the 14+ age group, because that is where the most readily identifiable focus for immediate change can be found. The consequences of such change

are, however, likely to be considerable, and not bounded by particular age, or stage, categories. The need to create inclusive
discourses around education and training, and to create a more
independent learner implies value shifts around 'learning' and
a greater status for learning of all kinds and at all ages.

Key questions remain, however, about how the very complex
vision implied by the 'learning society' can be realized. In the contested area of what curriculum should be – and the White Paper
Competitiveness demonstrates that contest internally in its own
tensions of discourse around educational choice – there needs to be
a debate about the role of education itself. There is no very clearly
defined body of people who would necessarily identify themselves
as representing 'education', and that perhaps is a problem. The
term might loosely be said to include all those teaching in whatever
sector of education including Adult and Higher Education,
those principally engaged in research in education and the Local
Education Authorities. Taking that breadth of definition, it might
be said that there is no single or proactive stance on curriculum in
the past that has united these groups. The current circumstances
are different. On the one hand there is the spectre of technicization
at all ages and levels of qualifications, and on the other there is
the challenge to widen definitions of learning to remove the discontinuities between life and learning, 'work' and learning, and
between learning at different ages and levels.

It is difficult to identify any grouping other than those working
in education (however ill-defined) of people that is so well placed
to attempt the definitions and reconceptualizations implied by the
learning society. Nor is it indeed easy to identify any group other
than education for whom a decision about whether to be proactive
and inclusive could be more important.

The real challenge then will be how to prevent a reassertion of
the professional role becoming merely professional self-protection,
or an attempt to entrench the culture of courses and to privilege
certain kinds of professional knowledge. For that is not what the
learning society is about. Personal agency is about empowerment,
and as has been suggested earlier, there may be fundamental
conflicts between learner-empowerment (whether conceived as
'students' or not) and professional traditions.

7

THE OBJECTIVES OF IMPOSED CURRICULA: DISSEMINATION, MEANINGS AND TEACHERS' WORK

A discussion of imposed curriculum objectives would not be complete without addressing the issue of whether the intended objectives can be understood as fixed and invariable, or whether in the process of dissemination and use, they become so variously interpreted that it is questionable whether it is appropriate to speak of a National Curriculum. The apparent simplicity of an objectives model is complicated by the processes which underlie its dissemination. Government imposition has chosen not to acknowledge the factors that lie between central prescription and the curriculum as experienced by the learner.

This chapter first of all considers the different kinds of objectives which operate at different levels within the work of individual teachers and of schools, and how these other objectives may interact with the notion of a common curriculum. Secondly, it explores arguments which might suggest that the only common meanings which we can attribute to the National Curriculum arise through the means of its introduction and dissemination, and through its assessment procedures, which are all about control. So that while we may not have a truly common curriculum, there is a common means of control of state education, the work of teachers, and possibly of the aspirations and outlook of students.

It has been suggested in previous chapters that the notion of the 'professional' is problematic, and part of a social order which current curricular and assessment arrangements are designed to contest. It is not the purpose here to construct a defence of teachers' professional autonomy, but rather to attempt to describe the micropolitical factors which are relevant to the processes of national prescription and national measurement.

Do we have a National Curriculum?

There are a number of ways in which this question could be approached. The purpose here is to focus specifically on the effect that schools as organizations, and teachers as individuals with professional identities, have upon the notion of a National Curriculum. There are a number of ways in which the Education Act 1988 and surrounding changes in education (such as the introduction of appraisal systems) have direct consequences for teachers' work. It is not suggested here that these particular circumstances create unique contexts in which to understand teachers' work, or have effects upon teachers that are inherently different from effects observed in other contexts. The argument is, rather, that although the Government believed itself to be introducing a package of measures which would ensure uniformity of curriculum, the reality is different.

We might retain in this discussion a focus on objectives. After all, the imposition of the National Curriculum presupposes that objectives in the form of attainment targets within curriculum subjects can exist in some uniform and unproblematic way. They are not, however, the only objectives in play, and it may be useful to try to refocus on the very wide and diverse sets of objectives to which teachers are working.

The discussion of educational objectives characteristically focuses upon one level at a time, so that, for example either political purposes are discussed, or the objectives of particular subject curricula or tasks. This separation is part of the process by which educational studies is fragmented into disciplinary and interdisciplinary parts. For the purpose of this discussion it is felt necessary to consider the various levels at which objectives are interacting with teaching and learning. The argument is that educational studies might focus upon this complexity; that by suggesting disparately to teachers that objectives are unidimensional and are operating in independent systems of the school, the work of teachers is being misrepresented. It might be argued that occupational stress is caused not by teachers being given overcomplex models of their job, but by their being given oversimple models which do not tally with their daily experience.

'Anxiety' is a repeated finding of the PACE research into teacher responses to National Curriculum assessment (Broadfoot *et al.* 1991a). Similarly 'guilt and anxiety' are identified as emergent themes of the study carried out by Gipps and others (Gipps *et al.* 1992). While these features of stress can be partly attributable to isolated features of National Curriculum assessment, and to unfamiliarity and innovation, the array of findings of the researches would also suggest that these features were attributable to the network of influences operating upon teachers. Chapter 11 gives a fuller outline and discussion of the findings.

The interrelationship of various levels of objective come together in the dissemination exercises associated with GCSE, with the National Curriculum and with NVQs. There are at the most obvious levels the stated curriculum objectives (i.e. GCSE assessment objectives; National Curriculum attainment targets and statements of attainment; NVQ statements, Units and Elements of competence).

At further levels there are the general objectives or aims of the curriculum innovation. As has been argued elsewhere, for GCSE these are explicit in the aims of the national criteria documents at a subject-specific level; for the National Curriculum there are none; and for NVQs they are expressed only instrumentally in terms of the roles and functions which the holders of a qualification have the requisite competencies to carry out. At another level there are the policy objectives (which may be multiple and in tension one with another). At another level there are the personal objectives of teachers, the institutional objectives of schools, and the fragile process of appraisal that supposedly provides an interface between the two.

Personal objectives

The personal objectives of teachers necessarily differ among teachers, and depend upon their own learning and career histories, as well as their views of teaching and learning, and their understandings of the role of the teacher. The most significant general influence operating within the teaching profession as a whole, however, may be the kinds of career expectations that have been established and sharpened through a new emphasis on school management.

This is a change created by the Education Act 1988, which places responsibility for management of budget and staffing with institutions. Further categorical funding of management training for staff has accompanied the introduction of the terms of the 1988 Act, and is planned into the future: 'From 1995–96 the Government will introduce a voucher scheme for training newly appointed headteachers in leadership and management skills in all maintained schools' (President of the Board of Trade *et al.* 1994: para. 4.43). These changes mark out management as a potentially separate and high status area of teachers' work, and create a potential division between management and curriculum process. Shipman identifies the problem that 'management training tends to be severed from the social sciences that could connect it to learning and its social conditions' (1990: 4).

In practice, curriculum and assessment coordination in schools is being delegated from headteachers, who might formerly have seen this as their distinctive role, to deputies and to classroom teachers with promoted posts. This does not always recognize the centrality of curriculum processes to the school, nor do the staff with coordination responsibilities necessarily have the time, the status or the leadership experience to give shape to this relatively new 'coordinator' role, itself fairly undefined (Butterfield 1993b). There appears to be a need for better descriptions of the role of curriculum management in schools and how this can be directly and effectively focused on curricular processes.

Different views about pedagogy also underlie teachers' work, and shape their personal teacher identities and objectives in teaching. The working philosophies about learning are often pragmatically and loosely based upon theory. Watts and Bentley (1991: 171–82), for example, discuss 'weak' and 'strong' versions of constructivism. The first involves what they call 'one-liners' such as 'start where the learner is at' and 'teacher as facilitator/enabler' (1991: 175–6). The 'strong' version is a 'theory of the limits of human knowledge, according to which all we can know is necessarily a product of our own cognitions', and which includes within a family of theories, views of knowledge as transitory and provisional, and which implies collegiality as fundamental: 'We believe that constructivism goes further than suggesting that all knowledge is simply the sum of cognitive-plus affective components: it is a humanistic, whole-bodied philosophy' (1991: 172–4). Their analysis also implies a tension between the attempts to engage with a constructivist 'pedagogic philosophy' and the organizational features of schools 'a curriculum built upon the criteria for strong constructivism would be very different from the National Curriculum as it is organized, and indeed would have far-reaching implications for the structural and organizational features of schools as they are now' (1991: 180). Watts and Bentley are arguing for the need to bring the strong and the weak versions closer together, so that teachers have more of an over-arching theoretical framework within which to justify their pedagogy. This could be seen to be especially relevant to the National Curriculum context, where although teachers and schools are nominally in control of curriculum process, there is 'the need to encourage a new kind of debate about primary education' (Alexander *et al.* 1992: para. 23) and in which genuine exploration of teaching approaches across all ages may be restricted by the pedagogical models implied by testing.

Institutional objectives

The 1988 Act creates a context in which, much more sharply than before, a school's objectives may be driven by a need for survival in a competitive marketplace. In this situation, schools are living with multiple contradictions. Their objectives in teaching and learning are being set at the outcome level by National Curriculum Attainment Targets, yet they have to find their own ways of managing the relationship with the market and their own processes of change. Frameworks for school development planning have been drawn up under DES sponsorship (Hargreaves and

Hopkins 1991). The resultant framework of rational planning (closely related to Tyler's curriculum planning model) has processes of evaluation as integral to processes of setting goals. It offers a framework for breaking general goals into more specific targets, the achievement of which can be identified through explicit success criteria. Thus at one level, it may now be easier than before to identify any given institution's objectives, though whether those objectives are shared and understood by the staff depends upon processes underlying the structure of planning.

The quality of those processes, however, is not automatically supported by the heavy workload of National Curriculum, or by the lack of non-contact time in primary schools. The culture of secondary school departments may also militate against shared planning processes. There may, moreover, be difficulties created by planning models which inadequately represent school realities. Schmidtlein (1988) questions the appropriateness of rational planning models, following a study of Higher Education institutions in the USA, in which the rhetoric of one kind of planning contradicted very different observed processes at work within the institutions, mainly because of size, individual autonomy and the unpredictable nature of external changes. Shipman (1983: 95) says of the application of systematic feedback models of school planning that 'The reality is often more messy'. Rational planning in schools may provide a context for guilt and for confusion of objectives if it is unable sufficiently to represent both the lived reality of school and the unpredictability of major and rapid governmentally imposed change.

Appraisal and target-setting

Teacher appraisal, introduced into schools as a part of the settlement of the 1984–87 industrial action by teachers, formally introduces another objective-setting process, 'targets for professional development' (DES 1989c: para. 64), into the complex web already suggested. The appraisal process has at its centre an apparently idiographic framework of target-setting and performance appraisal against these targets. Such a framework is problematic not only in the thin line between assessment and appraisal of teachers, but also in that it intersects with the teacher's personal objectives and also with institutional planning. It is unclear what the relationship between the institutional goals and the individual goals might be, or how the limited budgets held by individual schools for professional development are to be distributed between the conflicting demands of individuals. It is likely that such distribution will drive the system of target-setting, with staff increasingly suppressing aims that they know will attract no budgetary support. The appraisal process would appear inherently disingenuous if its supposed emphasis on the individual were in practice dominated by institutional (and ultimately government) objectives. Moreover, the appraisal process again questions the adequacy of the school development planning model, since there is no clear pathway by which the confidential discussions of appraiser and appraisee can be fed into a cycle of professional development planning for the school staff as a whole.

The selected areas of influence on teachers' work that have been discussed above may serve to illustrate something of the problem in trying to suggest that educational objectives (or objectives in education) can ever be singly understood. Moreover, there are internal contradictions in the way that the 1988 Act takes effect: the competition that is set in train between schools, and the hard-edged financial management necessary for school survival are not appropriate contexts to ensure curriculum access for students who will need additional resources. Two points arise from this: firstly that within diverse levels of objectives to which education is working, it cannot be assumed that the National Curriculum is experienced by all school pupils in the same way; secondly, that there is a need to reclaim the idea of curriculum as problematic and contested, if only because that more closely represents the reality.

Dissemination

It has been realised that if it is necessary to show discrimination in prescribing the different subjects to be taught, to transmit them in prudent dosages and to apportion them with care, it is even more essential to communicate to the teachers, who will be called upon to carry out this teaching, the spirit which is supposed to animate their work.

(Durkheim 1977 [1938]: 3)

Dissemination of curriculum change has been recognized in past development work as problematic. The Research, Development, Dissemination model developed by the Schools Council, for curriculum materials, led to study of the processes of innovation and implementation, and highlighted the complexity of those processes (Rudduck 1976). Interest increasingly focused upon school-based development (Skilbeck 1984; Oldroyd 1985). Fullan analysed the nature of change itself in educational settings highlighting organizational features and the key role of teachers acting collegially: 'if educational change is to happen, it will require that teachers understand themselves and are understood by others' (Fullan 1982: 117). Ball (1987) draws up a framework for understanding schools as organizations: a micro-political context embracing age, gender, the politics of leadership and career, and resources, as necessary in understanding the nature of schools.

Devolution of budgets to individual schools under the terms of the Education Act 1988 has included the devolution of that part of the budget formerly allocated for professional development and handled by Local Education Authorities (LEAs). Such school-based control and responsibility for staff development is in some respects in keeping with the general trend of research supporting school-focused development. However, in practice the distribution removes some of the economies of scale that Local Authorities were able to achieve, and further serves a model in which schools are to be seen as separate budget centres competing with each other. It therefore becomes essential to find other models which will reduce competitiveness. Partnerships (with LEAs and Higher Education) and consortia offer one way, it is suggested, in which individual schools can realize the benefits of in-house development while avoiding insularity (Clough *et al.* 1989; Rudduck 1992). Teachers' active participation in research, and initiation of research, also becomes central to this particular strand of thinking: 'a self-generating critical pedagogy is possible as a form of creative resistance to the hegemony of the state' (Elliott 1991: 117).

These shifts might be interpreted as part of a pattern of resistance to organizational features and to specific curricular interventions by central government or as a dialectical process of presenting oppositional models to the current Government's policy. The issue of whether the UK education system is 'best described as a national system locally administered or a local system nationally administered' (Simons 1987: 3) appears to be kept alive through this dynamic.

There are numerous types of meanings requiring consideration in the processes of dissemination. In the most obvious ways, the language of curriculum objectives is open to interpretation – meanings need to be interactively created. Language also surrounds the processes of curriculum change and seeks to legitimate them. The language of capitalism inhabits the language of education more palpably than previously: ownership and negotiation are potentially the empowering strands of Records of Achievement and other educational changes (PRAISE 1988). It is, of course, important to be clear about whether the adoption and colonization of this language is replacing the metaphors of growth in education as a temporary and conscious subversive strategy or whether it represents submission to the dominant ideology (Broadfoot 1990: 214).

Sikes analyses the strategies which teachers use to respond to centrally imposed change: carrying on as before, forming cliques, factions and enclaves, leaving, becoming more entrepreneurial about their career, resistance and sabotage, shifting the balance and grasping the opportunity (Sikes 1992: 46–8). Research into the effects of the introduction of the National Curriculum indicates the 'pressures and strains likely to be effected on both pupils and teachers' (Broadfoot *et al.* 1991b: 157), and that teachers see their role in SATs as protecting pupils (Gipps *et al.* 1992). Conditions of centrally imposed change and high levels of anxiety might be anticipated to create a complex array of response. HMI's review of training for the National Curriculum suggests a number of areas for further development, though it only hints at the multiple realities and subjectivities at work within this kind of change: 'Not all the training events inspected fully addressed the need to combine teaching and assessment, or were sufficiently clear about the separate purposes and techniques of assessment and recording. The main difficulty, even for skilled trainers, was the different starting-points of the teachers' (DES 1991b: 27). It appears that whether considered at the level of content of training, and different 'starting-points', or at the level of different responses to change and the effects of anxiety, the idea that the National Curriculum can provide a common curricular experience and common entitlement is flawed. The meanings that the National Curriculum and assessment take on in use will be created by a complex web of factors in teachers' histories and in the processes of dissemination.

The favoured model (by government) for the introduction of curriculum reforms has been the cascade model, which rests on assumptions that understandings can be hierarchically transmitted. This model was already identified as being profoundly inappropriate:

> It was fundamentally a rational model that had validity for transmitting purely technical information in a well-defined, stable and consensual context. For GCSE, both the task and the context were rather different. However smoothly the model had operated, it was almost inevitable that in practice teachers would have raised questions, taken alternative stances and interpreted the proceedings in different ways depending on their level of experience, knowledge and capabilities. It is questionable whether such a rational model would have had more than a limited effect. There was no guarantee that heads of department, left to their own devices and without any extra support or time, would have 'cascaded' down the underlying principles of the GCSE.
>
> (Radnor 1987: 55)

The cascading of specific understandings about curriculum may have been inadequate, but arguably that was not the only or the main kind of meaning being disseminated. The whole method of dissemination carried – and continues to carry – messages about the position of teachers in relation to the state. Grace (1987: 217) sees teachers used as 'a populist and simple explanation for Britain's contemporary and social ills'. The combination of political and bureaucratic imperatives have 'made serious inroads into their professional terrain' (1987: 218). In the cascade training model, a rhetoric of central control and information about curricular change accompanied a set of very generally stated assessment objectives requiring processes of interpretation. Anxiety characterized some training meetings and manifested itself by the time spent on administrative rather than curriculum questions (Butterfield 1989). That anxiety might be seen as related not only to change itself, but to particular kinds of change in the status of teachers. The reduction of the professional role of teachers in the National Curriculum is further illustrated through the changes between the moderation model for assessments advocated by TGAT, which essentially involved professional dialogue, and the introduction of an external

sampling process of quality audit (SEAC 1992a,b). All these processes set up a view that teaching is actually developed and
monitored by 'experts', a notion discussed by Apple (1986: 42),
rather than by practising classroom professionals. Moreover, professionals are increasingly isolated by the compartmentalization of
subjects. The trend of initial teacher education gives 'scarce attention to the personal development of new teachers, to reflection on
their values and purposes, and to the school cultures in which
teachers will learn their craft (Hargreaves 1991: 255). Hargreaves
sees teachers as becoming increasingly restricted to classrooms and
to subject knowledge.

While GCSE represented a new experience of imposed change for
secondary teachers it also gave them more curricular control than
previously at 16+. The National Curriculum, by contrast,
introduces a much more tightly defined curriculum and framework
for assessment. The form of curriculum conveys meanings: 'Currently of immense importance . . . is the way the logic and modes
of control of capital are entering the school through the form the
curriculum takes, not only its content' (Apple 1982: 31). Apple's
concerns in *Teachers and Texts* (1986) include 'the process by
which the curriculum gets to those teachers' (1986: 11). His definition of texts is relevant to the consideration of public understandings of education and teachers' work: '"texts" includes books and
proposals made available to educators and the general public by
specific groups to influence our decisions about what should be
taught in schools and what teachers' jobs should look like'. In this
analysis not only the curriculum documents of the National Curriculum and the various occupational standards being devised for
NVQs constitute texts, but also the speeches and interviews which
accompany the introduction of curriculum documents. The process
of dissemination also has a meaning and can be seen as a text, affecting understandings. Apple's major concerns are about the de-
skilling of teachers through 'the encroachment of technical control
procedures into the curriculum' (Apple 1986: 32) and through
intensification of workload.

Overview

Given the complexity of schools as organizations, and the importance of teachers individually and collectively in the processes of implementation, there is a difficulty with respect to whether we can talk of anything as monumental as a National Curriculum, or whether it is more appropriately understood as reinterpreted at individual school level. Bowe *et al.* (1992) use this process of reinterpretation and 're-creation' as the basis for arguing that the 'state control model is analytically very limited'. Hatcher and Troyna take issue with this, and locate their specific arguments with the testing associated with the National Curriculum: 'The imposition of national testing locks the National Curriculum in place as the dominant framework of teachers' work, whatever opportunities teachers may take to evade it or reshape it' (Hatcher and Troyna 1994: 165). This argument is in part developed through a discussion of whether Ball's discussion of 'readerly' texts (i.e. texts whose meanings are unequivocal) and 'writerly' texts (i.e. in which the reader is a co-producer of the meanings of the text) as defined by Barthes, is really a useful analytical framework for government policy, because readerly texts are so rare. 'None the less, we would stick our necks out here and suggest that the Standard Assessment Tasks (SATs) associated with the National Curriculum and the recent orders governing the dissolution of the binary system in Higher Education in Britain come close to this notion of a "readerly" policy text' (1994: 163).

It may indeed be the case, as Hatcher and Troyna argue, that national testing is almost uniquely unavailable to active reinterpretation by teachers, and that it makes the National Curriculum similarly unavailable to reinterpretation. If it is the case then we might see that as a very effective strategy for reducing professional authority over the curriculum, and truly allowing some uniformity of curriculum experience. However, it seems that it is unlikely that it is a common curriculum that is being disseminated in the context of National Curriculum, but rather a message about social control.

It has been argued in the previous chapter that professional power is a very difficult notion, since it cannot be automatically assumed that professional power is working in the interests of student power: the two may be in conflict. What we have to address is the relationship between a hierarchical view of national control of knowledge and work, and the impact of that upon students. It is difficult to see where student democracy will be modelled, or enabled within such a hierarchy. Just as it cannot be argued that professional power necessarily works to the advantage of students (arguments about protecting students from change and anxiety must be viewed with caution in so far as they may actually be used to extend traditional professional roles), nor can it be argued that removing professional authority automatically entitles or empowers students. Much may depend upon the messages of the medium of control.

8

CRITERION-REFERENCING: NOW YOU SEE IT, NOW YOU DON'T

It is not easy to give a definition of criterion-referencing. Indeed, much of this chapter will be concerned with just how slippery such a definition is. Criterion-referencing can more easily be described in terms of the rhetoric that surrounds it, than in terms of unambiguous examples of its use. Its appeal is, on the one hand, to the bureaucratic and on the other to the pedagogic interests in education. Once we have common, stated objectives in education then the success of individuals and of parts of the education service can, supposedly, be measured against those objectives. Thus it appears to offer much to those who seek greater accountability from the education service, and who seek to bring it under closer control. Criterion-referencing also has attractions for teachers since it superficially promises to give more meaningful information to learners about their progress. Whether it can satisfactorily address both of these interests, accountability and improved teaching/learning processes is, however, a key question. Does it truly provide an interface between the classroom and society? Can it really provide absolute information about standards and about progression?

Criterion-referencing is most usually contrasted to norm-referencing, or the determination of assessments by the attainment of an individual in comparison with others. Norm-referencing has been used in two main ways in assessment in the UK. Firstly, it has been used to determine grades in some public examination contexts. However, it has by no means been the only or the dominant method for determining grades. Far more use has been made of panel judgement of samples of examination scripts and of coursework, described by Christie and Forrest as 'limen-referencing': This

> is the model which characterises British examinations . . . The grades have at least the force of custom and the chief examiners can identify borderline grade performances in each year's examination paper with some accuracy. The grades do not, however, carry with them any explicit definition of the achievements they imply. We shall dub it a limen-referenced model to emphasize its role in dealing with fuzzy signals implying an interdependence of transmitter and receiver.
>
> (Christie and Forrest 1981: 57)

Despite the reality of grade-awarding procedures, the belief that norm-referencing has predominated has been difficult to budge, and teachers (and students) have felt that their efforts may not be individually judged on their merits.

Another context in which the education service has, at least historically, been familiar with norm-referencing is in its use in determining intelligence quotients in systems such as the 11+ examination used for selection to grammar, technical and secondary modern schools in the tripartite secondary education provision predating the widespread (but not national) establishment of comprehensive schools. The shortcomings of the selection process and of the subsequent differences of opportunity and outlook afforded to those either selected or deselected have left a legacy of mistrust of normative measures. The emphasis on ability (as a single measurable entity determining one's educational provision) created a powerful educational map. Criterion-referencing changes the map, by replacing the notion of ability (which by implication can be little altered by processes of teaching and learning) with a notion of achievements (the plural is important), which can be individually represented, and which will enable progress to be described.

The GCSE introduced to the everyday vocabulary of teachers the notion of criterion-referencing: 'Criteria-referenced grading is intended to describe a system under which grades are defined and awarded in terms of predetermined standards of performance specific to the subject concerned' (DES 1985b: 22). Similarly, it is the basis of the system advocated by TGAT: 'As defined in this report, an assessment system in which an award or grade is made on the basis of the quality of performance of a pupil irrespective of the performance of other pupils . . .' (DES 1987c: preface and glossary). It is now, supposedly, the basis for assessment in the National Curriculum, including the new Key Stage 4 GCSE, National Vocational Qualifications and the personal profiling element of Records of Achievement.

The limitations and possibilities of criterion-referencing, its theoretical robustness and its practical application on a national scale, require exploration.

The history of the term 'criterion-referencing' may serve to illustrate some of the discussion around what it might mean, as well as how it might be educationally applied. The term has been developed initially by psychologists concerned with the techniques of arriving at better – more valid and reliable – educational measurements. Within this arena of discussion are therefore to be found some of the technical debates, for example around what a criterion *is*, and around the nature of *mastery*.

Nedelsky (1954) developed in the 1940s a method of assessment applicable to multiple-choice test items, known as the Minimum Pass Level method. Experienced judges would identify the number of distractors that a student at a given grade level could identify as incorrect and the reciprocal of that number would give the cutting score for the item. This method has more to do with establishing the difficulty of an item than with ensuring its validity in terms of any particular criteria.

Robert Glaser's coinage of the term 'criterion-referenced measures' promises much: 'What I shall call criterion-referenced measures depend upon an absolute standard of quality, while what I term norm-referenced measures depend upon relative standard.' However, his exemplification of the difference does not in its immediate context resolve the difficulty of separating criteria from distributive judgements.

The scores obtained from an achievement test provide primarily two kinds of information. One is the degree to which the student has attained criterion performance, for example, whether he can satisfactorily prepare an experimental report, or solve certain kinds of word problems in arithmetic. The second type of information that an achievement test score provides is the relative ordering of individuals with respect to their test performance, for example whether Student A can solve his problems more quickly than Student B.

(Glaser 1963: 519)

The first example which depends upon satisfactory achievement begs the question of how that is to be defined. The likelihood is that the definition will formally or informally be derived from knowledge of performance of that age group, in other words from the normal distribution of results. The example of 'norm-referenced measures' does not help the distinction, since while the use of the word 'relatively' indicates that these will be viewed in terms of distribution, that distribution could equally be used in a subsequent test to create a 'criterion', i.e. the solution of a given problem in a given period of time.

Hambleton and others (1978: 2) attribute subsequent confusion to the misunderstanding associated with readings of Glaser's article. A domain of behaviours was meant, they assert, not a minimum proficiency level. In other words, in the example that Glaser gives, of 'satisfactorily preparing experimental reports', the criterion is not to be seen as 'satisfactorily' (however that would be defined) but the domain of 'prepare an experimental report'.

The National Curriculum in a sense side steps this debate by using both definitions. The Attainment Targets in themselves represent domains: 'Speaking and Listening' (one of five ATs in English); 'Scientific Investigation' (one of four ATs in Science); 'Shape and Space' (one of five ATs in Mathematics). The Statements of Attainment that constitute the level descriptors of each AT then represent another definition of criterion-referencing – the minimum proficiency definition. For example:

English
- describe an event, real or imagined to the teacher or another pupil;
- respond appropriately to a range of more complex instructions given by a teacher, and give simple instructions.

(Extracts from Speaking and Listening, English AT1, Level 2)

Mathematics
- use accurate measurement and drawing in constructing 3-D models;
- find areas of plane shapes or volumes of simple solids.
  (Extracts from Shape and Space, Mathematics AT4, Level 5)

This particular duality (between a domain definition and a minimum proficiency definition) may indeed go some way to explaining contradictions and tensions that teachers are experiencing in attempting to assess students against National Curriculum levels. They are trying to make assessments against two different models of criterion-referencing, both of which have their own inherent problems. Firstly, what are the problems in the minimum proficiency model? This draws upon the notion of mastery (Block 1971; Bloom *et al.* 1971). Mastery might be seen as a state (Bloom *et al.* 1971) or might be judged along a continuum (Ebel 1971). The state model which distinguishes only between mastery and non-mastery is typically concerned with structuring teaching and learning so that the great majority of students achieve mastery of each stage: 'Most students (perhaps more than 90 per cent) can master what we have to teach them, and it is the task of instruction to find the means which will enable them to master the subject under consideration' (Bloom *et al.* 1971: 43). The continuum model suggests that there may be stages or degrees of mastery.

Very close definition of each stage of mastery (as a state of mastery in itself) would suggest an enormous number of descriptors for any significant area of learning, and indeed this was the outcome in the search to find grade criteria for the GCSE. A continuum model might offer more flexibility, indeed the mastery could then be equated with the whole domain, and the degrees of mastery could be quite loosely defined. The National Curriculum appears unclear as to whether it is concerned with a state or a continuum model. Its statements of attainment are supposedly sufficiently independent and absolute in meaning that the whole public education system can be judged by these 'bench-marks' or states of mastery. The term mastery appears in training materials but is not really defined: under the heading 'Laying Foundations: The Idea of Mastery . . . Assessment in the National Curriculum is criterion-referenced. However it does not employ the notion of "mastery learning" which proposes that children should move forward as soon as an attainment is observed ... The National Curriculum does not follow this model, but relies on a balance between progression and consolidation' (SEAC 1990a: para. 6.3).

In practice, however, assessments rely heavily upon some definition of mastery. Teachers working with the statements of attainment are all too well aware that these statements require judgement and shared experience in order to be interpreted, and are far from being the technically precise system that national assessment appears to depend upon. The continuum model allows for degrees of mastery and therefore for a greater input of judgement, but professional judgement is precisely what National Curriculum assessment has (rhetorically) been designed to override.

The evidence for the educational success of the more rigid applications of mastery learning is anyway questionable. In an examination of both the theory of mastery learning and the experimental evidence which has been adduced to support it, Robert Slavin is unconvinced;

> In an extreme form, the central contentions of mastery learning are almost tautologically true. If we establish a set of learning objectives and demand that every student achieve them at a high level regardless of how long that takes, then it is virtually certain that all students will ultimately achieve that criterion.
>
> (Slavin 1987: 177)

His own analysis of seven methodically selected 'best-evidence' group-based mastery research projects points out that there is

> little support for the 'strong claim' that, holding time and objectives constant, mastery learning will accelerate student achievement ... Not one of the seven studies found effects of mastery learning that reached even conventional levels of statistical significance (even in individual-level analyses), much less educational significance.
>
> (Slavin 1987: 191)

Slavin suggests that where advantages do seem to have accrued from mastery learning their origins are in features such as regular feedback, rather than in instructional features distinctive of mastery learning.

Work conducted in Scotland led Sally Brown to warn that there are distinctly different definitions and expectations of what criterion-referencing can provide:

> anyone who adopts the following ... definition meaning of CRA [criterion-referenced assessment]
>
> > 'Criterion-referenced assessment provides an evaluative description of the qualities which are to be assessed (e.g. an account of what pupils know and can do) without reference to the performance of others.'
>
> will have quite different expectations from someone whose interpretation includes a requirement that criterion levels of achievement are defined. The former places few con-straints on how the assessment will be formulated: narratives, numbers, grades, or other forms will be acceptable in so far as they are appropriate to the quality which is being assessed. The latter interpretation, however, implies that the descrip-tion has to be in the form of something like grade-levels, and that the achievements can be described in some sort of step-wise progression.
>
> (S. Brown 1988: 4)

The further definition of criterion-referencing – that of referencing by domains – has its own range of problems. What constitutes a domain? A 'criterion-referenced test is used to ascertain an indi-vidual's status with respect to a well-defined behavioral domain' (Popham 1978). The following extract suggests that a domain may simply be something like 'giving impromptu speeches' and practice in the same is the key to success:

> One of the most powerful principles in instructional psycho-logy calls for providing the student with practice in perform-ing the types of behaviors being sought. For example, if you wish to have students become truly skilled at giving impromptu speeches, then you'd certainly better supply a ton of practice for them in giving impromptu speeches ...
>
> Essentially the teacher must generate practice exercises that call for the student to engage in the same kind of intellectual behavior as that specified in the criterion-referenced test's target behavior. Sometimes this practice can be conducted verbally, sometimes in writing, but the important thing is to

get the student to practice the intellectual operations called for in the test's domain of behaviors.

(Popham 1978: 221)

It is difficult not to feel frustrated by this example. The real key to the conceptualization of the domain appears to be not in the 'giving of impromptu speeches' but in the 'intellectual operations' (unspecified) which might underlie such performance. Popham's later comments appear to acknowledge the difficulty more fully:

> lacking solid research bases for our work with criterion-referenced test specifications, it seems necessary to rely on our best experience-based hunches about what sorts of test specification will prove serviceable ... At no point in the test development process for criterion-referenced measures is it more apparent that we are employing art, rather than science, than when the general nature of the behavioral domain to be tested is initially conceptualized.
>
> (Popham 1980: 19)

One way of avoiding the issues around mastery (and, possibly, around domain specification) is to use a system of cutting scores in looking at test performance. As such cutting scores can only really be determined by looking at performance of numbers of individuals on an item or on part of a test, as in the example earlier from Nedelsky, this begins to look indistinguishable from norm-referencing. Millman (1973) reviews the technical issues around this technique of criterion-referencing: 'but the authors' conceptualizations of the educational task facing the learners has not always been clear' (Meskauskas 1976: 134). In other words, there are problems in establishing validity of assessment from scores alone. Ebel (1962: 18) emphasized the need for reporting of raw scores and test content in order that meaningful information in terms of 'capacities, abilities and accomplishments' is available. In the development of National Curriculum assessment at the end of each Key Stage we are witnessing increasing moves towards pencil-and-paper testing. Such testing is not well adapted to covering the full content of the curriculum or its full range of objectives. It will be hard to relate performance on tests to specific ATs, far less to particular levels in terms of statements of attainment. Cutting scores are the only way to handle such tests in the allocation of levels, but such an approach sells teachers, parents and students very short of the promises with which a criterion-referenced system was heralded.

The changes in assessment introduced by government in the introduction of GCSE, and later the National Curriculum, did not exist in the absence of research and development, though such development was largely ignored in the Government's 'reforms'. Criterion-referenced assessment emphasizing diagnosis was explored by, among others, Black and Dockrell (1984). The work was largely focused upon classroom use and improvements in pedagogy. Brown warns against the application of such an approach outside specific contexts of learning:

> like many other educational ideas, criterion-referencing may have promised, or been interpreted as promising, much more than it could deliver. Secondly, by its very nature criterion-referenced assessment is intimately linked to a particular curriculum or to specific opportunities to learn; development of the assessment procedures, therefore, must be the responsibility of those who are closest to the curriculum and learning rather than of researchers.
>
> (S. Brown 1988: 1)

The graded assessment schemes in use in England and Wales such as the Graded Assessment in Mathematics (GAIM), Graded Assessment in Modern Languages (GOML) and Graded Assessment in Science Project (GASP) use the idea of mastery, and the objectives used are behavioural in nature. However, these schemes do not ally themselves with the terminology of 'behaviours' and 'instruction'. They are more characteristically concerned with 'pupil involvement', 'success', 'motivation' and 'development' (Harrison 1982: 42).

They are related, too, to developments in profiling, and the identification and mapping of areas and stages of achievement. This relationship with profiling raises possibilities of applying criterion-referencing in ways that are closely linked to individual progress, rather than to the technical issues of educational measurement.

> The principal contrast between graded assessments and profiles . . . lies in their stance towards quantification and measurement. Graded assessments are firmly within the

psychometric tradition of tests and examinations, while the advocates of profiles are often against measurement and the reductionism and trivialisation that all too often accompany measurement. So in the union of profiles and graded assessments, we see the exciting prospect of bringing together the humanistic and quantitative traditions in educational assessment. From this could emerge a most fruitful collaboration that could give a new rigour to humanistic assessment while preserving the pre-eminence of validity and curriculum relevance. [In regard to appropriate research] ... what is not needed is the sort of detailed technical research of the type that has been done for 50 years on existing examination systems, largely atheoretical and motivated by a desire to provide merely technical answers to essentially educational problems.

(Nuttall and Goldstein 1986: 200)

Another important area of research was that carried out by the Assessment of Performance Unit (APU) which was established in the 1970s to look at educational standards. It used light sampling to look at – or attempt to look at – changes over time in the performance of the school population generally. However, despite its contribution to test development and its insights into the difficulty of measuring change over time, its work did not match the Government's policies of the 1980s. General conclusions about standards might adversely reflect upon government provision, and could not be used to make judgements about individual schools and teachers. The emphasis on the testing of all students in state schooling introduced by the Education Act 1988 showed a very different engagement with educational standards from that embodied in the APU, whose last survey was undertaken in 1984.

Criterion-referencing as an arm of government policymaking has clear links to those same advantages that management by objectives (through assessment) has been argued to have. Despite the research evidence and the ambiguities in criterion-referencing outlined above, the model chosen by government – and recommended by TGAT – rests on the assumption that it is possible to define levels of achievement and to assess these levels nationally. This might have appeared to open up large questions about the relationship of levels and ages, and about the advisability, or otherwise, of teaching and assessing all students of a similar age together. Work on graded assessments in the UK focused attention on the need to consider stages rather than ages of learning, as a logical concomitant of criterion-referencing. Roger Murphy raised the matter in an early critique of National Curriculum assessment proposals: 'There is little justification for prescribing attainment targets in relation to fixed ages. Optimum attainment levels should be recorded and rewarded regardless of the age when they are reached by individual pupils' (Murphy 1988: 42). Cresswell and Houston, however, stress the importance of maturation as a context affecting performance, and see the National Curriculum model as disregarding research which shows that 'pupils of different ages make qualitatively different responses to the same task' (Cresswell and Houston 1991: 67). A question that arose when National Curriculum plans were first published was whether a student of say 10 or 11 could gain a GCSE certificate if they reached the requisite level. This was rapidly resolved by SEC who ruled that a GCSE was only available if one had studied the relevant course and taken the relevant examinations – it was not simply a matter of level. Already the boundaries of reform were visible: the tried and tested GCSE (and its longer pedigree in examining at 16 + through GCEs and CSEs) was not to be overturned, but may be only unsettled by its incorporation into the National Curriculum. The announcement by SEAC in 1993 that GCSE results would, after all, be awarded in grades as in the past, and not in National Curriculum levels, seemed further to endorse the existing rather than the new order.

Nervousness about age and stage may be further demonstrated in the discussion of the 10-point scale in the Dearing Report (Dearing 1993b: 56–71). One option explored there in some detail is end of Key Stage grades. The suggestion is that on a five-point grade scale, B and D might be 'criterion-referenced' and the other grades established by relation to those. This option would have further entrenched the pre-eminence of age as the anchor of progression, and the grading system might soon have drifted from criterion-referencing into some loosely normal distribution: 'Grade A would then indicate a performance significantly better than grade B; grade C a performance which lies between B and D . . .' (1993b: para. 7.40). This option was rejected by Dearing, but largely on the grounds of the amount of work that teachers had already done to try to make the 10-point scale work, rather than because of any view in principle about the appropriateness of giving Key Stages still further prominence in the assessment system.

The issue of ages and stages does not seem to have troubled policymakers and the reason for indifference may not be hard to find. Far more important in the current agenda is easing the route for schools to operate selection. So, if teachers and schools are having difficulty accommodating the wide variety of levels within a given age group, and in differentiating work sufficiently to meet the needs of all, they may be less likely to resist enticements to narrow their intake. The Key Stages correspond to traditional points of transfer between schools, or between schools and further education: in that way the National Curriculum could be used to facilitate selection or certainly would not impede such selection. Whereas teachers may have welcomed the promises of a criterion-referenced system (whatever its other flaws) in the hope of creating better individual-level information, for government the attraction of the National Curriculum model may (among other factors) have been that it would serve to highlight the gaps in achievement between individuals, and make mixed-ability groupings apparently unworkable.

Despite the many technical issues surrounding criterion-referencing, it may still seem to offer opportunities for structuring and reconceptualizing the work in classrooms. The central tension may be between a national system and an approach to pedagogy. A national system of criterion-referencing can only emphasize the technical issues without maximizing the opportunities that can be developed at a smaller scale and more informal level, in the school and in the classroom. To provide anything like precise descriptors the criteria, for anything as large as the whole of compulsory schooling, would stretch to even more volumes of paper than the already overweighty curriculum which Dearing has slimmed down. The tendency of criteria to proliferate out of control was seen in the search for GCSE grade criteria, and the rejection of them while in draft form because they would have been unworkably numerous in examining students. Yet the dilemma remained, for the principles of GCSE rested on a criterion-referenced system. Kingdon and Stobart saw grade criteria as essential if the principle of positive achievement was to be realized (Kingdon and Stobart 1988: 133–47). Cresswell and Houston (1991: 71–2) argue that because of the importance of context, criteria can only be task-specific.

Perhaps the problem is how much can be prescribed centrally. How far is central government creating unworkable systems by prescribing too much of the detail? Arguably the search for appropriate criteria is highly educational for the searcher, but a list of criteria handed down can be meaningless. The concept of 'ownership' which is gathering force in many assessment contexts, particularly in the development of Records of Achievement (PRAISE 1988: Part 1 1.3.4.{d}), has relevance here too, and, if we accept views based on long experience of development of criterion-referenced assessment in Scotland, small-scale and class-room use may be the appropriate context for such assessment.

The combining of a criterion-referenced system (in intention and description) with the reporting of overall performance of individuals, schools and LEAs, is, moreover, contradictory to the diagnostic purposes of this kind of assessment. Cresswell and Houston (1991: 72–8) argue that descriptive information can only be achieved by profiling which does not match with the policy intention of presenting information from National Curriculum assessment in league tables.

The question of the context in which criterion-referencing is developed may be central. Wood urges that the discussion of criterion-referencing should not be divorced from the purposes which it is enlisted to serve: 'Powerful though it may be as a mobilising emotion, it is subordinate to that of function . . . selection, or screening, or monitoring' (Wood 1986: 188).

The interaction of the politics of standards with criterion-referenced assessment in the context of competency testing in the USA is discussed by Ellwein and others. On the basis of their research they propose certain hypotheses in relation to competency testing. They suggest that normative influences underlie the setting of standards: 'anticipated fail rates influence standards when agencies must deal firsthand with the consequences of failure' (Ellwein *et al.* 1988: 5). They also draw attention to a feature of the micropolitics of change that is probably unrelated to any particular technical advantages in any large-scale assessment programme: 'Organizational efforts are most visible, intense, and detailed during early phases of competency testing reforms. Similar efforts are conspicuously absent during later stages' (1988: 7).

These views about purpose, about scale and about the political context have to be taken very seriously in appraising the worth of the introduction of large-scale 'criterion-referenced' systems in the UK. Firstly, it may well be the case that much of the so-called criterion-referencing is in fact norm-referencing, and trends towards that are already increasingly visible in National Curriculum testing. Secondly, resting a system of national league tables on a so-called criterion-referenced system cannot support the innovation and development needed at classroom level to explore its opportunities. Criterion-referencing is not so well developed a science (if science at all) that it can survive without the artistry of teachers.

Although the case for stated criteria in examinations was well developed prior to the introduction of GCSE, as was the classroom and diagnostic advantage of a criterion-referenced approach, the feasibility of carrying out national assessments according to criteria was not established. The pedagogic importance of the principle of criterion-referenced assessment may be capable of existence, and a fuller existence, outside the movements which would ally it to cutting scores, and which seek for a refinement of its principles to a point which works against educational validity.

The interest in criterion-referencing arises from a wish to find better ways of looking at – and assessing – individual progress and the effects of teaching upon learning. These are central matters. There is, however, currently a risk that schools and vocational training will be experiencing a great deal of measurement and not enough real feedback from that information. We would be in the position outlined by Wood (1986: 185) of having plenty of 'measurement in education' rather than 'educational measurement'.

National Curriculum progression and criterion-referencing

One of the advantages that could be claimed for criterion-referenced assessment built upon stated objectives and levels of achievement, is that it will provide for curricular progression. Indeed, 'progression' is one of the important legitimating concepts of the National Curriculum and its assessment. The models being introduced through the National Curriculum, and in vocational training, have contributed to bringing this very important area into prominence. However, the discussion above has tried to illustrate the very uncertain ground that criterion-referencing provides for any kind of measurement of levels on a national basis. There are of course also competing views of what constitutes progression.

During their work in the 1970s and 1980s, HMI were evolving a model of curriculum built upon areas of experience, elements – knowledge and skills, and characteristics including progression and continuity. Their definitions of progression and continuity were essentially drawn from a developmental tradition: 'there is a need to build systematically on the children's existing knowledge, concepts, skills and capabilities' (DES 1985c: 48). This fairly general statement bridges very different views of teaching and learning and does not breach the code either of child-centredness on the one hand, nor of mastery learning on the other. The report continues by identifying certain important transitional phases in school life when continuity can be most difficult to achieve: starting school, primary–secondary transition (in National Curriculum terms Key Stage 2) and the move from compulsory schooling at 16 + (now Key Stage 4). Underlying the National Curriculum, then, was an established area of concern with discontinuities caused by the different phases of education. However, the curriculum models which HMI were outlining in their Red Books did not suggest a technocratic answer like the National Curriculum. They were rather advocating broad principles which would inform educational planning.

In this matter of progression, as in others, the government policy for the National Curriculum took expediently the terms that HMI had established for educational discussion: the proposed curriculum would consolidate work on 'progression, continuity and coherence' from five to 16 and would raise standards of attainment by 'checking on progress' (DES 1987b). The policy for the new National Curriculum did not, however, address the underlying concepts of 'progression' or any history of debate.

There were of course important and conflicting traditions, characterizing and separating the two main phases of compulsory schooling. On the one hand secondary schools were strongly imbued with a subject oriented curriculum and culture, further strengthened by public examinations in those subjects at 16. Primary schools were influenced by developmentalist traditions, the need to contextualize learning and avoid what Donaldson called 'disembedded thought' (Donaldson 1978: 76–85).

The tension between a developmentalist view of curriculum and learning, and a knowledge-led view of curriculum is an established aspect of discussion of primary schooling, as a recent paper acknowledges in supplying its opinion of the resolution:

> The first, and longest established, focus of enquiry is the empirical study of how primary pupils develop and learn. To teach well, teachers must take account of how children learn. We do not, however, believe that it is possible to construct a model of primary education from evidence about children's development alone: the nature of the curriculum followed by the pupil and the range of teaching strategies employed by the teacher are also of critical importance. Teaching is not applied child development.
>
> (Alexander *et al.* 1992: 18)

This so-called 'Three Wise Men' report brought together three figures representing HMI, the National Curriculum Council (a government appointee) and Higher Education in its capacity of providing teacher training. It could be seen as an attempt to reconcile the developmentalist traditions and the new curriculum: certainly it engaged directly with the need (created by government policy) to establish a different balance in primary education between developmental theory, curriculum content and teaching strategy.

The developmentalist view linking cognitive, emotional and physical development implies a pedagogy based upon integration of these, and has been influential in pedagogy at primary level and especially in infant teaching. The shift forced by the National Curriculum was considerable. The National Curriculum initially removed itself from discussion of teaching method; it was 'not a description of how the school day should be organised or the curriculum delivered' (NCC 1989: 1). However, by suggesting a very heavily prescribed and content-led curriculum from age five, it has provided a changed working context in which teachers trained in developmentalist theories are working to a curriculum framework that has more in common with the subject-defined secondary curriculum. It is a long way from the very wide range of features of learning identified by Wood:

> desire and ability to attend, concentrate, and memorize, knowing how to apportion one's time and resources in order

to study and learn; understanding what people mean by what they say and do; possessing the confidence and expertise to explain oneself and knowing how to make what one has to say or write accessible to one's audience; the ability to evaluate and redirect one's efforts, to self-correct and self-instruct; and knowing how to make one's actions contingent upon the requests, demand and needs of others.

(Wood 1988: 214–15)

Although the lower levels of the National Curriculum model of progression may be compatible with theory about child development, the later levels are much more pragmatically, even arbitrarily linked to past practice in subject teaching. At later levels there is relatively little theory on which an overview of progression could have been based. However, some researches have attempted to apply Piaget's theory of cognitive development to subjects, and to identify a school-learning related model of adolescent and post-adolescent achievement. Such studies have particularly focused upon the abstraction and generalization consistent with the early formal and formal stages of Piaget's description (Piaget 1971: 1–12; Peel 1971; Wilkinson *et al.* 1980; Biggs and Collis 1982). Wilkinson, with his co-workers in the Crediton research project, attempted to devise a framework for assessing language development. The framework was devised from an 'interaction between our perceptions [i.e. the researchers' perceptions], teachers' judgements and theoretical considerations' (Wilkinson *et al.* 1980: 65). No such considerations affected the National Curriculum planning. Its overall view of educational purposes is signally lacking; its objectives were derived, deliberately, outside theoretical frameworks.

One further point needs to be made about the contribution that developmental theory might have made and should still make to National Curriculum and its assessment. The work of Donaldson (1978) and also of Light *et al.* (1979) has suggested the need to be aware of children's knowledge and understanding of the event structures in which they are asked to participate. The particular researches were carried out in a context of re-examining Piaget's experiments with young children. By repeating his experiments in different ways providing more 'real' contexts for the experiments which the children would recognize, a number of Piaget's theories about the limitations of early development have been reviewed. It is now considered that children have earlier capacities for conceptualization and understanding than Piaget suggested. The important factor for this discussion is that the repetition of Piaget's experiments throws light on what may happen in assessment situations (as well as in experimental situations) if young people are not confident about the event structures in which they are to respond to questions.

The extent to which National Curriculum and National Curriculum assessment facilitate the understanding of 'event structures' is dependent not only upon features inherent in learning and assessment tasks, but also in the understandings students have of purposes and their relationship to curriculum and assessment. If we accept the arguments outlined above about context, it must be supposed that the politics of curriculum is also part of that event structure and can be anticipated to affect what children and young adults appear to achieve.

GCSE was located within an attempt to redefine subjects with a taxonomy of learning objectives. Its relationship to Bloom's taxonomy is discussed in Chapters 3 and 4. Bloom's taxonomy 'is really intended to guide the selection of items for a test rather than to evaluate the quality of response' (Biggs and Collis 1982: 13). Hence the GCSE assessment objectives are not described in terms of levels; they do not inherently relate to levels of achievement or GCSE grades. It is intended that all who took the examination would perform at some level across all the objectives. It did not propose, from 1986–93, a system of progression through the two years of a course. The presentation of course work, accounting for between 20 and 100 per cent of the total assessed work (depending on the subject and syllabus chosen) was anticipated to span the course, and it was not felt necessary to devise any way for weighting work produced later in the course more heavily than that produced earlier. Hence in a National Curriculum model for GCSE, course work becomes problematic, because the National Curriculum is posited on a notion of progression, and an average difference of at least one GCSE grade would be suggested by the TGAT model of progression (DES 1987c: para. 104). The reduction (even elimination) of course work becomes logically necessary to sustaining the model of progression proposed by TGAT.

The TGAT model presents a very much simpler view than the

researches and theory about development would suggest. It rules out the influences of maturation as a context (Cresswell 1991) by supposing that levels of educational functioning can be plotted across ages irrespective of levels of emotional and physical maturity.

> In a criterion-referenced system there should be no distinction between the definition of the sequence of levels of a profile component to reflect progress between ages, and its use to differentiate progression at a particular age.
>
> (DES 1987c: para. 109)

The National Curriculum is thus explicitly distanced from a developmental model. Moreover, it also denies that the progression implied necessarily exists outside the definition of National Curriculum levels:

> It is not necessary to presume that the progression defined indicates some inescapable order in the way children learn, or some sequence of difficulty in the material learnt.
>
> (DES 1987c: para. 93)

Gipps questioned the apparent ease with which Statements of Attainment were devised within this model and warned that 'We do not yet know if they are in the right order . . .' (Gipps 1990: 94).

Schools are then working with a model which links progression firmly to fixed curriculum objectives and which effectively marginalizes alternative notions of progress or development. Questions of organization of teaching groups by age or stage become divorced from maturational/social dimensions of learning. Teachers are attempting to make formative assessments and keep assessment records that cannot always closely match summative SAT results if the system of progression is operating. Disparity between teacher assessment and SAT results may be used to legitimate the lower status of teacher assessment, rather than to reflect progression between the earlier times when teacher assessment is carried out, and the end of Key Stage SATs. Assessment as integrated, diagnostic and formative will be hard to sustain in a model of progression that is, in practice, dominated by Key Stage testing. The 'high stakes', identified as a problem in competency testing in the USA (Corbett and Wilson 1988), and also associated with the assessment arrangements here further weaken the possibility of the model of progression working.

There are organizational issues for schools too. Conducting (and teaching towards?) the SATs may come to be seen as the province of particular teachers within individual schools. It is possible that some teachers will be encouraged to become experts on the SATs. If teachers were repeatedly allocated to the end of Key Stage classes, because of their familiarity with the assessment arrangements, the professional climate and dialogue of the school is altered. The feed-forward and feedback of information between years would be less effective in the context of year-specialist teachers than in a context where teachers are annually changing their age group. An important context for progression and continuity would thus be lost.

The lack of interaction of the progression model with theory, and with the effects of the particular assessment arrangements is problematic. The need for the model to be closely evaluated by teachers was acknowledged by the NCC in the early development stages of the National Curriculum:

> Monitoring the National Curriculum is not just a matter of ensuring that the statutory requirements of Education Reform Act are carried out. It is an important part of the evaluation of the *appropriateness* of the National Curriculum itself, both *in general terms and in its details*. The National Curriculum Council is charged with the task of keeping the curriculum under review, and *evidence from teachers* will form an *essential* part of that process.
>
> （NCC 1989: 16) [italics added]

That evaluation is made increasingly problematic, however, by the dynamic of the argument about publication of results. Schools are under pressure to improve their results (against what may be a somewhat arbitrary scheme of progression) rather than to engage in professional dialogue with each other and with government about the validity of the curriculum and its assessment. Chapter 10 suggests that studies of school effectiveness find it difficult to articulate with detailed curricular and pedagogic matters. And yet, in this area of devising curricular change and improvements in assessment, there is a fundamental contradiction in supposing that both schools and the curriculum can be evaluated at the same time.

Outside the context of comparison, there are other examples of criterion-referenced assessment which are proving less contentious. In the personal profiling elements of Records of Achievement schools and students still have opportunities to develop useful frameworks for personal target-setting and review. Sometimes called 'ipsative assessment', that is a form of assessment which looks at progress in terms solely of oneself, this represents a form of criterion-referencing, and certainly fits the definition of not being based upon comparison with the performance of others. Of course, this is not educational measurement, but is concerned with self-awareness, personal responsibility in learning and motivation. The progression and the criteria may be personally defined.

The Records of Achievement National Steering Committee (RANSC) giving evidence to TGAT identified the contradictions in intentions and philosophy between National Curriculum assessment proposals and Records of Achievement. They stressed the importance of 'involvement of pupils in their own assessment by means of a dialogue between pupils and teachers' and of the principle of 'positive achievement'. They also went on to outline a more fundamental tension:

> ... the NC [National Curriculum] proposals, whilst aiming to raise the standards of individual pupils, are also concerned with the accountability of schools and local education authorities. This raises two possible tensions. First, certain pilot developments are strongly committed to the view that pupils are 'owners' of their ROA, having discretion about what to include and to whom to show them ... Secondly the recording and reporting of NC assessments in ways that fulfil the proposed evaluative and comparative purposes may sit uneasily within a pupil's individual record of his or her unique positive achievement, without reference to other pupils' achievements.
>
> (DES 1987c: Appendix 1)

The major issue is that the uncertainties and contradictions of the model of progression to which compulsory schooling is now working are driven by functional/political imperatives and used to support systems of accountability by results. This divides discussion between those who would wish to promote better models of progression, and those who would wish to use data evaluatively. Following either route independently of the other is likely to leave major questions unanswered.

9

ISSUES IN THE COMPARISON OF PERFORMANCE

One of the key arguments that might be adduced for the introduction of a core curriculum with specified objectives is the difficulty of making comparisons of performance (of standards) across assessments made against different curricular objectives. This difficulty was identified by the comparability studies carried out by the Schools Council and cited below. If judgemental accountability and measurement are at issue, as they are in the National Curriculum, then the system has to provide reliable and comparable information. Comparison is not, however, the main purpose of criterion-referencing, which is also part of the design of the National Curriculum. The problems and ambiguities surrounding the notion of criterion-referencing were discussed in Chapter 8. It is argued in that chapter that criterion-referencing does have a meaning as a pedagogic philosophy, but not as a technically established basis for large-scale testing. Teachers are working within a contradictory set of frameworks in implementing the National Curriculum: on the one hand attempting to carry out formative, 'criterion-referenced', individually focused classroom assessments and on the other working with a summative assessment system in which comparability of information is, in government policy, paramount.

Comparability therefore becomes an important issue in considering the introduction of the National Curriculum. This chapter identifies ways in which comparability has been considered in work on past assessment systems in the UK. Three main areas for discussion are identified and these are summarized below before being expanded in greater detail.

1 *Processes involved in the agreement of marking standards, between teachers, between schools and nationally.* The shift from the TGAT model of moderation meetings to agreement trials and visiting moderation has had profound implications for the role of teachers within the system and for the development of the National Curriculum itself.

2 *Comparability studies.* There is a history of comparability studies between different examination systems at 16+, and more recently across the various Examining Groups for GCSE. Characteristically, these studies have been inconclusive, and the most significant discussions to arise from them have been about the methodology of comparison. Arguably, the framework does not exist for establishing comparability of SAT results and Teacher Assessments, or of performance across subject areas.

3 *Performance and accountability.* The use of pupils' results as evaluative evidence about schools raises a number of questions about not only the wider educational purposes which can be devalued by an ethos of testing, but also the technical problems of reliability. The most useful models of comparison appear to be those which are referenced to progress. These offer important contributions to the debate about evaluation and planning at an institutional and local level, but also carry risks of appearing to legitimate assessment arrangements which may be based on inadequate curricular design and content.

Moderation

... the process of aligning standards between different examinations, different components or (most frequently) different centres or teachers responsible for the assessment of their own candidates.

(DES 1985b)

The process of checking comparability of different assessors' judgements of different groups of pupils.

(DES 1987c)

Moderation systems depend on common views of purpose, or of child development or of subject content, whichever is the defining characteristic of the assessment system in use.[5] The National Curriculum provides the statements of purpose in its attainment targets. It removes from the agenda any discussion of child development because it explicitly removes its progression from a claim to represent development in that sense (DES 1987c: para. 93) and it defines subject content. It provides, at least ostensibly, the conditions in which comparative, moderating judgements can be made, between one marker and another.

The picture is unlikely of course to be so simple. Stated objectives are not necessarily commonly interpreted but are more likely to become so with time and use and improved communication between teachers, but common understandings are established by relatively slow processes (Radnor 1987; Sadler 1987) and not by legislation. Furthermore, a factor that affects the way in which a stated objective (or attainment target) is understood, is the educational aim which the achievement of that objective could be said to serve. The National Curriculum has no educational aims as such. It has plenty of managerial aims – such as the raising of standards, increased accountability, and the monitoring of progress – but these are not in the commonly accepted sense educational aims, and they do not have any clear relationship to individual Attainment Targets in the way aims might have to their more specific objectives.

TGAT recommends a model (see Figure 9.1) that would involve a combination of input and outcome evidence,[6] a group and interschool structure within a pyramid structure to bring areas and regions into alignment, probably through meetings, and a combination of reference test and 'inspection' methods (DES 1988b: 4–7). Initially, SEAC's work was directed towards this model:

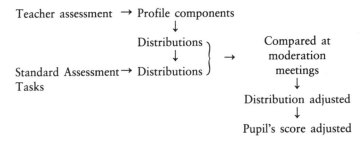

Figure 9.1 The TGAT model for moderation.
Source: Whetton (1989) 'The Development of Standard Assessment Tasks for Seven Year Olds,' *NFER Members Conference Papers.*

Towards the end of the relevant key stage for a group of pupils the teacher completes an assessment (TA) of each pupil's attainment against each attainment target, enters the results on a nationally prepared record sheet, and completes the aggregation process to provide levels of attainment for each profile component and subject. The record is then passed to the local moderating group, by, say, the end of the Spring term ... The teacher then administers the SATs, resulting in further assessments for each pupil, but possible only for some attainment targets. The teacher then reviews each pupil's attainment against each attainment target, entering in the record the SAT assessments where they are available, and the Spring term teacher assessment in other cases. The SAT assessment is thus 'preferred' to TA where it is available.

(Advice to the Secretary of State from SEAC, 13 July 1989: paras 22 and 23)

Moreover, the National Curriculum Council at this time made clear that teachers had a significant role in research and development. They were to provide evaluative information about the curriculum.

Monitoring the National Curriculum is not just a matter of ensuring that the statutory requirements of the Education Reform Act are carried out ... evidence from teachers will form an essential part of that process.

(NCC 1989: 16)

TGAT had offered, in the form of the proposed group moderation meetings, a means of carrying out that evaluative role:

> The group moderation meeting would first explore any general lack of matching between the overall teacher rating distribution and the overall distribution of results on the national tests. The general aim would be to adjust the teacher rating results to match the overall results of the national tests; if the group were to have clear and agreed reasons for not doing this, these should be reported to the LEA and eventually to the body responsible for operating the national assessment system. Such reports should lead to a new scrutiny for possible defects in the tests if enough agreed discrepancies were to be found.
>
> (DES 1987c: para. 74)

TGAT, moreover, emphasized the staff development aspects of group moderation, 'These professional deliberations' (DES 1987c: para. 76) and indicated the importance of establishing shared understandings of objectives. In existing examination systems it 'allows examiners to clarify in discussion both the objectives of their syllabus and the bases of their value judgements' (DES 1987c: para .72).

The trend of examinations at 16+ prior to 1994 towards increasingly large course work elements, towards greater teacher involvement and towards the use of more open-ended tasks is supported by research which has been directed to looking at the kinds of judgements and the processes for those judgements, that are made by groups of judges, rather than by individual markers, described by Christie and Forrest's (1981: 57) definition of 'limen-referencing': 'the model which characterizes British public examinations'. A significant body of work relates to the examining of English, where discrimination by outcomes is most vulnerable to criticisms of subjectivity. In climates other than the current one of government intervention, there has been investigation of results of multiple marking of English compositions (Britton *et al.* 1966) and of the qualities that can be deduced to be associated with grades in English examinations at 17+ (Dixon and Stratta 1981) and in A-level Literature examinations (Dixon and Brown 1984).

The deliberations of Dixon and Stratta (1981), arising from panel exercises with teachers and examiners, are illustrated here to exemplify the differences between the language of statistically achievable comparability and the range of judgemental factors felt to be operating within examination assessments:

> We have found in close scrutiny of the texts that the following four questions are central to our argument and effectively from a set of criteria:
>
> (a) What kinds of ordering or re-ordering occur as the writer imaginatively recovers the events of the past? – and to what effect? For example, is the sequence retraced in an elementary way, or are there more complex transformations? Are past events re-organised at any point from a later position, with the benefit of hindsight?
> (b) Is the writer automatically assuming or taking for granted a reader who is already acquainted with the setting, or the characters, or the events? Does s/he implicitly take into account readers without exactly similar experience and possibly with different attitudes or points of view?
> (c) Does the writer remain largely egocentric, or is there a more comprehensive perspective developing in which thoughts and feelings of other participants are more fully acknowledged or realised? (This is a question about authorial points of view, which may at times be ironically at odds with the 'I' of the story.)
> (d) What actual or potential understanding of the uses of language could be pointed to as significant? In what ways is the writer beginning to move from a relatively restricted range of choices (in the use of vocabulary and structure) and to develop a sense of appropriate forms and tacit or conscious rhetorical strategies to evoke more complex textures of experiences?
>
> (Dixon and Stratta 1981: 1–2)

Their conclusions are quoted here at some length to show that they offer a structured framework for the exercise of judgement, compatible with group moderation exercises, but difficult to represent adequately in mark schemes for individual use.

Against a background of increasing interest in the integrated possibility of curricular evaluation, staff development and setting of standards through group moderation, the change in policy for the National Curriculum introduces a restricted vision of moderation for Key Stage 3, which might be supposed as a potential model for other Key Stages. The pilots in Mathematics and Science in 1992 were subjected to a system of 'quality audit' (SEAC 1992a,b: 33–6); a sampling technique across and within institutions, designed to expedite the use of external assessors looking at light samples of work marked by teachers. The tests, the detailed mark schemes and the bureaucracy of audit prompted wide-scale refusal by teacher unions as they moved from the pilot to the full run in 1993 including, by then, tests in English too. There are complex differences of view amongst teachers about the nature of involvement that is, or is not, acceptable with this testing process. In response to complaints about additional workload, the then Secretary of State for Education, John Patten, announced that for 1995 the tests will be externally marked (thereby eradicating most of the problem of immediate workload, but reducing still further the autonomy and scope for professional judgement of the practitioner). Another body of opinion is, despite slimmed-down tests, pursuing the point of principle about the inadequacies of the tests themselves. The issue of 'audit' becomes somewhat side-lined within those differing considerations and within the practical strategies of protest that unions might adopt. It should not, however, be ignored in the longer term, for it marks a considerable turning point in the movement of educational activity into the language of commerce and industry, and in representing professional activity as technically measurable. In reinstating the importance of teacher assessment in the non-core subjects of the National Curriculum the Dearing Report recognizes that systems of moderation will be needed to support this (Dearing 1993b: paras 9.2 ff.). The return to the language of 'moderation' may yet signal further reinstatement of the teacher's role.

Comparability studies

Following the Beloe Report (Secondary Schools Examinations Council 1960) and the consequent introduction of the Certificate of Secondary Education, researches were directed towards the comparability of the co-existing systems of examining at 16. In 1963, the year when the first candidates began preparing for CSE examinations, the Secondary Schools Examinations Council spoke of the 'inevitability' of the new examination, and the 'mixed feelings' of the education service. It was feared that the 'formalising effect' of examinations would pervade the curriculum of Secondary Modern Schools as it had the grammar schools (Secondary Schools Examinations Council 1963: 1). In order to gain credibility the new examination had to be comparable to the GCE, and the studies which looked across the two systems, whatever their conclusions, could only endorse by the very act of comparison the public emphasis on comparability which allowed GCE to dominate styles of learning.

Comparability between examining boards and over time were studied. Willmott (1977) recording the results of the 1973 comparability study, and its possible relationship to the 1968 study, acknowledges the difficulties of finding unbiased reference tests of 'scholastic aptitude' and appropriate sampling procedures. Teachers' anxieties that public examinations did not match their own criteria of judgement (D. Hargreaves 1982), had been deflected into studies of reliability. A study of the effects of question choice (Willmott and Hall 1975) had to recommend that if a choice was to be given, facility adjustment would be necessary. Such devices could only, however, make the system more remote from the teachers. The authors' conclusions demonstrate tension between the wish to increase reliability and the knowledge that larger questions – of validity – have first to be addressed.

Accompanying the discussions from 1976 onwards specifically about the feasibility and then the shape of a common examining system at 16+, research was largely directed at determining technical matters of grade awards. Tattersall (1983) concluded that, with allowance for curricular considerations varying from subject to subject, differentiated examinations are an appropriate way of examining across the ability range at 16+, but recommended that differentiated options be separately considered by panel judgement since 'none of the known statistical methods – scaling, ranking or regression – is sufficient in itself to equate marks from options of varying difficulty'. Further experimental research on differentiation was carried out by Good and Cresswell for the Secondary Examinations Council. They, in common with Tattersall, recommended that further work should be done to find 'more comprehensive judgemental scaling techniques' (Good and Cresswell 1988: 76) in various differentiation patterns. Like comparability before it, differentiation and its associated problems play a dominant part in study of SEAC-sponsored research into GCSE examinations. The failure of GCSE to establish a common examination is considered by some to have duplicated or even worsened the previous system of differentiation (Gipps 1986: 12–15; Radnor 1988). The National Curriculum system of levels has reinforced the concern with differentiation, and may indeed be seen as having been introduced partly in response to concern that GCSE had been insufficiently able to differentiate. The criteria for the 1994 GCSE syllabuses include the requirement that 'Each scheme of assessment must involve papers . . . targeted at different ranges of levels . . . Candidates enter for a single tier in a syllabus in a particular examination sitting' (SEAC 1992c).

A further debate surrounds the effects of aggregated grades upon the representation of performance. The early and central claim of GCSE that it would provide more information about achievement is difficult to sustain since awards continue to be by grade. The aggregated grades that characterize public examinations are argued to be unsatisfactory vehicles for relevant profile information (Harrison 1983; Cresswell 1987). The National Curriculum assessments are aggregated for some reporting purposes, particularly the 'high stakes' evaluative purposes. How far teachers' judgements can be reliable when the survival of their schools depend upon the results is implicitly called into question by the increasing emphasis on external assessment. A more serious educational argument, however, is that the aggregation loses information thus suggesting similar attainment for students whose achievement – and future needs – are very different.

Comparability is made difficult by a range of sources of bias in assessments, brought about by factors such as teacher expectancy (Rogers 1982), presentation modes of assessment items (R. Murphy 1982) and gender differences in the understanding of question cues (P. Murphy 1988). Roger Murphy (1988) argues that TGAT underestimates the complexity of producing Assessment Tasks that will eliminate satisfactorily sources of gender bias, and sees a risk that the assessment tasks may 'compound gender and cultural influences' (1988: 171) despite the fact that the system 'presupposes homogeneity of outcome' (1988: 165) for purposes of accountability.

The issues relating to criterion-referencing also lie in uncharted areas so far as assessment development is concerned. The problems of promulgating standards and objectives were addressed in a study of the reliability of teachers' judgements of abilities tested by multiple choice items, using Bloom's taxonomy (Fairbrother 1975). While Fairbrother found the agreement of the teachers 'rather low' (1975: 202), he considers that a design weakness of the experiment was perhaps insufficient briefing of the participants. Fairbrother's experiment illustrates, through his critique of his methodology, that there are a number of factors being called into service to measure each other: a given classification of educational objectives; teachers' judgement; and test materials. The importance of briefing participants in such an experiment might be related to a more general need for discussion among assessors. Wilkinson (1980), in a study designed to find ways of assessing language (though not directly linked to public examinations) marries his framework to psychological models derived from, in the cognitive domain, Piaget, Peel (1971) and Bruner (1964), placing emphasis upon awareness of context and purpose as a criterion of communicative competence, and distinguishing between narrative and other forms, such as 'the essay', in terms of the analytical and other competencies called for in the writer. Study of levels of adolescent judgement (Peel 1971) and of the quality of learning outcomes (Biggs and Collis 1982) have some application in looking at GCSE prior to 1994. Such studies, however, have not provided readily transportable models for making assessments. Where their conclusions are open to question is in the single subjectivity on which qualitative judgements in their research have been based. Hence they indirectly point up the need for multiple judges in attributing levels.

The refinement of panel judgements may appear to offer a way forward. The introduction of the National Curriculum assessments has, however, seen a reduction in the amounts of teacher-assessed coursework (cf. Bowe and Whitty 1984), restriction of opportunity for group moderation (as for example in the Mode 3 schemes and consortia operating under GCSE), rejection of TGAT's proposals for group moderation, and a move to 'quality audit' (SEAC 1992, 1992a and 1992b: 34–7).

If further evidence were required that assessment is part of a macro-political struggle, the events surrounding the publication of the 1992 GCSE results would provide it. In July 1991 the Education White Paper *Choice and Diversity* celebrated the achievements of the GCSE which 'has enabled much higher proportions of 16 year olds – particularly those of around average ability – to show what they can do. As a result, the proportion of school leavers attaining 5 or more passes at grades A to C at GCSE or equivalent has gone up from 24 per cent in 1980 to 30 per cent in 1988 and 38 per cent in 1991' (DFE 1992a: 15). By September, the Secretary of State had issued a press release recording his concern at the 1992 results: 'In view of the HMI advice, I am now urgently considering what action is required to ensure that GCSE standards are maintained at as high a level as possible' (*Times Educational Supplement*, 4 September 1992). His press release was in advance of the publication of the HMI Report, which expressed 'limited confidence that standards are being maintained' (DFE 1992b: 2) and which appears anxious to re-open the already fruitless debate about grade criteria: 'The absence of criteria to define minimum standards for grades remains a major weakness'. (1992: 8). While the HMI report might appear to conform to current trends of attack upon the existing GCSE, it is silent about the detail of the processes by which Examination Boards do monitor standards and seems either unaware or forgetful of the history of comparability. The report and its reception illustrate the circularity of the standards issue: higher results can neither automatically be said to mean that standards are rising or falling. 'Results' are easier to exploit for rhetorical rather than educational purposes.

Accountability

The comparison of performance based on National Curriculum assessment results is intended to be used to provide information about how effective Local Education Authorities (LEAs), schools or 'classrooms' are (DES 1987c: paras 23, 38, 39). What background there is relating to the evaluative role of results suggests a complicated picture. HMI (1988) report that LEA policies and practices in respect of examination results were little developed and suggested that INSET planning might be related to identifiable areas of need signalled by results. In other words, although some judgemental evaluation might have arisen from the collation of results, there was inadequate evidence of evaluation for improvement.

HMI's own interpretation of results is questioned by Gray and

Hannon's (1986) argument that a model for comparison is needed which is able to show how far a school is enabling progress, rather than simply levels of achievement which may be arising from different baselines.

The argument about relative performance is further sharpened by a study in the Inner London Education Authority which suggests that students of different ethnic groups are achieving differently in different schools. Taking public examination results over the three years 1985, 1986 and 1987, and using multi-level modelling between students and within schools/between years and between schools, this study showed that there were significant differences between schools in the extent to which they narrowed the gap between the highest and lowest achieving pupils, between girls and boys and between ethnic groups (Nuttall *et al.* 1989: 769–76).

The Value-added option

As an alternative to raw results, systems which enable comparison according to progress, particularly which can look at pupil-level data (Nuttall *et al.* 1989; Woodhouse 1990: 63–71) appear to offer a better way forward. Fitz-Gibbon (1990b: 57–61; 1991) offers ways of making comparisons of A-level results with GCSE results, but feels that at a national level, progress in looking interpretively at results has been 'slow and patchy' (Fitz-Gibbon 1990b: 53). The arguments for finding good interpretive means of analysis appear to be good, especially within a context of misleading presentation of uninterpretive league tables. The Dearing review established a working group of the School Curriculum and Assessment Authority (SCAA)[7] to look at value-added options at the interim report stage. Value-added, as an alternative to raw results, seems at least to have a place on the policy agenda.

Nonetheless, there are reasons for looking carefully at the likely effects of value-added and other interpretive systems, which may serve to promote aspects of curriculum and assessment which are less than desirable, and to put certain aspects of innovation further beyond the influence of either academic research or school-based evaluation and development.

Firstly, progress and progression are defined in such systems entirely through the data available by existing examination and assessment arrangements. Their assumption has to be that the data is itself meaningful within terms of achievement and progression. These are questionable assumptions (see, for example, Torrance 1986). It is possible that research and evaluation of curriculum and of assessments is actually made harder if the results basis of comparison comes to be accepted. Value-added models could serve to legitimate features of the National Curriculum assessment which still require analysis in terms of reliability and validity, just as the curriculum on which they are based should still be regarded as provisional.

Secondly, all league tables, however derived, present a particular view of educational and institutional achievement in which comparison is paramount. Such a view runs counter to attitudes about self-esteem which many teachers are trying to promote through non-comparative and non-competitive means of assessment. There is a danger of going along the road of contrastive rhetoric, which claims value-added league tables to be a good thing simply because they avoid some of the worst features of raw result league tables.

Thirdly, the league tables which might be derived through value-added analyses might have serious weaknesses in offering information about school effectiveness, even leaving aside the objections outlined above. Goldstein (1991) presents a problem of time delay in looking at National Curriculum assessments in terms of relative degrees of progress, in so far as there would be an elapse of years before such measurements could be made. Schools change character in such periods, and the public, and teachers, could be receiving information about relative performance which was no longer applicable.

Fourthly, the progression of the children who are achieving highest at age seven is likely to be steeper on the TGAT 'graph' of progression (Figure 9.1) than the progression of children achieving as average or below average for their age group. Those children who are below level one at age seven may in some cases make little progression on the National Curriculum levels throughout their school careers. Therefore, schools with high proportions of the highest achieving pupils would expect to be able to demonstrate far more dramatic rates of progression than schools with a different mix of pupils. Calculations of value-added would need to be able to accommodate such different *rates* of progression. A procedure for banding schools according to their baseline results prior to attempting comparison of gains in grades was demonstrated by Nuttall, Thomas and Goldstein in an exercise carried out in *The Guardian* (20 October 1992). The participation of schools was entirely voluntary in this exercise, and it drew attention to the problems of different starting points when looking at anticipated educational progress. However, the use of a system capable of accommodating different rates of progress according to different baselines suggests a very sophisticated model if used compulsorily and nationally. The Government's past procedure of publishing raw results would have to undergo considerable modification to accommodate such an approach. Moreover, it is unclear whether such a model might place undue pressure upon schools with high achievers, while actually giving too little incentive to schools with large proportions of very low achievers.

Fifthly, the different ways in which league tables are calculated produce different kinds of curriculum backwash, little of which is necessarily beneficial. For example the release of information about A-levels in *The Times* (29 August 1992) ranked schools according to the average number of points achieved on the UCCA system. Were such a method of ranking to gain general currency, then the likely effect would be for schools to increase the number of subject entries per candidate as the simplest way to 'improve' such averages. This would not necessarily be in the interests of candidates, nor of the rest of their school populations from whom resources would be diverted. Value-added league tables would not necessarily interact with curricula in any more beneficial ways. The logic of National Curriculum progression-based league tables would suggest the advantage of depressing achievement at one Key Stage in order to demonstrate apparent progress at the next.

There are, then, a number of factors which surround the issue of 'value-added' reporting of results, some to do with the principle of reporting itself and whether any league table system will militate against good practice in teaching and learning, some to do with whether a technically satisfactory model of progress could be found and some to do with what the specific effects of value-added tables might be on schools' policies in assessment and organization.

Overview

There are therefore a number of important issues which arise in the area of comparability of performance. The moderation procedures which have been evolved over time, and accompanied by research, to support public examination systems rely heavily upon human judgement and appear to offer ways of reflecting the breadth of subject curricula. Statistical comparisons have played a part in comparability studies to highlight different patterns of achievement for large cohorts of students, but cannot alone determine questions of standards without detailed contextual information and direct comparison of work – and human judgement. The use of results to gather relative information about schools appears to be facilitated by the introduction of the National Curriculum but, as the research studies quoted above indicate, the use of raw results is inappropriate, since it can offer only restricted information on the extent to which schools are actually encouraging progress for their students, and indeed whether the school offers more to certain kinds of students – and why. Value-added comparisons on the other hand might actually compound some of the fundamental problems of National Curriculum assessment, simply by appearing to offer a better system while failing to engage with questions about the curriculum and about educational validity in assessment. Earlier chapters have considered the uncertain foundations of the National Curriculum assessments as a source of reliable and valid data and that argument is also highly relevant to matters of comparison. If the assessment results are not offering reliable and valid information about achievement, or about progression, then comparisons based upon them could be similarly fallacious.

EDUCATIONAL
STANDARDS
AND EFFECTIVENESS

This Chapter considers the interrelationships between school effectiveness, pupil performance and inspection of schools. The National Curriculum currently provides the means by which pupil performance is to be judged and is also to provide the keystone for judgements of school performance. There are two main reasons for questioning this very powerful arrangement for measurement. Firstly, there is inadequate evidence for relating assessment of individuals to judgements about school effectiveness, and secondly there is a danger that such processes entrench one particular view of curriculum at a time when a wider consideration of educational standards is needed.

Standards

The difficulty in talking about standards is that the concept is, like 'truth', or 'goodness', or 'beauty', both logically indispensable and yet impossible to define without considerable philosophical elaboration.

(Pring 1992: 21)

The term 'standards' has gathered around itself a web of meanings. Gipps (1990) suggests that the term 'standards' 'is probably more loosely used than any other in education', and she identifies its use in three separate ways, which as she points out, range from the very particular notion of the performance of an individual in a specific context to very large social and moral issues. She sees the three uses as attainment – either in basic skills or more widely across the curriculum, levels of educational provision and matters of conduct and social behaviour:

> referring to levels of *attainment* in basic skills such as reading or maths, or levels of attainment in a much wider range of school activities; we may be talking about standards of *provision*, e.g. the number of teachers and books per child, or we may be talking about behaviour, dress and other *social phenomena*.
>
> (Gipps 1990: 26)

In the absence of a clear or shared public view of what constitutes 'standards', the term may all too easily come to be equated with examinations and 'results'. *Better Schools* (DES 1985a), for example, allied the raising of standards closely to school examinations. As well as raising 'standards across the whole ability range', examinations should:

> ... support improvements in the curriculum and in the way in which it is taught;
> ... provide clear aims for teachers and pupils, to the benefit of both and of higher education and employers;
> ... record proven achievement;
> ... promote the measurement of achievement based on what candidates know, understand and can do;
> ... broaden the studies of pupils in the 4th and 5th secondary years and of 6th form students.
>
> (DES 1985a: 29, para. 93)

It is difficult to understand why the document separated out the notion of standards from those features which are listed above. Arguably, these are all to do with 'standards'. When *Better Schools* suggested that examinations would raise standards it apparently meant something like 'results'.

The National Curriculum Consultation Document (DES 1987b)

implied a definition of standards by setting out four ways in which a National Curriculum 'backed by clear assessment arrangements' would help to raise standards. The definition consists of:

curriculum breadth and balance – particularly related to flexible response 'to a changing world':

'. . . ensuring that all pupils study a broad and balanced range of subjects throughout their compulsory schooling and do not drop too early studies which may stand them in good stead later . . .'

realistic but challenging objectives to 'challenge each child to work to his or her potential';

'. . . setting clear objectives for what children over the full range of ability should be able to achieve . . . This will help schools to challenge each child to develop his or her potential . . . the national curriculum is intended to help teachers to set their expectations at a realistic but challenging level for each child, according to his or her ability . . .'

equal access to 'good and relevant education' – the emphasis of this paragraph then becomes relevance to 'adult and working life', suggesting that equal educational provision is really about labour supply, rather than fairness or opportunity

'. . . ensuring that all pupils, regardless of sex, ethnic origin and geographical location, have access to broadly the same good and relevant curriculum . . .'

diagnosis of strengths and weaknesses for formative teaching

'. . . checking on progress towards those objectives performance achieved at various stages, so that pupils can be stretched further when they are doing well and given more help when they are not . . .'

(DES 1987b: para. 8.i–iii)

These claims are offering a justification for a prescribed curriculum and for the use of what might be termed 'graded objectives'. The shape of the curriculum in its two dimensions is here established: the subjects and the way in which progress in each subject is to be defined. The kind of access outlined could be envisaged as an improvement in standards in its own right, an improvement in provision and entitlement. Here, however, access is linked only to attainment, and presumably to the idea that readily monitorable averages will rise.

Such a narrow view of access raises questions about whether uniformity of provision is truly opportunity, and whether the prescriptiveness of the National Curriculum is any more than a means of establishing bureaucratic accountability. The final point might serve to confirm this, as the term 'checking' hardly suggests any subtlety of pedagogic model. If, as the paragraph goes on to suggest, assessment truly yields formative information, then individual progress might reasonably be expected to improve; but if assessment is only perceived to be an exercise in accountability then there are no precedents for supposing that standards in any meaningful sense of the word can be raised.

> The idea that tests can measure standards in education is one thing. The idea that testing can raise standards is quite another, yet this has received even less critical attention.
>
> (Gipps 1990)

Hartnett and Naish (1990: 3–4) saw the main thrust of the National Curriculum arrangements as 'the claim to provide solutions to complex educational and social problems without additional resources'. They questioned the contention that testing can raise standards, and saw the particular model of standards being used as belonging to 'bureaucratic modes of evaluation' which may be at odds with 'the learning patterns of individual children' (1990: 5).

HMI's inspections of schools have been summarized in annual reports from the Chief Inspector on *Standards in Education* (e.g. HMCI 1990, 1991). These reports have focused on certain aspects of what might be termed 'input' – that is on accommodation and equipment, teacher training and supply, on processes (e.g. the teaching of reading), on outcomes (examination results) and on participation rates in post-compulsory education. Although the view of standards implicit in the reports ranges quite widely across input, process and results, there are quite narrow definitions of which results are important to highlight. Traditional high-status examination results (A-level passes and A–C grades in GCSE) are those which are headlined as indicators of standards (e.g. HMCI 1991: para. 6). Where that treatment of standards has focused upon results in examinations at 16+, it has been criticized for being oversimple and allowing schools with a strong academic intake of pupils to appear to be the best performing schools. Gray and Hannon's (1986) way of interpreting examination results identifies itself as distinct from that of HMI which they describe as decontextualized and unable to encompass the differences that particular schools make to children's achievement. They argued for, and have since further refined, ways of looking at results in relation to intake of particular schools, rather than simple comparisons of results across schools. The isolation by HMI not only of examination results, but of results which did not reflect the ability or advantage of schools' intakes would suggest a very simplistic approach to standards, based on the most accessible data. By 1988 HMI were looking at how education authorities used examination results where a number of comparative techniques are mentioned as 'rare', 'isolated instances' (DES 1989b: paras 11–18). They mention, with some circumspection, the possible value of examination results in monitoring performance and planning of INSET (para. 24). The report is, however, non-committal about how examination results should – or should not – be interpreted. In view of the National Curriculum 'there is much for LEAs to do in order to put themselves in a position . . . to make the best use of public examination results . . .' (para. 31).

The White Paper, *Diversity and Choice*, was in many respects a restatement of established strands of the Government's policy. It maintained the view that publication of results will somehow drive standards up, but combines this policy with the introduction of inspections. It viewed 'school autonomy and parental choice – combined with the National Curriculum' as the 'keys to achieving higher standards in all schools (DFE 1992a: 15). There would be increased school accountability through publication of results, providing information about schools' relative performance to inform parental choice (1992a: 17–18). There was to be a new 'School Curriculum and Assessment Authority' – a 'force for raising expectations and standards' (1992a; 16–17). The means by which standards were to be raised were, however, also 'regular inspection of all maintained schools' (1992a: 16).

The Education (Schools) Act 1992 established the arrangements for independent inspections of maintained schools by registered inspectors to be trained by and responsible to Ofsted (the Office for Standards in Education). These teams of inspectors, to include lay inspectors from outside teaching and education professions, are aimed to provide 'regular and rigorous inspection under the watchful eye of the new and powerful Chief Inspector for Schools' (DFE 1992a). Their terms of reference and arrangements for the conduct of inspections is detailed in a *Handbook for the Inspection of Schools*, a document which is available also to schools and for purchase by the public. Within the *Handbook*, the 'Framework for the Inspection of Schools' sets out in detail a wide range of indicators and criteria on which evidence is to be collected and judgements made, and hence addresses some of the past criticisms of HMI's treatment of standards in the past, on the grounds of their 'reluctance to explain their research procedures and methodologies' (D. Scott 1989: 283).

The Education (Schools) Act 1992, and the 'Framework' for inspection have established a very public set of criteria about effectiveness. These criteria may not satisfy all commentators on education, and may not successfully probe the ultimate questions about what education is for. They do, however, arguably broaden out the issue of 'standards' from a definition led by results. Moreover, they place the debate about educational effectiveness – and the basis for Ofsted judgements about schools – more firmly in the public arena than was the case with HMI practices of the past. Questions remain, however, about what effectiveness is, and about the meanings that are set up by particular definitions and by processes of inspection.

School effectiveness

The discussion about schools' effectiveness dates back well before the Government's introduction of legislation designed to impose certain models of effectiveness upon compulsory education. The influential, and controversial study, *Fifteen Thousand Hours* (Rutter *et al.* 1979), arose from a concern about whether the time pupils spend in school (the fifteen 15 000 hours of the title) actually makes a difference to their achievement and attitudes. The study was located in 12 Inner London Education Authority (ILEA) secondary schools. Its method was to relate individual school inputs, processes and outcomes, statistically. Its purpose was to look at whether particular aspects of school process actually made a difference to outcomes. It attempted to take into account differing intake factors in its analysis. It claimed to show that it had identified differences attributable to school processes. Its methods, however, attempted to apply statistical analysis to complex classroom processes and its modelling was open to criticism (Young 1980). Subsequent studies have tended to take more qualitative approaches, such as that carried out in 50 ILEA primary schools, set out to identify the characteristics, or 'key factors' of 'effective schools' (Mortimore *et al.* 1988).

Reid *et al.* (1987) drew together research from a number of studies to suggest characteristics of the effective school, but emphasize that the characteristics of effective schools (such as leadership, pupil participation, strength of teaching staff) are not simple hand-ons. They are guidelines which support certain essential commitments of the school to 'the improvement of teaching and learning', to the 'development of the school as a "learning institution"' and to 'the humanisation of schooling'.

The School Management Task Force, with a remit from the DES, identified a list of factors closely related to what might be seen as the emerging consensus of research and HMI reports: good leadership (i.e. vision and motivation of others); delegation and involvement of staff in policymaking; purposeful staffing structures; well-qualified staff (experience and expertise); clear aims and objectives; effective communication; clear systems of record keeping and assessment; high expectations; coherent curriculum including pupils' experience as a whole; positive ethos; orderly yet relaxed, suitable working environment; evidence of skills in deploying and managing material resources; good relationships with parents and the community; capacity to manage change, solve problems and to develop organically (DES 1990b: para. 15). More important than the characteristics themselves, however, are the statements of purpose: 'The focus of a good school is effective learning: this is the reason for its existence and therefore the final criterion against which its management is judged' (1990b: para. 16). Moreover, their report was centrally concerned with looking at processes for bringing about management development in schools, and saw roles for LEAs, for Higher Education, industry and professional associations; its language is that of 'support', 'collaborate', 'consultancy and training opportunities' (1990b:

paras 92–7) and it envisaged a network of regional Management Task Forces coordinating this development. It is a very different vision from that of external inspections; it establishes a framework for school-based but collaborative development, rather than a framework of judgements and sanctions.

There was also a flurry of work around performance indicators following the introduction of Local Management of Schools. Such 'indicators' are variously defined. They are part of the framework of audit (FEU 1989); they may be divided into input, process and outcome indicators (Coopers and Lybrand 1988: 51); they may need to be consciously eclectic of different models (CIPFA 1988: 3–4); they may be 'selected items of quantitative data which help in the evaluation of aspects of quality' in an inspection system (HMCI 1992: 2). There is a level of agreement among studies that indicators form a profile. This profile consists of 'major issue areas of significant and enduring educational importance' (NCES 1991: 9) – an 'outline' of 'the most important contexts within which those concerned with the management and appraisal of schools might need to identify key factors which contribute to the quality of their performance' (CIPFA 1988: 4).

Both CIPFA (the Chartered Institute of Public Finance and Accountancy) and Coopers and Lybrand in their reports of the late 1980s stress the importance of developing indicators within the working context. The indicators 'will, properly, vary with the perceptions of those in the particular school or LEA ... These papers do not prescribe a list of indicators but identify areas for schools and/or LEAs to use in developing *their own* [their emphasis] performance indicators' (CIPFA 1988: 4). Coopers and Lybrand suggest that LEAs will play a key role: 'LEAs will ... wish to specify minimum requirements for information on financial performance, resources and examination results and other performance indicators' (Coopers and Lybrand 1988: 42). Their report stands aloof from suggesting a list of indicators, and offers rather a 'List of factors *relevant to* performance indicators' (1988: 51–2) [author's emphasis].

Another, distinct, tradition of work on school effectiveness is concerned with looking at the processes for school and teacher development, through action research models of teacher involvement in school improvement. While action research involves targets and criteria (though the language may vary) they are derived at an institutional level, through professional discussion. This development tradition derives from the academic study and practice of evaluation, linked closely to the curriculum evaluations of the Schools Council and the increasing move from outsider/ objectivity-reliability focused evaluations to insider evaluations acknowledging multiple subjectivities. It addresses the need for illuminative research capable of representing a learning milieu a 'nexus of cultural, social, institutional and psychological variables' (Parlett and Hamilton 1987 [1972]: 62). It advocates action research by practitioners (Stenhouse 1980); extending a research approach within schools by teachers into recent educational change as 'a source of critical self-reflection and emancipatory action' (Elliott 1991: 116); and involving students in discussion about change (Rudduck 1991: 53–90). In the developmental tradition, involvement and participation become centrally important. The identification of success criteria and various levels of educational objective in evaluation becomes an important process in itself. This is also supported by other, more quantitative research:

> It appeared that an efficient system within which teachers worked harmoniously towards agreed goals was conducive to both good morale and effective teaching.
>
> (Rutter *et al.* 1979: 193)

By contrast to 'effectiveness' studies geared either to description or to measurement, the tradition which embraces evaluation, development and action research offers a participative engagement with questions of educational objectives at a generative level. Its central concern that educational development has ultimately to be understood at the level of the school, the classroom, the individual, is compatible with the view of Reid *et al.* about the importance of developing the 'learning institution' in which all are involved in processes of growth and an ethos of enquiry and development. Similarly, the School Management Task Force identified the need for the school to develop organically. The Education Act 1988 and the Education (Schools) Act 1992, however, so fundamentally change the context of accountability that a developmental approach is directly threatened by the assessment arrangements that are driving the machine, and by the influence that these arrangements will have upon schools' conceptions of purpose and values, or of what, pragmatically, are their priorities.

The publication of examination results and of National Curriculum assessment results has major implications for the way schools see their work, and how they understand their own capacities for judgement and action. Discussion of 'effectiveness', when engaging with the issue of results is in danger of becoming embroiled in discussion of the need for 'contextualization' rather than engaging with the whole issue of the effects of publication on school processes. The arguments for contextualization of these results take two main forms. Firstly, there is the argument that socio-economic factors should be considered: 'Great care is needed with ... comparisons of performance as the differences between schools and between their socio-economic environments are such that superficiality can be misleading if not dangerous' (Coopers and Lybrand 1988: 42)[8]. Secondly, it is suggested that more useful information about school performance is based on the progress that students make. The 'value-added' model and objections to it have been outlined in Chapter 9.

A further issue to address is how far there is a genuine articulation between the discourse of management (which is where discussion of school effectiveness studies are located) and a discourse about learning. How are the claims of the School Management Task Force that effective learning is the central focus of an effective school to be realized? Is there an organic relationship between 'management' and 'learning'? Mortimore and Stone (1990: 69) outline two views of education which are currently in contention in the discussion of quality: one of education as 'an essentially ethical activity', and the other as an instrumental activity designed to bring about the achievement of specifiable and uncontroversial educational goals, such that the key educational issues are technical and administrative. Reynolds (1988: 164) identifies some of the complexity in trying to make judgements about the effectiveness of teaching. He discussed the effect of 'teacher personality' and different educational philosophies, and 'whether different methods may be equally effective when used by different persons'.

How far, then, are effectiveness studies well placed to promote more than a 'technical and administrative' view of the educational task; how far are they engaged with the ethical/political/pedagogical questions of the classroom, and with the complex array of variables which may create the experienced curriculum of students? Shipman's *The Management of Learning* seeks to combine the discourse of management and the discourse of learning. This is an important enterprise, but the book overlooks very influential constructivist and interactionist theories of learning, and chooses rather to support its case by examples from psychologists who more readily fit the technical view of management. His central concern appears to establish a particular kind of management approach free of 'reactionary' or 'romantic' views of children (Shipman 1990: 95). Bloom is valued for demonstrating that 'learning can be managed' (1990: 102). This does not address the concern that some educational practices are being preferred because they are overtly managerial and not because they represent best educational practice (Apple 1979: 128–9; Apple 1982: 90).

The fact that discourses about effective learning are separate from discourses about school management and school effectiveness has implications. It raises the possibility that within the micro-politics of schools, teaching, learning and curriculum content may be increasingly marginalized as legitimate centres of interest, while management attention focuses upon the outward expressions of the ethos of the school as a whole. There is no automatic relationship between the 'ethos' of a school and the details of interpersonal relationship which may actually create for students an understanding of the 'event structures' of which they are part as learners.

Another element in this already complex problem of the appropriate mode of study for the work of schools, is the introduction of inspection. Whereas the work cited earlier on the characteristics of effective schools, or performance indicators for looking at schools was conducted in a context in which these might act as general guides to schools in their development, the external inspections established by the 1992 Act provide a very different context.

The 'Framework' for the Inspection of Schools reflects some of the differing constituencies which have voices about education. The Government's concern about efficiency is most sharply focused in the part of the 'Framework' which looks at financial management – the 'efficiency of the school'; that is,

> the quality of the financial management and decision-making; the efficiency and effectiveness with which resources are deployed to attain the school's aims and objectives and to

match its priorities; the efficiency of financial control'; 'the assessment of any steps that are taken by the school to evaluate its cost effectiveness.

(HMCI 1993: 19)

The opening sections of the Education Act 1988 and the long-standing concerns of HMI for wide personal development of pupils are reflected in that part of the 'Framework' which sets out criteria for judging the school's effectiveness in promoting 'Pupils' spiritual, moral, social and cultural development': for example,

Spiritual development relates to that aspect of inner life through which pupils acquire insights into their personal existence which are of enduring worth. It is characterised by reflection, the attribution of meaning to experience, valuing a non-material dimension to life and intimations of an enduring reality.

(HMCI 1993: 21)

The 'Framework' does incorporate a very considerable amount of inspection of 'process' (indeed the definition above of spiritual development is unlikely to be accessible to any cross-sectional inspection), and therefore may offer a counterbalance to a results-dominated assessment of schools' performance.

It does, however, require an 'analysis' of results, but the associated technical paper is very unspecific on some key points of analysis.

Schools should be asked to provide any quantified data on the intake's ability or attainment. Standardised test results, for those pupils whose examination results are being analysed, may give inspectors *some insight* [italics added] into the value added by the school as shown in its overall GCSE results.

(HMCI 1993: 33)

Given the difficulty that expert statisticians are finding in drawing up suitable models for value-added analysis, 'some insight' may even be an overstatement. In the absence of its own method for interpreting results, the paper says: 'Schools should be asked to provide details of any of their own initiatives to analyse value-added factors in their results, and any other evaluations of their own results' (1993: 34). Similarly,

The LEA in whose area the school lies may undertake its own analyses of examination results for that area. Such analyses may be, at present, the only source of information on value-added ... Registered Inspectors may wish to seek access to any such analyses ...

(HMCI 1993: 33)

There is a suggestion here that 'value-added' is relatively unproblematic, and a possible danger that results will be interpreted to mean more – or less – than they do.

However, it also gives considerable emphasis to other aspects of assessment, particularly to the kinds of formative information about pupils' progress which will affect lesson and curriculum planning, and which will affect appropriate access to the curriculum. 'Quality of Learning' is to include

progress made ... learning skills, including observation and information-seeking, looking for patterns and deeper understandings and ideas in various ways, posing questions and solving problems, applying what has been learned to unfamiliar situations, evaluating work done ... attitudes to learning, including motivation, interest and the ability to concentrate, co-operate and work productively.

(HMCI 1993: para. 3.2)

The inspection of 'Assessment, Recording and Reporting' includes the criteria that 'the outcomes are constructive and helpful to pupils, teachers, parents and employers ... the outcomes inform subsequent work' and among the evidence looked for are 'procedures for reviewing and monitoring the progress of individual pupils' (HMCI 1993: para. 7.2). In the inspection of the curriculum emphasis is placed on 'its capacity to meet the needs of all pupils' (HMCI 1993: para. 7.3i), and that 'all pupils, irrespective of gender, ability (including giftedness), ethnicity, and social circumstance, have access to the curriculum and make the greatest progress possible (HMCI 1993: para. 7.3ii). The 'Framework' thus underlines the importance of good information about achievement and capacities as appropriate access to curriculum and best possible progression for individuals are predicated upon good formative assessment evaluation.

The principles enshrined in the 'Framework' are not at variance with a growing consensus in effectiveness studies about the characteristics which typify 'good schools'. Moreover, it retains a high status for process characteristics of schools (and hence for such otherwise fragile values as formative assessment) in a climate where league tables based on summative assessments are still intended to be the driving force behind school improvement.

The 'Framework' also fulfils the Government's project of 'demystification' (DFE 1992a), and not least for teachers in demystification of the criteria on which schools are judged by inspectors. In making explicit, however, it also attempts to separate out various aspects of schools' work and ethos: it presents a different view from the more holistic 'professional' one. Nixon and Rudduck draw attention to the need for criteria and also the possible problems, in an account of research into the transformed role of Local Authority advisers/inspectors:

> advisers/inspectors emphasise the strong element of progressive focusing implicit in the process of school inspection. They tend to shift from ascertaining what 'bits' of desirable practice are in place to exploring the quality of those 'bits' and the extent to which they add up to something coherent and worthwhile [and] ... Concerns about teaching and learning in the classroom might ... occasion a lateral shift of focus to different aspects of school practice – shifts that is that presuppose a strong sense by advisers/inspectors of the complex and indeterminate relation between different aspects of school practice.
>
> If advisers/inspectors are to retain this element of professional judgement – and at the same time retain their credibility with schools – they will need to articulate it with much greater clarity and coherence than at present. The skilful use ... of tacit criteria can all too easily appear to be a failure to make those criteria explicit – rather than the sensitive exercise of a particular kind of professional judgement.
>
> (Nixon and Rudduck 1992: 432)

It is that tension, between the unstated (or unpublicized criteria of past inspection practices) and the very explicit statement of criteria for Ofsted inspections, that marks out the territory in which schools now find themselves. 'Teachers generally welcomed the

'Framework' and its display of the criteria for good teaching and learning' (Coopers and Lybrand 1994: para. 15). Nevertheless, what is less clear is whether their processes of policymaking are now being dictated by the inspection process; are teachers welcoming the 'Framework' for its explicitness (in that they know what they will be inspected upon) or are they welcoming it for the content and appropriateness of its criteria? Coopers and Lybrand are able to be more specific about what proportion of teachers received the 'Framework' (81 per cent) than they are about what proportion actually welcomed it. 'Headteachers regarded the *Handbook* as thorough, comprehensive and *invaluable to schools preparing for inspection*' (1994: para. 14; italics added), by-passing the issue of whether the 'Framework' was intrinsically useful to the work of the school or only instrumentally useful in coping with inspection.

Moreover, there is a mismatch between the usefulness of the 'Framework' as the basis for public discussion about schools' effectiveness and criteria for that effectiveness, and the 'Framework' as an instrument of a conception of judgement about schools that has very powerful meanings of its own. The Ofsted inspections are very deliberately separating in their work the previously mixed responsibilities of Local Education Authorities for inspection and for improvement of schools. Ofsted inspects. Schools identified as 'at risk' will be taken over by an 'Education Association' if the schools governors and LEA fail to make or carry through appropriate action plans to improve performance. Such schools would be temporarily in the position of a grant-maintained school, under the stewardship of an Education Association appointed by the Secretary of State. These are fairly radical plans. While the 'Framework' may represent an established and research-based body of evidence about school effectiveness, the plan to have schools effectively taken over and managed by a sort of task team is an untested procedure. Does such a procedure create the possibilities for a 'learning school', or does it merely address some short-term problems?

There may have been (or have been perceived to be) various layers of professional self-protection in past inspection practices. Schools may not have been rigorously and regularly inspected, and both Local Authority and HMI inspectors were less than explicit to schools about the criteria for judgement. Where criticisms were made it was unclear what actions or sanctions could apply. Local

Authority inspectors were both the inspectors and the advisers of schools, so in an inspection context they were in one sense inspecting their own work. Such practices are not very robust when viewed from the vantage point of accountability to taxpayers, to community and to students. However, the central dilemma is that schools are complex communities in themselves, and the processes of improvement are not readily reducible to the procedures of inspection. Schools need to grow and develop before and after inspections and development is likely to involve a sense of self-direction and self-worth. It is not clear whether external inspection can provide that. Inspection processes and procedures, and the meanings that schools draw from inspection about their own capacity for self-direction may be creating more extreme discontinuities between schooling and life.

Further, inspection processes may just be establishing a further layer of assessment/management by objectives. Far from counterbalancing the effects of an assessment-driven culture for education, inspection may be entrenching such a culture more firmly.

Changing the structures

A different approach to the issue of standards is illustrated through discussion of how we move from a monumental kind of education system into a more flexible, diverse and responsive one.

> Most of us have inherited a British (perhaps English?) tradition whereby the good life is to be lived in the mono-cultural, unitary and largely segregated institutions of family, work, leisure and religion, and life-courses take the form of single life-long careers between the end of schooling and the beginning of retirement. This neat, linear, predictable pattern is familiar and comforting, but it is giving way to a far more complex mosaic of institutions and life-patterns ... Schools remain as in the first picture, protruding from the changed landscape like carcasses of the factories on which they were modelled, out of their time and beyond anybody's power to make them efficient.
>
> (Hargreaves 1994: 56)

The ideas that Hargreaves puts forward for realizing this change are challenging, not least because of the shift they represent in his own biography and beliefs. He argues for schools that are 'smaller, differentiated and specialised' (1994: 53), for teachers with a 'portfolio occupational pattern' (1994: 26) in which time working in industry is combined with other periods in schools, and fixed-term contracts; for headteachers to be clearly leading professionals promoted through excellence in teaching and working alongside a professional manager; and for more thoroughgoing use of new technologies:

> IT [information technology] opens up new interactive communication between home and school, and between students and distant peers and mentors. Here are the seeds of a major challenge to teachers' monopoly over teaching . . .
>
> (Hargreaves 1994: 41)

Much of Hargreaves' argument is uncomfortable for a professional audience, and is meant to be. But the issues he raises, and his proposed solutions, are a contribution to the very wide debate about ways in which the curriculum needs more structurally – and through the very occupational patterns of teachers and the organization of schools – to reflect the wider world.

In spirit this chimes in with the message of *Competitiveness* (President of the Board of Trade *et al.* 1994) and suggests a vision for schools that would accord more closely with the changing structures in Further Education. A similar message for Higher Education is promoted by the CAT (Credit Accumulation and Transfer) Development Project (HEQC 1994), which looks to modular credit accumulation, supported by voucher entitlements for learners as the way to increase access, choice and mobility. The report acknowledges the very wide frameworks of interest and theoretical commitment that it is taking on in suggesting a credit accumulation pattern for Higher Education. It presents the possible conflict in terms of the identification of credit systems with a post-modern assault upon the modernist universities;

> Following this analysis it may be clearer why some informed opinion in universities remains suspicious of the introduction of credit systems and modularity. Their concerns go beyond a superficial antipathy to markets or a collectivist opposition to the individualisation of the curriculum in higher education.

They believe that what is at stake is the place and purpose of the university in the modern world. Is it to retain its principal purpose as a centre of intellectual rationality, coherence and moral integrity? Or is it to join other organisations of the 'post-modern' world in intellectual fragmentation, 'consumerist' superficiality and moral relativism?

(HEQC CATS Development Project 1994: para. 1089)

These issues are taken up here because the discussion of standards is incomplete without thinking of the wider context of educational debate in which the specifics of National Curriculum assessment – and of school inspections – may be quite transitory, even idiosyncratic, parts. A redefinition of the relationship of education and society is under way.

Overview

The Government has established what it believes to be the mechanisms for the monitoring and control of standards in maintained schools. However, the inspection of schools is still heavily involved in looking at the teaching of the National Curriculum, and so in some ways bound within its assumptions about standards. Inspection, like assessment, may serve to entrench the prescribed curriculum, and prevailing Government policies for the control of teachers. It is unlikely that questions about school accountability or the measurement of achievement will go away, but there are also pressures requiring other kinds of response. Secondary education, for example, is likely to experience considerable opportunity and change in the re-established priority of vocational education in the post-14 curriculum. That shift begins to reflect on the whole National Curriculum model; sometimes characterized as a secondary curriculum enforced on primary schools, it seems already very outmoded for the secondary sector. For a short time there seems to have been a growing consensus about the features of effective schools and the criteria for inspecting schools. However, the 'Framework' presupposes a fairly stable and uniform pattern of educational provision, and – the argument is here – that may be set to change.

The most clear and persistent definition of standards coming through the Government's legislation for education in the 1980s and 1990s is that standards are reflected by (even enshrined in) examination results. (Nor, as has been indicated in the case of GCSE, is there even any clarity about whether better results show declining standards of measurement or genuine improvement.) The very close identification of standards with achievement in the National Curriculum sets up a potentially very narrow and circular view of standards, only engaging with a single dimension of the complex work of schools. There are, on the one hand, arguments about the reliability of assessment information, and the problems of creating suitable models for fair comparison of schools. Inspections and other studies of school effectiveness have to acknowledge the inadequacy of methodologies for analysing results. On the other hand, there is the even more fundamental question of whether the results are themselves meaningful (is the curriculum on which they are based meaningful) in terms of objectives for education which may not be encompassed in the National Curriculum. As has been argued in previous chapters, there is a risk that educational activity becomes tied through assessment to an unquestioning, non-evaluative relation to fixed objectives.

Moreover, there is a risk (because of the location of the study of effectiveness within a management discourse) that the discussion of school effectiveness becomes divorced from discussion about the adequacy of the curriculum and the validity of assessments on which judgements might be made. The study of effectiveness is not necessarily good at engaging in detail with issues of purpose, either at the level of individual learning (how does effective management articulate with effective learning?) or at the level of the overall purposes of education (effective in terms of what ultimate goal?). The study of school effectiveness needs for the future to be very closely linked, not only to discussion of the reliability and validity of the National Curriculum assessments, but also to wider discussions of the overall aims of education.

The reason for introducing the idea of possible changes in structures of educational provision is to emphasize that standards include access and participation and relevant opportunities for student choice. It is difficult to equate these standards with what Hargreaves sees as the 'custodial' use of schools. National Curriculum and its assessment arrangements, together with the model of inspection, may serve to reinforce such a custodial culture. The search for 'effectiveness' may become a fairly barren one, entrenching existing cultures and celebrating conformity rather than opportunity.

The rationale for the National Curriculum does not provide a thorough or consistent definition of the educational 'standards' that the curriculum seeks to establish, and as Chapter 4 has argued its aims are linked to the management of educational provision, not to learning aims. There is some emphasis on individual attainment, some on provision in the notion of equal access and some implied attitudinal benefit through mentions of increased 'confidence' and 'challenge' (DES 1987b: para. 8). Another emphasis is the importance of providing adequate suitably skilled labour to meet the challenge of 'competitor countries'. If the aim is to make the UK more economically competitive, then there is no obvious path to that through increased parental choice of schools, or through a curriculum which is remarkable for its echoes of the past (Aldrich 1988: 22–3), and which may by the very rigidity and detail of its framework make close educational and qualifications links with the European market countries the harder to achieve. The hegemonic projects of the 'New Right', however, are concerned with the re-establishment of a distinctive national rather than international identity (Quicke 1988).

The worst case is that we have an education system for schools which reduces standards, for individuals and schools, to the meeting of narrow objectives, with a wholly inadequate description of the purposes of that process other than to bring professionals more closely under public (in practice governmental) control. If that is the case then there is a very large omission in educational planning.

It has been argued in relation to curricular objectives (Chapters 1, 3 and 4) that implicit objectives protect a broadly liberal humanist, professional control of education, whereas explicit objectives challenge the professional mode of control. The same could be argued at the level of objectives (for that is in effect what the Ofsted inspection 'Framework' establishes) for schools themselves. Reductionist though such a statement of objectives and criteria are, they do begin to deconstruct the professional role, and control, and thereby allow space for reconstruction. It is taking advantage of that space that is difficult, and involves finding the means for education as a whole to address the issues. It may be that education has now the space to engage not only at the level of changing its own role, and the specifics of curriculum, but also at the level of the purposes and policy direction of the education system.

11

THE RESEARCH
AGENDA

Broadfoot and others (1991b) outline two levels of issue – the
macro level relating to whether the new assessment system is
meeting the purposes assigned it, and the micro level relating to
classroom issues of implementation. Both require attention. The
macro level, they state, 'is more than equally matched in significance by the more micro issues of the actual quality of any of
the assessment information generated' (1991b: 157). R. Murphy
(1988), responding to the National Curriculum assessment proposals, identified issues of classroom practice, curriculum coverage, use of results and the reductive effects of a system designed
to produce 'simple' information (1988 39–45). The tension between
the levels on which the National Curriculum assessments operate
is a problem for research, firstly in that it generates so many
research questions to be addressed within the very rapid period of
introduction of the new system, and secondly because attention to
individual issues or to levels of issue may appear to legitimate
rather than question decisions taken at other levels. For example,
research findings which identify undue expenditure of teacher time
in preparing and administering SATs, is equally capable in itself of
justifying either a reduction in the complexity of the tasks, or a

greater reliance on teacher assessment. These decisions would represent very different interpretations of the evidence related to different views of the purpose of the National Curriculum assessments. This chapter gives an overview of the fields of research and evaluation in which the National Curriculum assessments are being developed and investigated, and the extent to which different levels of issue can be addressed within the constraints which operate.

The speed of introduction of the National Curriculum has been, and continues to be, a very important constraint upon research and evaluation. The Report by the National Foundation for Educational Research (NFER) and Bishop Grosseteste College (BGC), commissioned by SEAC, acknowledged the problem in making its recommendations: 'At the time of writing, decisions about the 1992 Standard Assessment task [*sic*] have already been taken . . .' (1991b: 87). Hence, there is restricted likelihood of detailed research having a meaningful impact upon policy in the short term.

The scale of change, affecting all maintained schools in England and Wales, is a further factor. Small-scale studies, able to identify some of the processes of classrooms, may produce very specific information related to teachers and pupils, but may not be easy to generalize to the majority of schools. On the other hand, questionnaire research has restrictions in its ability to reach classroom processes.

The sources of information below have each used a variety of methods to arrive at their findings, and such triangulation again demands studies of some scope and scale. Observation of the SATs themselves is a key element in Key Stage 1 researches, and because of the limited window of time within which the SATs are administered, there are physical problems in large-scale sampling for observational research.

Development of Standard Assessment Tasks and tests

The development of standard task and subsequently test materials for respectively Key Stages 1 and 3 has been one sponsored area of research/development. Such development has worked closely to specifications by SEAC. The early work for Key Stage 1 and the 1990 pilots suggested ambitious schemes, with a high concentration on construct and content validity. The Standard Tests and

Assessment Implementation Research (STAIR) consortium used a network of teachers to develop and trial activities for each Statement of Attainment (SoA) at Key Stage 1. All three Key Stage 1 development consortia were required to conduct a 2 per cent sample pilot nationally using their materials and to publish reports on these across specified areas including relative performance by gender and ethnicity (SEAC 1991d). The ambitiousness of some of the early development work has been progressively reduced through the concerns with 'manageability' (Robinson 1990), and 'the question of what it is most efficient to assess' (SEAC 1991c: para. 133). Assessing all pupils appears to have been a priority for SEAC in its monitoring of the pilots. This coverage is essential to a programme of national testing to provide school league tables but not necessary to the expressed purposes of training teachers and providing them with a means of checking their standards (SEAC 1991c: para. 131).

LEAs' role in providing training, support and moderation of Key Stage 1 SATs is complemented also by an evaluative role of its own arrangements (SEAC 1991a: 11). SEAC has gathered information by proforma from LEAs. Moderators (later called 'auditors') are advised to gather information on the training and support given to teachers, on the assessment procedures, teachers' perceptions of the reliability of results, the 'consistency between one school and another' and on whether the National Curriculum assessment is 'proving beneficial to the children's education' (SEAC 1991b: 14). The matter of 'consistency' is not defined, and it is unclear whether it refers to consistency of standard of assessment or procedural consistency in carrying out assessments, or even consistency in curricular practice.

HMI reports

HMI in a *Survey of 100 Schools* reported on the implementation of the National Curriculum in primary schools in 1989, and commented upon strategies for observation, methods of record keeping and attention to progression. Records they noted were generally improving in their standardization and curricular coverage, and some schools were recording not only the work that whole classes had covered, but also individual progress. They also, however, noted a proliferation of checklists providing 'only superficial information' (DES 1990c: 9, paras 35–8).

Subsequent reports covering Key Stages 1, 2 and 3, and relating to core subjects individually and to Special Educational Needs, were more searching in relation to progression and continuity. In relation to special needs students in ordinary schools they again criticize the checklist approach: 'Such systems rarely influenced the planning of future work' (DES 1992d: 18, para. 22). The Science report draws attention to the fact that recording has been a priority at the expense of 'ways of matching performance to levels in a consistent manner . . .' and recommends that schools give more attention to 'using the results of assessment to guide the planning of future work' (DES 1992c: 30, para. 75). The Mathematics report emphasizes the need to 'ensure that information obtained is used to plan the next stage in the pupils' development . . .' (DES 1992a: 38, para. 65). The English report focuses upon poorly differentiated work and the fact that 'Some departments confused the recording of experiences with the assessment of what had been achieved'. This report too is concerned with progression: 'A lack of connection between assessment and subsequent planning was widespread.' The use of written comments for diagnosis was also generally lacking (DES 1992b: 22, para. 28).

Ofsted had taken over this reporting role by the 1993 report on the 1991–92 year. Its report on *Assessment, Recording and Reporting* is based on 2600 inspections across primary and secondary schools. Their claims that Key Stage 1 assessment is now firmly established . . .' and 'In Key Stage 3, teachers and pupils came successfully through the national pilot tests, despite a good deal of public anxiety . . .' (HMCI 1993: 3) give no indication of the tensions that led to industrial action and a widespread boycott of SAT and test procedures in 1993, and again in 1994. There is a general message (relating to Key Stage 1) that there were improvements over the previous year, but the basis of these improvements is often on grounds of administration and manageability: 'Many Year 2 teachers were better prepared to administer the Standard Assessment Tasks in 1992 than in 1991. Schools benefited from the previous year's experience' (1993: para. 5). 'Schools found the 1992 Standard Tasks easier to manage than those used in 1991' (1993: para. 9). 'The decision not to assess investigative work in Science and Mathematics through the Standard Tasks simplified administration and reduced the overall time needed' (1993: para. 10). 'Teachers generally made more reliable assessments than in 1991. This was partly because the 1992 Standard Tasks were more manageable' (1993: para. 15). Where there were matters to criticize, these were apparently problems with teachers not with the Tasks: 'Administering the Tasks to small groups at a time also showed up the wider weaknesses in teachers' ability effectively to manage learning in small groups' (1993: para. 9).

The reporting on Key Stage 3 refers to pilot tests run in Science and Mathematics in 1991. The report does not directly address the issue of how far the Key Stage 3 tests are intended to mirror the practices of examinations at 16 +, though there is some assumption of an examination culture:

> Most schools provided opportunities for pupils to practise for the tests, although the amount of preparation and revision varied significantly from school to school. Some departments prepared revision materials and class work tests that were clearly linked to relevant ATs, sometimes using SEAC's sample materials as a guide. This kind of preparation had a beneficial effect on pupils' subsequent results . . . A few teachers overdid the pupils' preparation and undertook intensive cramming which caused unnecessary anxiety . . .
>
> (HMCI 1993: para. 24)

The report does not engage with whether the revision and preparation that stopped short of 'cramming' had beneficial effects on students' motivation for learning or their longer term understanding of the material. There is a section devoted to 'Managing the tests' concerned with arrangements for secure storage and for invigilation, and arrangements for pupils needing additional support.

The difficulties are, in short, seen in a predominantly administrative light, with limited exploration of how the process or content of external testing really interacts with teacher development and teaching process. A few potential problems are acknowledged:

> There is a danger that the Tasks may be replicated in lessons and give too narrow a focus to the work . . . not all teachers recognised the potential of good assessment for

raising standards, nor used assessment to modify their planning and teaching.

(HMCI 1993: 19)

These could be seen as fairly fundamental problems in the system, undermining the supposed diagnostic and developmental purposes of the testing.

Reports on pilots and the 1992 Key Stage 1 assessments commissioned by SEAC

The Evaluation of the National Curriculum at Key Stage 1 (ENCA) project based at the University of Leeds expands the brief to take account of contextual school and classroom factors, 'to provide explanations as to why any discrepancies of scores between TA, SAT and ENCA re-assessment occurred' (ENCA 1992a: 5).

The study sampled 96 schools from 16 LEAs with some balance of metropolitan/non-metropolitan location and geographical location defined by North, South, East and West regions of the country. Within that sample, numbers of children were identified according to age, gender, ethnic background, first language and social background. The study also collected as contextualizing information details of teachers' and headteachers' length of service and qualifications.

The strands of data collection were observational studies, ENCA re-assessments, questionnaires to LEAs, to teachers, pupils and parents, and pupil record sheets. Their report concludes that there was some unevenness of preparation for assessment across the country between LEAs. They found discrepancies between teachers in their understandings of terms in SoAs, most particularly in English where in such terms as 'fluency' and 'understanding' they found 'little agreement' (ENCA 1992b: 7). In Mathematics and Science a more common area of discrepancy was between teachers and SAT developers in their interpretation of 'or' in SoAs. Teachers commonly took this to mean that items were alternatives whereas SATs treated the listings as inclusive of its items.

This study found higher correlation between SAT scores and teacher assessments in schools which had experience of the 1990 pilots, suggesting the importance of experience and familiarity.

Table 11.1   SEAC specification for evaluation of the 1991 Key Stage 1
Assessments

The original specification from SEAC, the commissioning body,
required that the evaluation should carry out in-depth assessment of a
national sample of children (England and Wales) to provide evidence
from which it would be possible to:

- compare the NCA results with those obtained from the in-depth
  studies;
- consider the range of achievements of individuals and groups in
  different assessment tasks;
- highlight aspects of NCA that could be improved by modifications
  to SAT or TA procedures;
- explore the validity and reliability of attainment level scores as
  indicators of progression;
- investigate the effects of combining SAT and TA information and
  the validity of the single scores derived;
- explore the stability of NCA results across different groups of
  pupils.

Source: ENCA 1992a

Such findings appear to endorse the need for further LEA coordination and training, and that agreement about interpretation of
such statements is the result of shared experience over time rather
than of written publication or single training events. They also
attribute some of the discrepancies between SAT scores and TAs
to unfamiliarity of teachers with levels (ENCA 1992b: 53–4).

The report gives, however, support to the TAs and offers its
judgement that some of the discrepancies between sets of scores
arose from the greater curriculum coverage of TAs (1992b: 53–4).
Furthermore, they cast doubt on the extent to which conditions can
be 'standard' for SATs: 'If this [i.e. standard] is taken to imply that
the activities, procedures and performance requirements were the
same for all children then the 1991 SAT fell considerably short of
this' (1992b: 52). They found that while the majority of parents (57
per cent) favoured reporting of TA and SAT results, less than 1 per
cent favoured the reporting of the SAT result only; 37 per cent
favoured the reporting of the TA assessment and not the SAT, a
finding that also relates to the teachers' own confidence in their
assessments (1992b: 20). This confidence is, however, questioned

by the discrepancies found between TAs and SAT results where the SAT result was most frequently one level (and sometimes two levels: this study found somewhat more discrepancy than the NFER study) higher than the TA (ENCA 1992a: 95–105).

ENCA found that in the opinion of headteachers the SAT exercise had a positive effect on relationships between the schools and their governors and parents, but a negative effect on general behaviour. There was concern by teachers and others about the non-challenging nature of work for those children not involved in SATs (1992a: 10ff.). Children's perceptions of the tasks and of their performance suggested some positive views (1992a: 66–9) but this information is not cross-referenced with information about actual performance, and therefore is unable to shed light on questions about the extent to which pupils' understandings about assessment may affect the curricular impact of assessments.

The study also found that age of children appeared to be affecting their achievement of levels (ENCA 1992b: 23). There were also gender differences, particularly in English where girls were achieving significantly better than boys, as also in some ATs in Science and Mathematics (1992b: 22). Performance in English and Mathematics they found to be significantly better in pupils who had nursery experience (1992b: 23). They found differences in groups according to ethnic origin with the lowest performance among Asian children and the highest among white children (the groupings for this were very broad) (1992b: 24) and that there was 'a declining pattern of attainment for children from high status neighbourhoods to low status neighbourhoods' (1992b: 25).

The ENCA re-assessments do not appear to have contributed greatly to the study with the most important sources of data coming from questionnaires, SAT and TA information. The ENCA re-assessments were not able to sample validly across the curriculum and therefore offer data which can only be considered alongside the other data rather than as a reference point from which to judge it. They were carried out later than the other assessments and by people unknown to the children and the report acknowledges that it is not possible to know whether this would have had positive or negative effects upon performance (ENCA 1992a: 109–22).

The study carried out by NFER/BGC retained some distinction between the strands of its research into teacher assessment on the one hand and the SATs on the other. The research into teacher assessment was conducted by questionnaire, nationally (England and Wales), and by visits to 38 schools from 24 LEAs. The schools were selected to 'elucidate particular issues' (NFER/BGC 1991a: 25). The consortium's study of SATs also sampled nationally by questionnaire to teachers and by requesting a stratified sample of schools to send pupil record sheets, pupil information and assessment record booklets, and had response rates of between 50 and 70 per cent for various materials and parts of the sample.

The study gives attention to workload, collecting information about the additional hours spent by teachers on planning for SATs, administering them and preparation during the SAT period (NFER/BGC 1991b: 15–18). The overload identified is offered as a possible explanation for some of the incorrect routes taken through the SATs (1991b: 12–13). They also collected information about relative levels of confidence of teachers before and during the SATs and found that levels rose in the course of the exercise (1991b: 27–9). Since they identified high levels of anxiety before the SAT exercise it is difficult to equate the SAT procedures with an increase in confidence when what may have been experienced is relief rather than professional growth.

They found acceptable facility values, but with some discrepancy in performance across SoAs (1991b: 46–7). There was general correlation between ATs the notable exception being handwriting which correlated poorly with other English ATs and with Science and Mathematics performance (1991b: 46–8). They found there were discrepancies in level between TA and SAT results, 'the most frequent discrepancy was for the Standard Assessment task result to be one level higher than the TA' (1991b: 58). They found that there was an improvement in match of TA and SAT levels compared with the 1990 pilots, with an average match of 57 per cent in English, 41 per cent in Mathematics, 31 per cent in Science and 63 per cent in Welsh. Familiarity would again seem to be important, but, unlike the ENCA study they found that the match in assessments among the 1990 pilot schools was no greater than among other schools (1991b: 58).

The study used resolved results (i.e. TA and SAT) to consider whether there were significant differences among groups. (ENCA attempted to use unresolved data for this purpose, presumably to identify whether teachers were advantaging or disadvantaging any groups of pupils in their assessments; they concluded that they should have used resolved data; ENCA 1992a: 105.) They found a similar pattern to ENCA with girls performing higher across the English ATs than boys and in some ATs in the other core subjects. They too found an age advantage (NFER/BGC 1991b: 67). Asian and Afro-Caribbean children were more frequently achieving at Level 1 than white children (1991b: 74–6). They point out, however, that the sample size in relation to ethnicity is too small to permit reliable inferences. Unlike the ENCA study they found no consistent evidence of advantage from nursery experience (1991b: 70–1). They also present tentatively some findings on small classes in which there appeared to be an 'increased likelihood of achievement at Level 3', but suggest that this would require further investigation using multi-level modelling (1991b: 77).

NFER and Brunel University carried out a study of the Key Stage 3 pilot assessments in Mathematics and Science in 1992 (NFER/ Brunel University 1993). Their sampling matrix consisted of school type, size of age group and location (metropolitan/non-metropolitan, and by one of four broadly defined regions of the country – North, Midlands, South, Wales). Schools were surveyed by questionnaire, with a pupil sample of 12 per school providing the data for analysis of performance. There were also case-study visits related to particular topics such as reactions to the testing process.

Their study identified a number of points for development, both in relation to the support needed for teacher assessment, and in relation to coverage, validity and reliability of tests. There is attention to administration, to sources of bias, and to teacher and pupil reactions to the tests. It is a detailed report, mainly concerned, in accordance with its brief, with fine-tuning of a system intended to be fully operational for the following year. It does also engage, however, in some more wide-ranging discussion of the 'State of Development of National Curriculum Assessment'.

The original TGAT concept of a parallel formal assessment to those made by teachers for all attainment targets has been lost. As currently operating, the formal test element of National Curriculum assessment at Key Stage 3 can now be seen to be the result of a series of decisions to reduce the amount of time needed for assessment and to focus on summative purposes. In our view a reappraisal is needed of the purposes of the Key Stage 3 tests so that all are clear on these purposes and the tests are designed to meet them . . . . Highly aggregated data available for all pupils could be acquired by simpler tests designed to produce a subject level. More detailed monitoring of standards could be accomplished by an effective strategy of sampling schools. . . . We recommend that SEAC consider in detail the level and nature of the information required from the Key Stage 3 testing programme and ensure that clearly stated purposes are met by producing an assessment framework designed to produce this information as efficiently and reliably as possible.

(NFER/Brunel University 1993: 230–2)

Reports on the implementation of Mathematics in the National Curriculum (SCAA 1993a,b,c), Science (SCAA 1994a,b,c) and English (SCAA 1994d) were also commissioned, based on national surveys and more detailed case-study research. Though these reports have curriculum as their central focus they also, naturally, identify a number of issues relating to assessment: 'many of the problems relate to the dual nature of the current Mathematics Order in attempting to provide a framework to guide teaching and a prescription for assessment arrangements' (SCAA 1993b: para. 6.3.2). The Science reports include detailed consideration of progression (1994b) and differentiation (SCAA 1994c), both closely related to good formative assessment practice. 'The prevailing debate and concerns about assessment tend to place the summative functions of assessment to the fore. There has been relatively little discussion about the development and use of diagnostic tests that support the on-going teaching of science' (SCAA 1994b: para. 7.2). Moreover, the development of Key Stages (essentially driven by the idea of key reporting stages for summative results) 'has probably resulted in a greater within-phase introspection. There is a paradox here, since one of the National Curriculum innovations was to set out the courses of study that would enhance the possibility of continuity across the Key Stage 2–Key Stage 3 divide'. Such continuity, the report suggests, requires processes to support it, and it advocates the kinds of study groups that had been established for the research as a model for such development. The report on differentiation identifies similarly the need for processes of teacher support to realize the curricular aims of assessment.

> Formative assessment provides an essential underpinning to effective differentiation. This is a skill which is part of good classroom practice, but which teachers need support in developing (SCAA 1994c: para. 2.5). This should be addressed by in-service training, but further there is a need for more active and participatory forms of teacher development. Effective differentiation cannot proceed simply by prescribing a list of strategies for teachers to adopt ... Teacher involvement in empirical classroom-based research should be undertaken in order to explore approaches towards differentiated provision. Such research should help to identify successful teaching strategies that can improve the quality of learning experiences offered to all pupils. The research outcomes would inform professional guidance an INSET provision.
>
> (SCAA 1994b: para. 7.5)

The Dearing Report

Following the substantial boycott of the Key Stage 3 tests in England and Wales in 1993, as well as a widespread boycott of Key Stage 1 SATs, Ron Dearing was charged by the DFE with the task of reviewing the National Curriculum and its assessment arrangements. The terms of reference of the review were:

(i) the scope for slimming down the curriculum;
(ii) how the central administration of the National Curriculum and testing arrangements could be improved;
(iii) how the testing arrangements might be simplified; and
(iv) the future of the ten-level scale for recognising children's attainment.

(Dearing 1993b: para. 1.1)

The review was conducted through consultations ranging across teacher associations, parents groups and industry, and also through regional conferences for consultation with teachers. Although the

Dearing proposals have met mixed reactions from those in education, the involvement of teachers so actively in the consultation was in itself a significant shift in the policy of implementation and review by government. In a letter from Ron Dearing to the Secretary of State for Education:

> I have been deeply impressed – at times moved – by the strong commitment of everyone concerned in education to serve our children well . . . the last thing our schools need is precipitate, ill-thought through change.
>
> (Dearing 1993b: 1)

The slimming down of the curriculum opens the way for much more variety in the post-14 age group and for the introduction of vocational qualifications. It also reduces the workload elsewhere. After a circumspect discussion of the 10-level scale, it is decided that it should be retained, as preferable to Key Stage gradings which were proposed as the main alternative. It has been suggested in Chapter 10 that the increased flexibility in the curriculum brought about by the slimming down will in itself be significant in establishing the context for other kinds of curriculum development in the later 1990s. The other area of significance is the whole change in tone about the role of teachers, and the acknowledgement that there may need to be a more active role for teachers in moderating processes for teacher assessment in non-core subjects for which statutory tests are not now to be developed. Although he envisages a role for non-statutory tests and guidance materials, and for inspection visits in the moderating process, he also makes the 'assumption that schools in a locality come together to form groups to moderate their assessments' (Dearing 1993b: para. 9.2).

ESRC research and evaluation studies

Two ESRC (Economic and Social Research Council) -funded projects will be briefly outlined here: The Primary Assessment, Curriculum and Experience Project (PACE) based at Bristol Polytechnic and Bristol University and National Assessment in Primary Schools Evaluation Project based at the London Institute of Education.

The PACE project was a longitudinal study, giving it greater depth and continuity of contact with study schools than the SEAC-commissioned work. Its sample of 50 schools across eight LEAs is for the purposes of some strands of its methodology reduced to a sub-sample of 10. Its sampling is described as drawing on a range of schools, by geographical location; in terms of strategies of LEA support and coordination and in terms of socio-economic factors (PACE 1989: 1–7). Its methodology comprised: structured interviews with headteachers and infant teachers; classroom observation and discussion of the sub-sample of schools; detailed monitoring of assessment within that sub-sample; an ethnography to identify features of the schools as a whole; and a federated approach to collating the outcomes of action research projects of teachers offering to be attached to the project as a whole (1989: 8–13).

The findings of the project, as well as its developing practice (for it is also engaged in exploring methodological issues in relation to the study of national assessments) have been published in a series of working papers. One of these is outlined here to indicate key themes that emerged in the research.

Broadfoot and others (1991a) identify a range of issues which could loosely be categorized as pedagogic, organizational, technical (in relation to making assessments), and concerning relations with colleagues and parents.

The paper focuses upon time pressures, support needed to carry out SATs effectively in the classroom, disruption of normal practice, the tensions caused by a shift from collaborative and teacher-supported work, neglect of non-SAT children and teachers' emphasis on the need to protect children from stress. These issues represent organization matters but are also a great deal deeper, as they interrelate with closely held views about the nature of classroom relations and the way those support effective learning. Views of teachers about the assessments made using SATs showed a concern about the following: the absence of formative/diagnostic information; lack of faith in resolved levels in some cases; lack of standard conditions; wide variety of achievement in some levels – the tasks not differentiating effectively); problems in making decisions about level; and some issues of validity, for example that the time constraint in a Mathematics task did not appear to be relevant to the SoA. Teachers also identified that the SATs presented new features in their relationship with parents, in terms of parental perceptions of SATs' purposes, the need to calm some parents' anxieties about testing, and the problems some parents perceived when other parents were helping in SAT classrooms. Relationships with colleagues were feared by some to be affected, since there were anxieties that there might be disagreements over levels (Broadfoot *et al.* 1991a: 1–10).

The study of SATs is, of course, only one element in the much larger developing picture of national assessment addressed by the PACE project, though some of the themes identified are common to the whole of the National Curriculum assessment procedure. Broadfoot and others (1991b: 160–7) give prominence to record-keeping and pupils' involvement in the process of recording, and to ownership, themes which are consonant with Records of Achievement (Broadfoot *et al.* 1988) and suggest an integrated way forward, and 'evidence that we might be at the beginning of a very creative phase of development in the use of assessment' (Broadfoot *et al.* 1991b: 163).

The project questions the reliability of the SATs at Key Stage 1, and finds evidence contrary to the views of Ofsted that experience is necessarily making assessments more valid and reliable:

> During the 1992 assessment process too, all PACE schools were visited while the Mathematics 3 SAT, which seems to purport to be more reliable that those used in 1991, was carried out. Observation suggested, however, that this apparently more standardised task was equally vulnerable to variations in the way teachers present the activity.
>
> (Abbott *et al.* 1994: 171)

The London Institute study involved four LEAs, with a stratified random sample of eight schools within each. The research was conducted by discussion, interview and observation (Gipps *et al.* 1992). The issues identified for interim discussion were: school organization; teaching and ancillary support; support by head-teachers; quality of support; stress, especially of Year 2 teachers and headteachers; curricular implications of assessment practices; school development; changes in classroom practice, for example there was greater use of group-work; and the degree of integration of SATs into normal classroom practice. The emergent themes identified from the findings under these headings are teachers' emphasis on protecting children, encouraging best performance, feelings of guilt and anxiety and a sense of raised professionalism.

What we can say is that the 1991 KS1 SATs were designed on an authentic assessment model. Despite anxiety over the quality of the worksheets, they matched the active process-based tasks which children do in good infant classroom practice much more closely than do traditional standardized tests. As our data shows, these assessment tasks not only gave our teachers direct ideas for areas of the curriculum which they had not covered, but also, for some, pointers towards a wider view of teaching and learning. This is the opposite of a traditional view of teaching to the test – which is typically viewed as narrowing and negative – in that it widened teachers' practice rather than narrowed it. Thus, from this experience we can say that the introduction of high-stakes, authentic assessment can broaden teachers' practice . . . On this basis, we can hypothesize that the move away from using process-based tasks and any attempt to return to narrow paper and pencil test of the traditional, standardized type will effect a narrowing of teaching again.

(Gipps *et al.* 1992: 79)

An administrative, technical, pedagogic and political issue?

The reports from HMI and Ofsted, and those reports working to SEAC terms of reference, give considerable attention to administration and manageability of the SAT, testing and teacher assessment arrangements. That focus tends to cast other more fundamental issues aside, and does not address the validity of the exercise which is to be made less time-consuming. There is a danger that some reporting on assessment looks at manageability, at the expense of purpose.

The technical issues surrounding assessment, particularly of the validity and reliability of the assessments, of whether there are any sources of bias in the assessments and how results should be interpreted, are clearly important ones. Apart from the critical attention received in some of the work quoted here, there have also been other studies addressing the principles of assessment and reporting. For example, Cresswell and Houston (1991: 63–78) argue that the problems of decontextualized assessment, and of aggregation of levels, indicate the appropriateness of a profiling of National Curriculum assessments at Key Stage 4. M. Brown (1991) discusses the inappropriateness of reporting the subject level as the median of the levels achieved across Attainment Targets as likely to give a very inaccurate picture of achievement. These are clearly very important matters, central to retaining the vitality of the claim that national assessment arrangements can truly provide valid diagnostic information.

The ESRC-sponsored projects outlined above, together with those reports published by SCAA regarding implementation of the curriculum in specific subjects, have a strong concern with pedagogy, the effects of assessments upon classroom activities and the extent to which assessment arrangements do – or can – inform the processes of teaching and learning.

The key issue that the research on National Curriculum assessment raises, however, is one of level. The context for National Curriculum assessment is not easy to reduce. The political and social change of the late twentieth century give a new prominence to education as a principal site of a complex struggle between professional privilege, commercial pragmatism and community rights. To locate assessment research within particular issues, or (as may increasingly happen in the secondary range) within subject-discipline-based areas of study, risks removing it from its centrality in such a struggle. The use of research on Key Stage 1 pilots (showing them to be unwieldy, time-consuming and subject to unequal amounts of school-based resourcing) to justify governmentally prescribed simplification of the tasks to timed tests is indicative of the political context in which such research currently operates.

McNamara, outlining an 'agenda for research', draws attention to the political context: educational researchers are only noticed 'where it is convenient for those who determine events to quote "research" to justify policies which they are determined to pursue in any event' (McNamara 1990: 225). He suggests that in such a context

there is little point in continuing to challenge the philosophical and educational basis of the National Curriculum;

the way forward for educational research is rather to engage with the Government's claim that the Education Reform Act will improve the quality of learning in schools but lays down a National Curriculum which is eloquently silent on how such an aspiration is to be attained.

(McNamara 1990: 226)

Gipps argues that there is a lack of fundamental research particularly accompanying the introduction of assessment: 'Millions of pounds have so far been spent on national assessment and yet the programme itself is in a shambles' (Gipps 1992a: 277). She outlines the areas, spanning fundamental research and development and monitoring, which should, she argues, be the focus of the research effort: process-based criterion-referenced assessment, performance assessment, organization and pedagogical issues, learning hierarchies, the use of assessment results and equal opportunities (1992a: 277–86). Brown makes a similar defence of the importance of fundamental research 'within the framework of the current, somewhat frenetic, activity' (S. Brown 1991: 238).

Fundamental research is, however, seriously challenged by current policy, and not only by funding allocation, but also because of the way in which research findings are seen through the lens of policy. There are also features of current change which are consciously designed to challenge the strongholds of Higher Education, and to expose the weaknesses of the fragmentation that specialization can cause within institutions, and indeed nationally in research. The question remains of whether the National Curriculum assessment can or should be considered out of the context of radical change in schools brought about by Local Management of Schools, and whether teaching and learning are indeed separable from the entire social context in which education is currently a central and embattled part.

12

AGAINST FRAGMENTATION

The history of the introduction of the National Curriculum shows a powerful political agenda, which is about far more than adjusting the content of what school students learn. A redefinition of the relationship of teachers, at all levels and ages of the education process, to society is attempted. The motives for this shift are not unitary – there are different threads within government thinking, and there are different kinds of attacks coming from different directions upon the control that teachers as professionals have traditionally had over their work and their students.

> The Conservative government in Britain is in two minds and talks with two voices. One voice suggests that the future will reflect a devolution of power to the clientele of the schools ... The other voice says that curriculum control will be more centralized. Both voices agree on one thing: the professional autonomy of teachers that has for so long been the hallmark of the rhetoric of curriculum control will be curtailed.
>
> (Simons 1987: 4)

The argument presented in Chapter 1 is that the 'two-voice' argument to an extent obscures the variety of possibility within the neo-liberal positions. There is a great difference between the educational future suggested by league-table driven market forces, and that suggested by an enterprise culture which can be translated into greater educational participation. It is not easy to characterize the projects of the New Right singly, or simply to defend professional privileges against government interference.

The professional ethic in education has come to be identified with the liberal humanist ethic, and this has been exemplified at points in the discussion of HMI's work which repeatedly resists schematization of its curricular ideas, or specification of level or type of educational 'objectives'. Such an approach is liberal humanist in so far as it assumes the possibility of consensus through tradition, common experience and values. It does, however, place great faith in teachers and in continuity, and is arguably inadequate to meet the challenge of an increasingly participatory and pluralist society. Chapter 6 points out that some commentaries which are critical of right-wing reforms could be regarded as preserving the notion of professional power, rather than seeking an agenda for social change through education. Yet there are other sources of opposition, very different from those of the New Right, to the 'professional' stance.

> The impressive corpus of radical and Marxist analysis of American, Canadian and British education has accumulated evidence, from many angles, against the liberal vision of schooling as a broad preparation for life, as an effective means to reproduce the kind of society and individual consistent with western humanist traditions ... According to left education theory, schools cannot truly serve workers and other subordinate groups because they are ... reproducers of the dominant relations of production. Consequently, Marxism has found its critique and even its language appropriated by the right which ... is entirely sympathetic to an economic interpretation of the function of schools ...
>
> (Aronowitz and Giroux 1986: 5–6)

Within such a context, the interest among the New Right in 'objectives' poses a number of challenging questions. Objectives, on the one hand serve a technicist-managerial function, 'management by objectives'. Since behavioural objectives characterize NVQs and to some extent the National Curriculum also, and since behavioural

objectives are essentially technicist in their view of mental functioning, the objectives of the current curriculum changes can be viewed
as existing within this particular dimension of control. However,
objectives may also serve to demonstrate 'what is at stake': they can
be deconstructive of the prevailing order and its assumptions.
Defining objectives is an inherently political act, making assumptions open to scrutiny. Moreover, the setting of objectives permits
clearer identification of the Machereyan 'not said', the silences and
gaps in the curricular projects of the New Right (and of course in
the previous curricular projects of liberal humanism). The National
Curriculum makes its content objectives plain – they are open to
view and to criticism. It also structurally changes the work of
teachers. A third, and again distinct, opportunity presented by
objectives is that they can form a personal process of idiographic
motivation, which may be capable of co-option by managerial
designs, but by remaining individual is not necessarily part of an
external process of control.

The fact that there are at least three ways of interpreting the
social and educational functions of objectives, undoubtedly com-
plicates response. All three positions would cooperate with a move
to reduce or change the traditional role of teachers. A technicist
vision makes the teacher a functionary, replaceable in many ways
by a computer. If we follow through the deconstructive argument
then we might see objectives as a means of questioning and reducing the power of teachers. The idiographic use of objectives, as
translated in personal target setting and recording of achievement,
suggests a role for teachers which places greater emphasis on
counselling and facilitating, thus reducing the emphasis on the different epistemological status of teacher knowledge and student
knowledge.

In terms of the effects that such changes might have upon
students it could be conjectured that a technicist teaching force
would be designed to produce a programmed and predictable
workforce. If we see the deconstructive power of objectives as
reducing the power of teachers then it is open to argument whether
this increases the power of students, or whether students then
become an even less empowered group. This depends upon who
is setting the objectives, for what purpose and whether they are
truly open to negotiation. Some commentators see teachers as
having a key role in protecting and promoting the welfare of

students (the position adopted by Apple 1986) while others see teachers as often acting as agents of cultural hegemony (Mac an Ghaill 1988). Does the removal of teacher power give students more or less power? Does bringing teachers' work much more closely under governmental control suggest a new hierarchy with students at the bottom of a process of transmission, or does the government act as an agent to release students from the control of teachers by inhibiting the power of professionalism? The third way of interpreting the changes, the idiographic vision, has been critiqued by Hargreaves (1989) and by Broadfoot (1990) as cited in Chapter 5, as having potential for good or ill: having potential to motivate students but also being capable of incorporation into a project of surveillance and control.

Objectives and assessment

Objectives are closely associated with assessment in the current government-directed change. Once objectives are specified their achievement can be assessed, and if all school students are working to the same objectives, then superficially it seems possible to advance the possibility of making standard assessments across the school population. The issues arising from such a view have been discussed in Chapters 5, 6, 7 and 10. The difficulties surrounding criterion-referencing, standardization and notions of progression are not readily resolvable at a national or any large-scale level. It is argued in Chapter 6 that criterion referencing is an important pedagogical notion, releasing teachers from normative notions of attainment promulgated by ability-oriented models of measurement. It gives teachers support in thinking about individuation of curriculum, and provides a rationale for a greater focus upon the processes of teaching, learning and progression. Criterion-referencing is, however, impossible to define rigorously, in any way that satisfies both the need for an elaborated curriculum and a reliable national system of measurement. It is not possible to turn the rhetoric of criterion-referencing into absolute standards of performance on which schools and teachers can be judged. What appears to be emerging in the development of national testing at Key Stages 2 and 3 is a system that may be no more or less normatively judged than past examination systems, and which can be anticipated to have the same effects throughout the compulsory school years as examination systems geared to timed tests have had in the past.

The largest danger in this diverse array of uncertainties, is that league tables of schools will remove the possibility of pursuing the debate which deconstruction of the curriculum (and of teachers' work) has opened up. The focus upon results, exaggerated by comparison of results, sets in motion a machinery which excludes curricular debate or reform, and which marginalizes what should be fundamental discussions, such as those about access and participation in Higher Education and training. League tables which contextualize information, be it in terms of socio-economic factors or in terms of 'progress', legitimate the activity of comparison for competition in education, and also accept the validity of the underlying structures of curriculum and assessment. Such activities close the debate that at its best the defining of objectives has opened, and entrench the use of objectives as a means of control.

Democracy, citizenship and empowerment

These three related, but not identical, principles are suggested as keys to organizing alternative but achievable aims in education within the policies of New Right governments. Issues which persist are the extent to which democracy is advocated as a collegial democracy among teachers, as opposed to a democracy truly offering equality of participation to students, and the extent to which education which proposes to be culturally analytical is in fact geared more to an inculcation of existing social and cultural forms than to what Giroux terms a 'critical pedagogy'. In such a pedagogy 'in addition to treating curriculum as a narrative whose interests must be uncovered and critically interrogated, teachers must promote pedagogical conditions within their classrooms that provide spaces for different student voices' (Giroux 1989: 165). Applying such a pedagogy to the National Curriculum would involve uncovering the processes by which the National Curriculum in broad and in particular terms was instituted, and the interests that are represented within its statements of attainment. As the most visible curriculum to which teachers in England and Wales have worked, it is particularly available for this kind of interrogation and deconstruction. Its objectives being at least in part explicit are part of a potentially deconstructive process.

What part objectives play in opening up opportunities for truly participative democracy must depend a great deal on the part that students have in such processes. It is possible to see the current use of objectives as the imposition of a 'systems' approach upon educational process, 'behavioral objectives as tacitly preserving in an unquestioning manner the dominant modes of institutional interaction in an unequal economy' allied to 'a penchant for order in the curriculum' (Apple 1979: 114). In such an interpretation of the use of objectives, teachers and students are reduced to uncritical functionaries in the social plans of others. The key difference between the role of pre-specified objectives, and that of the process of identifying and formulating objectives at an institutional or personal level, has been outlined in the discussion of school-effectiveness studies. In that context the emphasis is largely upon teachers' role in examining their objectives, but 'the pupils too have "objectives", beliefs and values which must influence the effective curriculum just as much as do the teacher's planned objectives' (Barnes 1976: 187–8).

The National Curriculum establishes a context in which neither teachers nor students have control over the curriculum objectives. Central to whether objectives act as a further layer of external control and a further means of cultural reproduction, or whether they permit a truly critical and emancipatory pedagogy will be the interpretation that teachers place upon their role in the implementation of the National Curriculum. Curriculum may come to be seen as a 'given', a matter for degrees of acceptance or incorporation within past practice, or it may be increasingly a site for interrogation of the cultural narrative of which it is a part. These interpretations would suggest very different definitions of how democracy, citizenship or empowerment were to be achieved through education.

If schools were to engage increasingly in a critical pedagogy, and one in which the voice and 'objectives' of students maintained equal privilege with those of teachers and of national prescription, the challenge to Higher Education to provide leadership in these activities would be considerable. Arguably, it is the control of Higher Education over access and participation post-16 which provides the competitive context in which schools and students have traditionally worked. Higher Education has to some extent within its own grasp the means to change fundamental characteristics of education, which are at least in part attributable to its own entry and access rituals, and their reverberation not only throughout the school system, but also throughout the social systems of prestige within which schools operate. Even commentators who speak of the 'seamless web' of education (Warnock 1989: 135) claim that different degrees of academic freedom should characterize degree-awarding institutions as opposed to schools and tertiary colleges (1989: 135–70). The current wave of education-by-objectives is, however, unlikely to be confined to the school and to basic vocational training. A very real issue exists about how Higher Education responds, and its preparedness to respond.

The power and weakness of disciplines

The disciplinary organization of the academic system may be seen as 'the dominant form of social organization of legitimate intellectual knowledge today' (Aronowitz and Giroux 1991: 145). It is, as a survival of western post-Platonic culture, marked by its 'penchant for classification (1991: 146), against which one might set non-classificatory, non-taxonomic frameworks such as deconstruction, Marxism, or phenomenology. What the writers are advocating here is an intellectually integrative activity, rather than a taxonomic, disciplinary separation of culturally defined knowledge. More pragmatically, considering the barriers to quality issues within Higher Education, Scott identifies 'the inner life of disciplines' as a key factor preventing institution wide processes: 'the development of the academic profession(s) has received little attention' (P. Scott 1989: 13).

Such arguments have relevance to Higher Education's role in relation to education itself in two ways. Firstly, it could be said that education as an area for study is disciplinarily isolated from other fields or disciplines within the academy. Higher Education treats education as one of its disciplines, rather than as a structurally central concern to its own enterprise. As long as the role of education departments, with their necessary engagement in the education of the whole population, is marginal, then the academy is the better able to detach itself from the social effects of its social isolation.

They [the universities] seek to preserve their cognitive rationality not by combat and friction with establishments but by maintaining distance, by lying low rather than by rising up ... cognitive rationality is subverted by complacency, by the drift toward the maintenance of creature comforts, by security from accepting the establishment and the friendly discourse with it, and by immersal in narrow problem-solving which blocks a view of larger contexts.

(Gouldner 1985: 299)

Education departments have contributions to make, and opportunities for larger involvement in the life of the institutions of which they are a part. A fuller engagement in Higher Education and school education simultaneously could provide a vital bridge in opening opportunity and access.

Secondly, the power of disciplines also operates within education departments themselves. Bernstein makes the distinction between two discourses 'a general discourse concerned with a body of knowledge called 'education' and specific discourses called professional subjects' (Bernstein 1990: 161). Moreover, he traces stages in the move away from the general to the specialized discourse: from a single lecturer teaching both 'education' and professional subjects, to the development of specialized discourses of philosophy, psychology, sociology and history taught by specialists, to the insertion of 'curriculum studies', 'together with the rise of the dominance of policy, management, and assessment' (1990: 163). However one interprets these shifts, they do represent an increasing movement towards disciplinarity in one sense, to be replaced in the current stage by school-based teacher training, which will assert the dominance of the subject or subjects (as defined by the National Curriculum). The question then remains of how successfully a fragmented view of education and professional preparation for teaching (fragmented in the sense of being identified as a series of disciplines or subjects) can address the very wide range of issues associated with current curricular change. If, as Giroux or Apple or Bernstein warn, education is becoming increasingly reduced to a technical conception of teaching, how well placed are any of the separate disciplines within 'education' to address that matter? It has been suggested in Chapter 10 that a satisfactory model of educational management and its relationship to pedagogy

does not appear to exist, that the discourse of educational management, of school effectiveness and indeed of educational policy does
not easily relate to a discourse about individual learning experience
within the classroom. Yet, these very different areas are all crucially
involved in the issues surrounding the National Curriculum and its
assessment arrangements.

Assessment itself has no central place within the first set of
disciplines identified by Bernstein as the elements of professional
studies. In relation to current change there may be difficulty in
organizing an adequate response to assessment because of its uncertain past in terms of academic disciplines. It is locatable as an issue
of interest to the history, the sociology, the psychology and the
philosophy of education yet none of these individually can encompass all the dimensions of the issue of national assessment as it
currently presents itself to schools and to society. As an entirely
school-subject-based issue, it begins to close the discussion of the
content of subjects as well as to restrict discussion between them.

Assessment and research

The Education Act 1988, as well as UK government policy on
education and training generally, make assessment a key issue. Its
study, however, may be inhibited by a number of factors: one is
certainly the instrumental interests of government, and another
may be the difficulty of finding satisfactory levels and breadth of
engagement with the issues involved.

Broadfoot, in discussing the general principles of educational
research in current contexts, cites a warning by Neville Bennett of
'the dangers of research findings being corruptly used by "ideologies" if it happens to be relevant to prevailing public concerns'
(Broadfoot 1988: 12).

There are a number of ways in which the danger of such corrupt
use appears particularly applicable to National Curriculum assessment. Chapters 4 and 11 have suggested that initial evaluation
of SATs and teacher assessment has been diverted into matters of
'manageability', that is, that classroom convenience has been of
greater importance than considerations of validity of results or
of staff development opportunities for teachers in determining how
evaluations findings are interpreted by sponsors. The TGAT

report, while not representing research, nonetheless represented a considered public presentation arising from substantial educational research experience. The model for assessment it proposed has been used to support an objectives/assessment-led curriculum change but without the key educational features which were recommended, and which have been successively removed in the process of introduction. Such an abandonment of expert advice might carry with it strong messages:

> The point to be underlined is not that TGAT lost the argument. We won the argument. The chilling feature is that in the world of political pressure to which education is now subject, that was of no consequence . . . Those who gave dire warnings that the Education Reform Act would be an instrument for direct government control in which the opinions of ministers would be isolated from professional opinion and expertise have been proved correct . . . the terms 'expert', 'academic' and 'researcher' have been turned into terms of abuse.
>
> (Black 1992: 8)

In such a context, the need for interdisciplinary research, and inter-institutional research, appears to be all the more pressing, since research which looks at any one feature of the National Curriculum assessment in isolation may be the more subject to 'corrupt' use. The PRAISE project is outlined by Broadfoot (1992) as an example of a multi-level evaluation, involving an important relationship between local and national evaluation and between individual evaluations and the meta-evaluation. The advantage that wide-ranging and cumulative research studies may have is that in crossing disciplinary boundaries, and finding common discourses, they may also better achieve what Hartnett and Naish (1990) and Grace (1991a) have identified as the need for academics to communicate better with the wider world.

The politics with which education has to engage to meet the current challenge are not only the politics of a particular government. The politics of professionalism, the politics of disciplinary division in Higher Education, and the politics of division between parts of the education service are equally important, if education as a whole is to take the initiative in formulating its own objectives, and in presenting a unified alternative to the domination by competitive assessment.

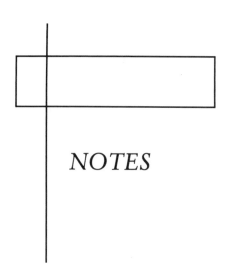

NOTES

1 The term 'reform' may have value implications. Maclure calls his discussion of the 1988 Education Act *Education Re-formed* (Maclure 1989) implying an examination of the rhetorical use of the term.
2 The tension in language implies different views of style and content.
3 The nine areas are: aesthetic and creative; human and social; linguistic and literary; mathematical; moral; physical; scientific; spiritual; technological.
4 A further player is the Department of Trade and Industry which has recently shown its hand in the publication of a White Paper on *Competitiveness* which incorporates new plans for education and training under its general banner of 'Helping Business to Win'.
5 In the studies across GCE and CSE cited in this chapter the examinations had specified subject content and unspecified objectives. It was possible that where content appeared similar, the objectives were nonetheless different, with CSE examinations placing more stress, for example, on ability to sustain independent work.
6 Input evidence might, for example, involve basing moderation judgements on the teacher's account of the work covered, tasks set and assessment criteria. Such evidence might exist in the form of lesson plans, schemes of work, observation schedules for classroom-based assessment, etc.). Outcome evidence would involve the actual work

produced by pupils, and for moderation purposes this might exist in the form of written work or taped work.

7 The School Curriculum and Assessment Authority, under the chairmanship of Sir Ron Dearing, subsumed the previously separate National Curriculum Council and the School Examinations and Assessment Council in 1993.

8 Chubb and Moe's book, *Politics, Markets and America's Schools* (Chubb and Moe 1990) which has been influential in legitimating moves to devolution of school management in the USA, used statistics of differential school performance to advance an argument that bureaucratic management appeared to be the cause of poor performance in schools. The low-performance schools were predominantly in deprived city areas where school boards were active in directing the affairs of the schools. Schools in suburban and more affluent areas were performing much better and had greater freedom. The inference was drawn that it was the autonomy of schools (i.e. rather than their socio-economic intake and favoured locations) that was the basis for success.

REFERENCES

Abbott, D., Broadfoot, P., Croll, P., Osborn, M. and Pollard, A. (1994) Some Sink, Some Float: National Curriculum Assessment and Accountability. *British Educational Research Journal* 20(2): 155–70.

Aldrich, R. (1988) The National Curriculum: an historical perspective. In D. Lawton and C. Chitty (eds) *The National Curriculum*. London: University of London.

Alexander, R., Rose, J. and Woodhead, C. (1992) *Curriculum Organisation and Classroom Practice in Primary Schools: A Discussion Paper*. London: DES.

Apple, M. W. (1979) *Ideology and Curriculum*. London: Routledge and Kegan Paul.

Apple, M. W. (1982) *Education and Power*. London: Routledge and Kegan Paul.

Apple, M. W. (1986) *Teachers and Texts: A Political Economy of Class and Gender Relations in Education*. London: Routledge and Kegan Paul.

Aronowitz, S. and Giroux, H. (1986) *Education Under Siege*. London: Routledge and Kegan Paul.

Aronowitz, S. and Giroux, H. (1991) *Postmodern Education: Politics, Culture and Social Criticism*. Minneapolis: University of Minnesota Press.

Aspin, D. (1986) Objectivity and assessment in the arts – the problem of aesthetic education. *Inspection and Advice* 22(1): 21–7.

Atkins, M. J. (1987) The pre-vocational curriculum: a review of the issues involved. *Journal of Curriculum Studies* 19(1): 45–53.

Audit Commission (1989) *Losing an Empire. Finding a Role: The LEA of the Future*. London: HMSO.

Baker, E. L. (1976) Beyond objectives: domain-referenced tests for evaluation and instructional improvement. *Educational Technology* 14(6): 10–17.

Ball, C. (1993) *Towards a Learning Society*. London: RSA.

Ball, S. J. (1987) *The Micro-Politics of the School: Towards a Theory of School Organization*. London: Methuen.

Ball, S. J. (1990) *Politics and Policy Making in Education*. London: Routledge.

Ball, S. J. and Bowe, R. (1992) Subject departments and the 'implementation' of the National Curriculum. *Journal of Curriculum Studies* 24(2): 98–115.

Barnes, D. (1976) *From Communication to Curriculum*. Harmondsworth: Penguin Education.

Barrett, E., Barton, L., Furlong, J., Galvin, C., Miles, S. and Whitty, G. (1992) *Initial Teacher Education in England and Wales: A Topography*. London: Institute of Education.

Bernstein, B. (1977) *Class, Codes and Control*. Volume I. London: Routledge and Kegan Paul.

Bernstein, B. (1990) *The Structuring of Pedagogic Discourse Class, Codes and Control*. Volume IV. London: Routledge.

Biggs, J. B. and Collis K. F. (1982) *Evaluating the Quality of Learning*. London: Academic Press.

Black, P. (1992) Presidential Address to the British Association for the Advancement of Science (Education Section). Edited version reprinted in *Times Educational Supplement*, 28 August 1992.

Black, H. D. and Dockrell, W. B. (1984) *Criterion Referenced Assessment in the Classroom*. Edinburgh: SCRE.

Block, J. H. (ed.) (1971) *Mastery Learning: Theory and Practice*. New York: Holt, Rinehart and Winston.

Bloom, B. (ed.) (1956) *Taxonomy of Educational Objectives: Book 1, Cognitive Domain*. London: Longman.

Bloom, B. (ed.) (1964) *Taxonomy of Educational Objectives: Book 2, Affective Domain*. London: Longman.

Bloom, B., Hastings, J. and Madaus, G. (1971) *Handbook on Formative and Summative Evaluation of Student Learning*. New York: McGraw-Hill.

Bobbitt, F. (1918) *The Curriculum*. Boston: Houghton Mifflin.

Bobbitt, F. (1924) *How to Make a Curriculum*. Boston: Houghton Mifflin.

Bourdieu, P. and Passeron, J. C. (1970) *La Reproduction.* Paris: Les Editions de Minuit.

Bowe, R. and Whitty, G. (1984) Teachers, boards and standards: the attack on school-based assessment in english public examinations at 16 + . In P. Broadfoot (ed.) *Selection, Certification and Control.* Lewes: Falmer Press.

Bowe, R., Ball, S. and Gold, A. (1992) *Reforming Education and Changing Schools.* London: Routledge.

Brighouse, T. and Moon, B. (1990) *Managing the National Curriculum.* Harlow: Longman, in association with the British Educational Management and Administration Society.

Britton, J. N., Martin, N. C. and Rosen, H. (1966) *Multiple Marking of English Compositions: An Account of an Experiment.* London: HMSO.

Broadfoot, P. (1979) *Assessment, Schools and Society.* London: Methuen.

Broadfoot, P. (1988) Educational research: two cultures and three estates. *British Educational Research Journal* 14(1): 3–15.

Broadfoot, P. (1990) Cinderella and the ugly sisters: an assessment policy pantomime in two acts. *Curriculum Journal* 1(2): 199–215.

Broadfoot, P. (1992) Multilateral evaluation: a case study of the national evaluation of records of achievement (PRAISE) project. *British Educational Research Journal* 18(3): 245–60.

Broadfoot, P., Murphy, R. and Torrance, H. (1990) *Changing Educational Assessment: International Perspectives and Trends.* London: Routledge.

Broadfoot, P., Abbott, D., Croll, P., Osborn, M. and Pollard, A. (1991a) 'Look Back in Anger?: findings from the PACE project concerning primary teachers'. Experiences of SATs. Bristol: PACE working paper.

Broadfoot, P., Abbott, D., Croll, P., Osborn, M., Pollard, A. and Towler, L. (1991b) Implementing national assessment: issues for primary teachers. *Cambridge Journal of Education* 21(2): 153–68.

Brown, M. (1991) Problematic issues in national assessment. *Cambridge Journal of Education* 21(2): 215–29.

Brown, S. (1988) Criterion-referenced assessment: what role for research? In H. D. Black and W. B. Dockrell, New developments in educational assessment. *British Journal of Educational Psychology,* Monograph Series no. 3, 1–14. Edinburgh: Scottish Academic Press.

Brown, S. (1991) The Influence on policy and practice of research on asessment. *Cambridge Journal of Education* 21(2): 231–44.

Bruner, J. S. (1960) *The Process of Education.* Cambridge, Massachusetts: Harvard University Press.

Bruner, J. S. (1964) The course of cognitive growth. *American Psychologist* 19(1): 1–15.

Bush, T. (1986) *Theories of Educational Management.* London: Harper and Row.

Butterfield, S. (1989) *GCSE Objectives and Outcomes*. Birmingham: The West Midlands Examinations Board.

Butterfield, S. (1992) Whole school policies for assessment. In P. Ribbins *Delivering the National Cirriculum*. Harlow: Longman.

Butterfield, S. (1993a) *Pupils' Perceptions of National Assessment: Implications for Outcomes*. Birmingham: University of Birmingham.

Butterfield, S. (1993b) National Curriculum progression. In S. Butterfield, I. Campbell, C. Chitty, (eds) *et al. The National Curriculum: Is It Working?* Harlow: Longman.

Butterfield, S., Campbell, I., Chitty, C. (ed.), Mac an Ghaill, M. and Ribbins, P. (1993) *The National Curriculum: Is It Working?* Harlow: Longman.

Chanan, G. (1974) Objectives in the humanities. *Educational Research* 16(3): 198–205.

Chitty, C. (1988) Two Models of a National Curriculum: origins and interpretations. In D. Lawton and C. Chitty (eds) *The National Curriculum*. London: University of London.

Chitty, C. (1989) *Towards a New Education System: The Victory of the New Right*. London: Falmer.

Chitty, C. (ed.) (1993) *The National Curriculum: Is It Working?* Harlow: Longman.

Christie, T. and Forrest, G. M. (1981) *Defining Public Examination Standards* (Schools Council Research Studies). London: Macmillan Education.

Chubb, J. E. and Moe, T. M. (1990) *Politics, Markets and America's Schools*. Washington DC: Brookings Institute.

CIPFA (Chartered Institute of Public Finance and Accountancy) (1988) *Performance Indicators for Schools*. London: CIPFA.

Clough, E., Clough, J. and Nixon J. (1989) *The New Learning*. London: Macmillan.

Cohen, D. (1990) Re-shaping the standards agenda: from an Australian's perspective of curriculum and assessment. In P. Broadfoot, R. Murphy and H. Torrance (eds) *Changing Educational Assessment: International Perspectives and Trends*. London: Routledge.

Coopers and Lybrand (1988) *Local Management of Schools: A Report to the Department of Education and Science*. London: DES.

Coopers and Lybrand (1994) *A Focus on Quality*. London: Ofsted.

Corbett, H. D. and Wilson, B. (1988) Raising the stakes in mandatory minimum competency testing. *Journal of Education Policy* 3(5).

Cox, B. (1991) *Cox on Cox: An English Curriculum for the 1990s*. London: Hodder and Stoughton.

Cresswell, M. J. (1987) Describing examination performance: grade criteria in public examinations. *Educational Studies* 13(3): 247–65.

Cresswell, M. J. and Houston, J. G. (1991) Assessment of the National Curriculum – some fundamental considerations. *Educational Review* 43(1): 63–78.

CVCP (Committee of Vice Chancellors and Principals) (1993) Note to Vice Chancellors and Principals.

Dale, R. *et al.* (1990) *The TVEI Story: Policy, Practice and Preparation for the Workforce.* Milton Keynes: Open University Press.

Dale, R. and Pires, E. (1984) Linking people and jobs: the indeterminate place of educational credentials. In P. Broadfoot (ed.) *Selection, Certification and Control.* Lewes: Falmer Press.

Dearing, R. (1993a) *The National Curriculum and its Assessment: Interim Report.* York/London: NCC/SEAC.

Dearing, R. (1993b) *The National Curriculum and its Assessment: Final Report.* London: SCAA.

Debling, G. (1989) The Employment Department/Training Agency Standards Programme and NVQs: implications for education. In J. W. Burke, (ed.) *Competency Based Education and Training.* London: Falmer.

Department for Education (1992a) *Choice and Diversity: A New Framework for Schools.* London: DFE/WO.

Department for Education (1992b) *GCSE Examinations: Quality and Standards.* A report by HM Inspectorate. London: DFE.

Department of Education and Science (1977) *HMI: Curriculum 11–16.* London: DES.

Department of Education and Science (1978) *School Examinations*: report of the Steering Committee established to consider proposals for replacing the GCE O-level and CSE examinations by a common system of examining (Waddell Report). London: HMSO.

Department of Education and Science (1979) *HMI: Aspects of Secondary Education.* London: HMSO.

Department of Education and Science (1982) *Mathematics Counts*: report of the Committee of Inquiry into the teaching of Mathematics in schools (Cockcroft Report). London: HMSO.

Department of Education and Science (1984) *Records of Achievement: A Statement of Policy.* London: DES.

Department of Education and Science (1985a) *Better Schools* (Cmnd 9469). London: HMSO.

Department of Education and Science (1985b) *GCSE: The National Criteria.* London: HMSO.

Department of Education and Science (1985c) *The Curriculum 5–16.* London: HMSO.

Department of Education and Science (1986a) *English from 5–16 (Curriculum Matters 1)*, second edition incorporating responses. London: HMSO.

Department of Education and Science (1986b) *Working Together*. London: HMSO.

Department of Education and Science (1987b) *The National Curriculum 5–16: A Consultation Document*. London: DES.

Department of Education and Science (1987c) *National Curriculum: Task Group on Assessment and Testing – A Report*. London: DES.

Department of Education and Science (1988a) *Report by HM Inspectors on The Introduction of the General Certificate of Secondary Education in Schools 1986–1988*. London: DES.

Department of Education and Science (1988b) *National Curriculum: Task Group on Assessment and Testing – Three Supplementary Reports*. London: DES/WO.

Department of Education and Science (1989b) *HMI: The Use Made by Local Education Authorities of Public Examination Results*. London: DES.

Department of Education and Science (1989c) *School Teacher Appraisal: A National Framework*. London: HMSO.

Department of Education and Science (1990b) *Developing School Management: The Way Forward. A Report by the School Management Task Force*. London: HMSO.

Department of Education and Science (1990c) *HMI: The Implementation of the National Curriculum in Primary Schools*. London: DES.

Department of Education and Science (1990d) *English in the National Curriculum*. London: HMSO.

Department of Education and Science (1991a) *History in the National Curriculum*. London: HMSO.

Department of Education and Science (1991b) *In-Service Training for the Introduction of the National Curriculum: A Report by HM Inspectorate 1988–1990*. London: DES.

Department of Education and Science (1991c) *Education and Training for the 21st Century* (Cm 1536). London: HMSO.

Department of Education and Science (1992a) *HMI: The Implementation of the Curricular Requirements of the Education Reform Act: Mathematics Key Stages 1, 2, and 3*. London: HMSO.

Department of Education and Science (1992b) *HMI: The Implementation of the Curricular Requirements of the Education Reform Act: English Key Stages 1, 2, and 3*. London: HMSO.

Department of Education and Science (1992c) *HMI: The Implementation of the Curricular Requirements of the Education Reform Act: Science Key Stages 1, 2, and 3*. London: HMSO.

Department of Education and Science (1992d) *HMI: The Implementation of the Curricular Requirements of the Education Reform Act: Special Needs and the National Curriculum 1990–1991*. London: HMSO.

Department of Education and Science (1992e) *Reform of Initial Teacher Training: A Consultation Document.* London: DES.

Dewey, J. (1916) *Democracy and Education.* New York: Macmillan.

Dixon, J. and Stratta, L. (1981) *Criteria for Writing in English.* Southampton: Southern Regional Examinations Board.

Dixon, J. and Brown, J. (1984) *Responses to literature – What is being assessed. Part 1. Literary response – What counts as evidence? Part 2. What evidence of appreciation in coursework and set papers? Part 3. Representative corpus of students' essays and readers' commentaries.* London: School Curriculum Development Committee.

Dockrell, W. B. (1988) *Achievement, Assessment and Reporting.* Edinburgh: SCRE.

Donaldson, M. (1978) *Children's Minds.* London: Fontana.

Duke, C. (1992) *The Learning University.* Milton Keynes: Open University Press.

Durkheim, E. (1977 [1938]) *The Evolution of Educational Thought*, trans. P. Collins. London: Routledge and Kegan Paul.

Ebel, R. L. (1962) Content standard test scores. *Educational and Psychological Measurement* 22: 11–17.

Ebel, R. L. (1971) Criterion-referenced measurements: limitations. *School Review* 69: 282–8.

Eisner, E. W. (1985) *The Art of Educational Evaluation.* Lewes: Falmer Press.

Elliott, J. (1991) *Action Research for Educational Change.* Milton Keynes: Open University Press.

Ellwein, M. C. (1988) Standards of competence: propositions on the nature of testing reforms. *Educational Researcher* 17(8): 4–9.

ENCA (1992a) *The Evaluation of National Curriculum Assessment at Key Stage 1 – Final Report.* London: SEAC.

ENCA (1992b) *The Evaluation of National Curriculum Assessment at Key Stage 1 – Final Report (Synopsis).* London: SEAC.

Eraut, M. (1989) Initial teacher training and the NCVQ model. In J. W. Burke, (ed.) (1989) *Competency Based Education and Training.* London: Falmer.

Evans, N. (1992) *Experiential Learning: Assessment and Accreditation.* London: Routledge.

Fairbrother, R. W. (1975) The reliability of teachers' judgements of the abilities being tested in multiple choice items. *Educational Research* 17(3): 202–10.

Fitz-Gibbon, C. (1990b) Analysing examination results. In C. Fitz-Gibbon (ed.) *Performance Indicators.* Clevedon: Multilingual Matters.

Fitz-Gibbon, C. (1991) Reporting on Quality. Conference paper, University of Birmingham conference series 'Improving Education', 30 October.

Fullan, M. (1982) *The Meaning of Educational Change.* New York: Teachers College Press.

Fullan, M. and Hargreaves, A. (1992) *Teacher Development and Educational Change.* London: Falmer.

Further Education Unit (1992) *Vocational Education and Training in Europe: A Four-Country Study in Four Employment Sectors.* London: FEU.

Further Education Unit (1994) *Examining Assessment.* London: FEU.

Gagne, R. M. (1965) *The Conditions of Learning and Theory of Instruction*, 4th edn. London: Holt, Rinehart and Winston.

Gipps, C. (ed.) (1986) *The GCSE: an Uncommon Examination*, Bedford Way Papers 29. London: Institute of Education, University of London.

Gipps, C. (1990) *Assessment: A Teachers' Guide to the Issues.* London: Hodder and Stoughton.

Gipps, C. (1992a) National Curriculum assessment: a research agenda. *British Educational Research Journal* 18(3): 277–86.

Gipps, C., McCallum, B., McAlister, S. and Brown, M. (1992) National assessment at seven: some emerging themes. In C. Gipps *Developing Assessment for the National Curriculum.* London: Kogan Page.

Giroux, H. (1989) *Schooling for Democracy: Critical Pedagogy in the Modern Age.* London: Routledge.

Glaser, R. (1963) Instructional technology and the measurement of learning outcomes: some questions. *American Psychologist* 18: 519–21.

Gleeson, D. (1989) *The Paradox of Training.* Milton Keynes: Open University Press.

Goldstein, H. (1991) Educational Quality and Student Achievement. Conference paper, University of Birmingham conference series 'Improving Education', 30 October.

Good, F. and Cresswell, M. (1988) *Grading the GCSE.* London: SEC.

Goodson, I. (1987) *School Subjects and Curriculum Change: Studies in Curriculum History.* Lewes: Falmer.

Gouldner, A. W. (1985) *Against Fragmentation.* Oxford: Oxford University Press.

Grace G. (1987) Teachers and the state in Britain. *Teachers: The Culture and Politics of Work.* London: Falmer.

Grace, G. (1991a) *The New Right and the challenge to educational research. Cambridge Journal of Education* 21(3): 265–75.

Grace, G. (1991b) The state and the teachers: problems in teacher supply, retention and morale. In G. Grace and M. Lawn *Teacher Supply and Teacher Quality.* Clevedon: Multilingual Matters.

Gray, J. and Hannon, V. (1986) HMI's interpretation of schools' examination results. *Journal of Education Policy* 1(1): 23–33.

Gribble, J. (1970) Pandora's box: the affective domain of educational objectives. *Journal of Curriculum Studies* 2(1): 10–24.

Grundy, S. (1989) Beyond professionalism. In W. Carr *Quality Teaching: Arguments for a Reflective Profession.* London: Falmer.

Hambleton, R. K., Swaminathan, H., Algina, J. and Coulson, D. B. (1978) Criterion-referenced testing and measurement: a review of technical issues and developments. *Review of Educational Research* 48(1): 1–47.

Harber, C. and Meighan, R. (eds) (1989) *The Democratic School: Educational Management and the Practice of Democracy.* Ticknall: Education Now.

Hargreaves, A. (1989) *Curriculum and Assessment Reform.* Milton Keynes: Open University Press.

Hargreaves, A. (1991) Curriculum reform and the teachers. *The Curriculum Journal* 2(3): 249–58.

Hargreaves, D. (1982) *The Challenge for the Comprehensive School.* London: Routledge and Kegan Paul.

Hargreaves, D. (1994) *The Mosaic of Learning: Schools and Teachers for the Next Century.* London: Demos.

Hargreaves, D. and Hopkins, D. (1991) *The Empowered School.* London: Cassell.

Harland, J. (1987) The TVEI experience: issues of control, response and the professional role of teachers. In D. Gleeson (ed.) *TVEI and Secondary Education: A Critical Appraisal.* Milton Keynes: Open University Press.

Harrison, A. (1982) *A Review of Graded Tests.* Schools Council Examinations Bulletin 41. London: Methuen Educational.

Harrison, A. (1983) *Profile Reporting of Examination Results.* Schools Council Examinations Bulletin 43. London: Methuen Educational.

Hartnett, A. and Naish, M. (1990) The sleep or reason breeds monsters: the birth of a statutory curriculum in England and Wales. *Journal of Curriculum Studies* 22(1): 1–16.

Hatcher, R. and Troyna, B. (1994) The 'policy cycle': a ball by ball account. *Education Policy* 9(2): 155–70.

Hazlitt, W. C. (ed.) (1952) Montaigne, M. E. (1580) *Essays.* C. Cotton, (trans.). London: Benton.

Her Majesty's Chief Inspector of Schools (1989) *Standards in Education 1987–88.* London:HMI/DES.

Her Majesty's Chief Inspector of Schools (1990) *Standards in Education 1988–89.* London: HMI/DES.

Her Majesty's Chief Inspector of Schools (1991) *Standards in Education 1989–90.* London: HMI/DES.

Her Majesty's Chief Inspector of Schools (1992) *Framework for the Inspection of Schools: Paper for consultation.* London: HMCI.

Her Majesty's Chief Inspector of Schools (1993) *Framework for the*

Inspection of Schools (Handbook for the Inspection of Schools, Part 2). London: HMCI.

Higher Education Quality Council (1994) *Choosing to change: extending access, choice and mobility in higher education – the report of the HEQC CAT project*. London: HEQC.

Hillgate Group (1986) *Whose Schools?: A Radical Manifesto*. London: Hillgate Group.

Husen, T. (1974) *The Learning Society*. London: Methuen.

Jamieson, I. (1990) TVEI and the management of change. In D. Hopkins (ed.) *TVEI: At the Change of Life*. Clevedon: Multilingual Matters.

Jessup, G. (1989) The emerging model of vocational education and training. In J. W. Burke (ed.) *Competency Based Education and Training*. London: Falmer.

Joseph, K. Speeches reprinted in *Secondary Examinations Council Annual Report 1983–84*. London: SEC.

Keohane Report (1979) *Proposals for a Certificate of Extended Education*. London: HMSO.

Kingdon, M. and Stobart, G. (1988) *GCSE Examined*. London: Falmer.

Lawton, D. (1986) Curriculum and assessment. In S. Ranson and J. Tomlinson (eds) *The Changing Government of Education*. London: Allen and Unwin.

Lawton, D. (1988) Ideologies of education. In D. Lawton and C. Chitty (eds) *The National Curriculum*. London: University of London.

Lawton, D. (1989) *Education, Culture and the National Curriculum*. London: Hodder and Stoughton.

Light, P. H., Buckingham, N. and Robbins, A. H. (1979) The conservation task in an interactionist setting. *British Journal of Educational Psychology* 49: 304–10.

Mac an Ghaill, M. (1988) *Young, Gifted and Black: Student–teacher Relations in the Schooling of Black Youth*. Milton Keynes: Open University Press.

Mac an Ghaill, M. (1992) Student perspectives on curriculum innovation and change in an English secondary school: an empirical study. *British Educational Research Journal* 18(3): 221–34.

Maclure, S. (1989) *Education Re-Formed*, 2nd edn. London: Hodder and Stoughton.

Mager, R. F. (1962) *Preparing Instructional Objectives*. Belmont: Fearon.

Mansell Report (1979) *A Basis for Choice*. London: FEU.

McNamara, D. (1990) The National Curriculum: an agenda for research. *British Educational Research Journal* 16(3): 225–35.

Meskauskas, J. A. (1976) Evaluation models for criterion-referenced testing: views regarding mastery and standard setting. *Review of Educational Research* 46(1): 133–58.

Millman, J. (1973) Passing scores and test lengths for domain-referenced measures. *Review of Educational Research* 43(21): 205–16.

Moon, B., Murphy, P. and Raynor, J. (eds) (1989) *Policies for the Curriculum*. London: Hodder and Stoughton.

Moon, B., with Isaac, J. and Powney, J. (1990) *Judging Standards and Effectiveness in Education*. London: Hodder and Stoughton.

Morris, N. (1961) An historian's view of examinations. In S. Wiseman (1961) *Examinations and English Education*. Manchester: Manchester University Press.

Morrison, K. and Ridley, K. (1989) Ideological contexts for curriculum planning. In M. Preedy (ed.) *Approaches to Curriculum Management*. Milton Keynes: Open University Press.

Mortimore, P. and Stone, C. (1990) Measuring educational quality. *British Journal of Educational Studies* 40(1): 69–82.

Mortimore, P., Sammons, P., Stoll, L., Lewis, D. and Ecob, R. (1988) *School Matters: The Junior Years*. London: Open Books.

Murphy, P. (1988) Gender and assessment. *Curriculum* 9(3): 165–71.

Murphy, P. and Moon, B. (eds) (1989) *Developments in Learning and Assessment*. London: Hodder and Stoughton.

Murphy, R. (1982) Sex differences in performance in examinations at 16 + . *British Journal of Educational Psychology* 52: 213–19.

Murphy, R. (1988) Great Education Reform Bill proposals for testing – a critique. *Local Government Studies* 14(1): 39–45.

National Association for the Teaching of English (1988) *A Response to the Committee of Enquiry into the Teaching of English Language*. Sheffield: NATE.

NCC (1989) *Curriculum Guidance 1: A Framework for the Primary Curriculum*. York: NCC.

NCES (National Center for Education Statistics) (1991) *Education Counts: An Indicator System to Monitor the Nation's Educational Health*. Washington DC: NCES.

NCVQ (1993) *General National Vocational Qualifications: NCVQ Information Note*. London: NCVQ.

Nedelsky, L. (1954) Absolute grading standards for objective tests. *Educational and Psychological Measurement* 14: 3–19.

NFER/BGC (1991a) *National Curriculum assessment: A report on teacher assessment*. London: SEAC.

NFER/BGC (1991b) *National Curriculum assessment at Key Stage 1: 1991 evaluation*. London: SEAC.

NFER/Brunel University (1993) *Report on the 1992 National Pilot Assessment of Mathematics and Science*. London: SEAC.

Nixon, J. and Rudduck, J. (1992) Agents of change. *Education*, 27 November.

North, J. (1987) *The GCSE: An Examination*. London: Claridge Press.

Nuttall, D. (1971) *The 1968 CSE Monitoring Experiment*. London: Evans Methuen Educational.

Nuttall, D. (1988) The implications of National Curriculum assessments. *Educational Psychology* 8(4): 229–36.

Nuttall, D. and Goldstein, H. (1986) Profiles and graded tests: the technical issues. In P. Broadfoot (ed.) *Selection, Certification and Control*. Lewes: Falmer Press.

Nuttall, D., Goldstein, H., Prosser, R. and Rasbash, J. (1989) Differential school effectiveness. *International Journal of Educational Research* 13: 769–76.

O'Hear, A. (1987) The GCSE philosophy of education. In J. North *The GCSE: An Examination*. London: Claridge Press.

Oldroyd, D. (1985) The management of school-based staff development: an example. *British Journal of In-service Education* 11(2): 82–90.

Otter, S. (1992) Competence or competences? Holism or vocationalism in Higher Education? *The New Academic* 1(3): 6–7.

PACE (1989) A Study of Educational Change Under the National Curriculum: Working Paper 1. Bristol: PACE.

Parlett, M. and Hamilton, D. (1972) Evaluation as illumination: a new approach to the study of innovatory programmes. Reprinted in R. Murphy and H. Torrance *Evaluating Education: Issues and Methods*. London: Harper and Row.

Peel, E. A. (1971) *The Nature of Adolescent Judgment*. London: Staples.

Piaget, J. (1971) Intellectual development from adolescence to adulthood. *Human Development* 15: 1–12.

Pietrasik, R. (1987) The teachers action 1984–1986. In M. Lawn and G. Grace (eds) *Teachers: The Culture and Politics of Work*. London: Falmer.

Pollitt, A., Entwistle, N., Hutchinson, C. and de Luca, C. (1985) *What Makes Exam Questions Difficult? An Analysis of O-Grade Questions and Answers*. Edinburgh: Scottish Academic Press.

Popham, W. J. (1978) *Criterion-Referenced Measurement*. Englewood Cliffs, New Jersey: Prentice-Hall.

Popham, W. J. (1980) Domain specification strategies. In R. A. Berk (ed.) *Criterion-Referenced Measurement: the state of the art*, pp. 15–31. Baltimore: Johns Hopkins University Press.

PRAISE (1988) *Records of Achievement: Report of the National Evaluation of Pilot Schemes*. London: HMSO.

President of the Board of Trade, Chancellor of the Exchequer, the Secretaries of State for Transport, Environment and Employment, The Chancellor of the Duchy of Lancaster, the Secretaries of State for Scotland, Northern Ireland, Education and Wales (1994) *Competitiveness: Helping Business to Win* (Cm 2563). London: HMSO.

Pring, R. (1990) *The New Curriculum*. London: Cassell.

Pring, R. (1992) Standards and quality in education. *British Journal of Educational Studies* 40(1): 4–22.

Quicke, J. (1988) The 'New Right' and education. *British Journal of Educational Studies*, 36(1): 5–20.

Radnor, H. (1987) *The Impact of the Introduction of GCSE at LEA and School Level*. Slough: NFER.

Radnor, H. (1988) GCSE – does it support equality? *British Journal of Educational Studies* 36(1): 37–48.

Ranson, S. (1984) Towards a tertiary tripartism: new codes of social control and the 17 +. In P. Broadfoot (ed.) *Selection, Certification and Control*. Lewes: Falmer Press.

Ranson, S. (1988) From 1944 to 1988: education, citizenship and democracy. *Local Government Studies*, January/February 1988.

Ranson, S. (1993) Markets or democracy for education. *British Journal of Educational Studies* 41(4): 333–52.

Ranson, S. and Tomlinson, J. (eds) (1986) *The Changing Government of Education*. London: Allen and Unwin.

Reid, K., Hopkins, D. and Holly, P. (1987) *Towards the Effective School*. Oxford: Basil Blackwell.

Reynolds, D. (1988) School effectiveness and school improvement: a review of the British literature. In B. Moon *et al. Judging Standards* and *Effectiveness in Education*. London: Hodder and Stoughton.

Ribbins, P. (ed.) (1992) *Delivering the National Curriculum*. Harlow: Longman.

Robinson, C. (1990) Issues in Public Examinations. A paper given to the International Association for Educational Assessment, 16th Annual Conference, Netherlands, 18–22 June 1990.

Rogers, C. (1982) *A Social Psychology of Schooling*. London: Routledge and Kegan Paul.

Rosen, H., Britton, J. N. and Martin, N. C. (1966) *Multiple Marking of English Compositions: An Account of an Experiment*. London: HMSO.

Rudduck, J. (1976) *The Dissemination of Innovation: The Humanities Curriculum Project*. London: Evans/Methuen.

Rudduck, J. (1991) *Innovation and Change*. Milton Keynes: Open University Press.

Rudduck, J. (1992) Universities in partnership with schools and school systems: les liaisons dangereuses? In M. Fullan and A. Hargreaves, (eds) *Teacher Development and Educational Change*. London: Falmer.

Rutter, M., Maughan, B., Mortimore, P. and Ouston, J. (1979) *Fifteen Thousand Hours*. London: Open Books.

Sadler, D. R. (1987) Specifying and promulgating achievement standards. *Oxford Review of Education* 13(2): 191–209.

Schmidtlein, F. A. (1988) Campus Planning in the United States: Perspectives from a nation-wide study. Paper presented at the Tenth European Association for Institutional Research Forum, Bergen, Norway.

Schön, D. A. (1983) *The Reflective Practitioner*. New York: Basic Books.

School Curriculum and Assessment Authority (1993a) *Evaluation of the Implementation of National Curriculum Mathematics at Key Stages 1, 2 and 3. Research for the National Curriculum Council by the Centre for Education Studies, Kings College, London; The School of Education, University of Birmingham; and the University of Cambridge Institute of Education Volume 1: Report*. London: SCAA.

School Curriculum and Assessment Authority (1993b) *Evaluation of the Implementation of National Curriculum Mathematics at Key Stages 1, 2 and 3. Research for the National Curriculum Council by the Centre for Education Studies, Kings College, London; The School of Education, University of Birmingham; and the University of Cambridge Institute of Education Volume 2: Appendix*. London: SCAA.

School Curriculum and Assessment Authority (1993c) *Evaluation of the Implementation of National Curriculum Mathematics at Key Stages 1, 2 and 3. Research for the National Curriculum Council by the Centre for Education Studies, Kings College, London; The School of Education, University of Birmingham; and the University of Cambridge Institute of Education Volume 3: Summary Report*. London: SCAA.

School Curriculum and Assessment Authority (1994a) *Evaluation of the Implementation of Science in the National Curriculum at Key Stages 1, 2 and 3. Research for the National Curriculum Council by the Centre for Research in Primary Science and Technology, University of Liverpool Volume 1: Executive Summary*. London: SCAA.

School Curriculum and Assessment Authority (1994b) *Evaluation of the Implementation of Science in the National Curriculum at Key Stages 1, 2 and 3. Research for the National Curriculum Council by the Centre for Research in Primary Science and Technology, University of Liverpool Volume 2: Progression*. London: SCAA.

School Curriculum and Assessment Authority (1994c) *Evaluation of the Implementation of Science in the National Curriculum at Key Stages 1, 2 and 3. Research for the National Curriculum Council by the Centre for Research in Primary Science and Technology, University of Liverpool Volume 3: Differentiation*. London: SCAA.

School Curriculum and Assessment Authority (1994d) *Evaluation of the Implementation of English in the National Curriculum at Key Stages 1, 2 and 3. (1991–1993) Research for the National Curriculum Council by the University of Warwick*. London: SCAA.

School Examinations and Assessment Council (1988) Initial Report on the GCSE to the Secretary of State for Education and Science. London: SEAC.

School Examinations and Assessment Council (1990a) *A Guide to Teacher Assessment* (Packs A, B, C). London: SEAC/Heinemann Educational.

School Examinations and Assessment Council (1990b) *National Curriculum Assessment Key Stage 1. Responsibility of LEAs in 1990–91.* London: SEAC.

School Examinations and Assessment Council (1991a) *National Curriculum Assessment Key Stage 1. Responsibility of LEAs in 1991–92.* London: SEAC.

School Examinations and Assessment Council (1991b) *National Curriculum Assessment Key Stage 1. A Moderator's Handbook 1991–92.* London: SEAC.

School Examinations and Assessment Council (1991c) *Key Stage 1. Pilot 1990: A Report from the Evaluation and Monitoring Unit.* London: SEAC.

School Examinations and Assessment Council (1992a) *Key Stage 3. School Assessment Folder (Part Two) Mathematics.* London: SEAC.

School Examinations and Assessment Council (1992b) *Key Stage 3. School Assessment Folder (Part Two) Science.* London: SEAC.

School Examinations and Assessment Council (1992c) *GCSE/Key Stage 4. Standards for Assessment and Certification. General Criteria.* London: SEAC.

Scott, D. (1989) HMI Reporting on the GCSE. *Journal of Education Policy* 4(3): 281–8.

Scott, P. (1989) The power of ideas. In C. Ball and H. Eggins (eds) *Higher Education into the 1990s.* Milton Keynes: Open University Press.

Secondary Schools Examinations Council (1963) *Examinations Bulletin, no. 1. The Certificate of Secondary Education: some suggestions for teachers and examiners.* London: HMSO.

Seddon, G. M. (1978) The properties of bloom's taxonomy of educational objectives for the cognitive domain. *Review of Educational Research* 48(2): 303–23.

Shepard, L. A. and Smith, M. L. (1988) Escalating academic demands in the kindergarten: counterproductive policies. *Elementary School Journal* 89(2): 135–45.

Shipman, M. (1983) *Assessment in Primary and Middle Schools.* London: Croom Helm.

Shipman, M. (1990) *In Search of Learning: A New Approach to School Management.* Oxford: Basil Blackwell.

Sikes, P. (1992) Imposed change and the experienced teacher. In Fullan, M. and Hargreaves, A. *Teacher Development and Educational Change.* London: Falmer.

Simons, H. (1987) *Getting to Know Schools in a Democracy.* Lewes: Falmer Press.

Skilbeck, M. (1984) *School-Based Curriculum Development.* London: Harper and Row.

Skilbeck, M. (1990) *Curriculum Reform: An Overview of Trends*. Paris: OECD.

Slavin, R. E. (1987) Mastery learning reconsidered. *Review of Educational Research* 57(2): 175–213.

Spencer, H. (1861) *Education: Intellectual, Moral, and Physical*. London: Williams and Norgate.

Stenhouse, L. (ed.) (1980) *Curriculum Research and Development in Action*. London: Heinemann.

Tattersall, K. (1983) *Differentiated Examinations: A Strategy for Assessment at 16 +*. Schools Council Examinations, Bulletin 42. London: Methuen.

Taylor, W. (1991) Ideology, accountability and improvement in teacher education. In G. Grace and M. Lawn (eds) *Teacher Supply and Teacher Quality*. Clevedon: Multilingual Matters.

Thatcher, M. (1987) Speech to the Conservative Party Conference.

Thomas, N. (1986) The inspectors. In S. Ranson and J. Tomlinson (eds) *The Changing Government of Education*. London: Allen and Unwin.

Thomas, H., Kirkpatrick, G. and Nicholson, E. (1989) *Financial Delegation and the Local Management of Schools*. London: Cassell.

Torrance, H. (1986) What can Examinations Contribute to School Evaluation? *Educational Review* 38(1): 31–40.

Tyler, R. (1949) *Basic Principles of Curriculum and Instruction*. Chicago: University of Chicago Press.

Warnock, M. (1989) *A Common Policy for Education*. Oxford: Oxford University Press.

Watts, M. and Bentley, D. (1991) Constructivism in the Curriculum. *The Curriculum Journal* 2(2): 171–82.

Webster, F. (1991) *MCI Management Competencies Project: Evaluation Report*. London: MCI.

Whale, E. and Ribbins, P. (1990) Quality development in education. *Educational Review* 42(2): 167–79.

Whitty, G. (1990) The New Right and the National Curriculum: state control or market forces? In M. Flude and M. Hammer *The Education Reform Act 1988. Its Origins and Implications*. Basingstoke: Falmer.

Wilkinson, A., Barnsley, G., Hanna, P. and Swan, M. (1980) *Assessing Language Development*. Oxford: Oxford University Press.

Williams, R. (1962) *Communication*. Harmondsworth: Penguin.

Willmott, A. S. and Hall, C. G. W. (1975) *O-Level Examined: The Effect of Question Choice* (Schools Council Research Studies). London: Macmillan.

Willmott, A. S. and Nuttall, D. L. (1975) *The Reliability of Examinations at 16 +* (Schools Council Research Studies). London: Macmillan.

Willmott, A. S. (1977) *CSE and GCE Grading Standards: The 1973 Comparability Study* (Schools Council Research Studies). London: Macmillan.

Wolf, A. (1989) Can competence and knowledge mix? In Burke, S. *GCSE Objectives and Outcomes*. Birmingham: The West Midlands Examinations Board.

Wolpe, A. (1988) *Within School Walls: The Role of Discipline, Sexuality and the Curriculum*. London: Routledge.

Wood, D. (1988) *How Children Think and Learn*. Oxford: Basil Blackwell.

Wood, R. (1986) The agenda for educational measurement. In D. Nuttall *Assessing Educational Achievement*. Lewes: Falmer Press.

Woodhouse, G. (1990) The need for pupil-level data. In Fitz-Gibbon, C. (ed.) *Performance Indicators*. Cleveland: Multilingual Matters.

Worthen, J. (1987) English, in North, J. *The GCSE: An Examination*. London: The Claridge Press.

Young, M. (1980) A case study of the limitation of policy research. In B. Tizard *et al*. *Fifteen Thousand Hours: a Discussion*. London: University of London Institute of Education.

Young, M. (1993) A curriculum for the 21st Century? Towards a basis for overcoming academic/vocational divisions. *British Journal of Educational Studies* 41(3): 203–22.

INDEX

A FAIR TEST?
ASSESSMENT, ACHIEVEMENT AND EQUITY
Caroline Gipps and Patricia Murphy

How far is assessment fair? In this evaluation of research from a wide range
of countries the authors examine the evidence for differences in performance among gender and ethnic groups on various forms of assessment.
They explore the reasons put forward for these observed differences and
clarify the issues involved. The authors' concern is that assessment practice
and interpretation of results are *just* for all groups.

This is a complex field in which access to schooling, the curriculum offered,
pupil motivation and esteem, teacher stereotype and expectation all
interact with the mode of assessment. This analytical and comprehensive
overview is essential reading in a field crucial to educators.

Contents
*Introduction – Defining equity – Sex differences in intellectual abilities –
Intelligence and intelligence testing – International surveys of achievement
– National assessment programmes 1: the Assessment of Performance Unit
in the UK – National assessment programmes 2: the National Assessment
of Educational Progress in the USA – National Curriculum assessment –
Examination performance – Conclusions: beyond the concept of a fair
test – References – Index.*

320pp   0 335 15673 8 (paperback)   0 335 15674 6 (hardback)

ASSESSING AND RECORDING ACHIEVEMENT
IMPLEMENTING A NEW APPROACH IN SCHOOL

Christopher J. Pole

Records of Achievement are meant to provide school students, parents and future employers with a document recognizing personal development and practical achievement; they are also seen as a challenge for teachers and pupils. Christopher Pole gives us an account of how Records of Achievement actually work through a case study of a particular school, and pays particular attention to the whole school nature of the endeavour and to pupil responses. He shows that there seems to be an almost irresistible pressure to bureaucratize the process of recording achievement in order for it to be integrated into the usual routines of schooling. This is then a cautionary tale for those who believe that schools are easily changed or controlled by changes in assessment. It makes fascinating reading for all those in schools and teacher training who are engaged in introducing new methods of assessment.

Contents
Introduction – Setting the scene – Fitting it all in: it's a question of time – Battering down and middling out: pupil-teacher discussions – Challenging the teachers – Hitting the target – What's the use? – Conclusion – Appendix 1: descriptor sheets – Appendix 2: parent's page and pupil page relating to activities out of school – References – Index.

176pp   0 335 09960 2 (paperback)   0 335 09961 0 (hardback)

ASSESSING ACHIEVEMENT IN THE ARTS

Malcolm Ross, Hilary Radnor, Sally Mitchell and Cathy Bierton

Largely absent from current assessment practice in the arts is any serious encouragement of the student's own act of self-appraisal: it is unusual for arts teachers to make time to sit down with individual students to talk about their creative work and help them weigh up their achievement. This is precisely the proposal made here. Following an intensive programme of collaborative research in ten secondary schools the authors set out the case for a fresh approach to assessment in the arts, an approach which gives the student a voice and at the same time allows the teacher access to the student's subjective world – that world in which particular aesthetic projects arise and unique aesthetic judgements are made. The vehicle of assessment becomes student-teacher talk: the reflective conversation. The research raises serious questions about the focus, emphasis and direction of the arts in education within the framework set out by the National Curriculum in the UK.

Contents
Contextualising the project – The project's history – Theoretical – Case studies – Conclusion – Notes – References and bibliography – Index.

192pp   0 335 19061 8 (Paperback)   0 335 19062 6 (hardback)